Spiritual Practices
in Psychotherapy

Spiritual Practices in Psychotherapy

Thomas G. Plante

American Psychological Association

Washington, DC

Published by
American Psychological Association
750 First Street, NE
Washington, DC 20002
www.apa.org

To order
APA Order Department
P.O. Box 92984
Washington, DC 20090-2984
Tel: (800) 374-2721; Direct: (202) 336-5510
Fax: (202) 336-5502; TDD/TTY: (202) 336-6123
Online: www.apa.org/books/
E-mail: order@apa.org

In the U.K., Europe, Africa, and the Middle East, copies may be ordered from
American Psychological Association
3 Henrietta Street
Covent Garden, London
WC2E 8LU England

Typeset in Goudy by Stephen McDougal, Mechanicsville, MD

Printer: Edwards Brothers, Inc., Ann Arbor, MI
Cover Designer: Minker Design, Bethesda, MD
Technical/Production Editor: Devon Bourexis

The opinions and statements published are the responsibility of the authors, and such opinions and statements do not necessarily represent the policies of the American Psychological Association.

Library of Congress Cataloging-in-Publication Data
Plante, Thomas G.
  Spiritual practices in psychotherapy : thirteen tools for enhancing psychological health /
Thomas G. Plante. — 1st ed.
     p. ; cm.
  Includes bibliographical references and index.
  ISBN-13: 978-1-4338-0429-8
  ISBN-10: 1-4338-0429-8
  1. Psychiatry and religion. 2. Spirituality—Psychological aspects. I. American
Psychological Association. II. Title.
  [DNLM: 1. Psychotherapy—methods. 2. Religion and Psychology. 3. Spirituality.
WM 420 P713s 2009]
  RC455.4.R4P63 2009
  616.89'14—dc22   2008033092

British Library Cataloguing-in-Publication Data
A CIP record is available from the British Library.

Printed in the United States of America
First Edition

This book is dedicated to Gerdenio M. "Sonny" Manuel, PhD, SJ, a dear friend, colleague, clinical psychologist, professor, Jesuit priest, and godfather to my son, Zachary, who has best modeled spiritually and religiously integrated psychotherapy for me and for so many others.

CONTENTS

PREFACE

In my quarter century of conducting psychotherapy with clients from all walks of life, I have found that time and time again many of the issues clients wish to discuss in psychotherapy are related to religious–spiritual concerns, very broadly defined. For example, clients often come to mental health professionals feeling empty, isolated, directionless, and depressed. They often focus on relationships or careers that are unsatisfying and frustrating. They are frequently upset about the lack of ethical and moral behavior among family members and colleagues. Some are trying to find meaning and purpose in their lives or make sense of stressful life events such as the loss of a loved one or something they valued dearly. So many of the issues these clients are concerned about have roots in religious–spiritual questions, and many clients bring up religious–spiritual issues when they feel that I am open to them. Furthermore, as a researcher who focuses on the relationship between spirituality, religion, and both mental and physical health outcomes, I am aware that religious–spiritual issues can be closely related to positive or, sometimes, negative health outcomes. Because the American Psychological Association's (APA's; 2002) "Ethical Principles of Psychologists and Code of Conduct" demands that psychologists be mindful of diversity, including religious diversity, psychologists have an obligation to be respectful and responsible in this area and can no longer afford to ignore religious–spiritual concerns among their clients.

As far as I can tell, few books that are both practical and high in quality are available to therapists to help them better integrate religious–spiritual principles and tools into psychotherapy and other professional psychological services. Although this topic has become popular, most books can be categorized into one of three areas.

First, some books are very research focused, with perhaps little practical help for the typical clinician. They are flying at clinical altitudes of 35,000 feet above the ground, discussing in great detail the various research projects on spirituality, religion, psychology, and health, with emphasis on research methodology and statistics. These books are generally written by academics at top universities who may not treat psychotherapy clients. Clinicians may learn about research in this area but are not likely to have much direction or particular tools to use with their clients after reading these books.

Second, other books tend to avoid research results and offer a variety of clinical stories of how religious–spiritual principles and experiences were helpful to their clients. These books tend to be written by clinicians flying at a much lower clinical altitude who are usually spiritual themselves, highlighting their clinical experiences without much attention to research and empirical support. These books may be enjoyable and even inspirational to read, but in the end, they may be of modest value to the average practicing clinician because they often do not address solid research findings that support clinical interventions. The various clinical perspectives and stories from one clinician who writes a book on this topic may not translate into helpful techniques, principles, or tools for other clinicians.

Finally, some books discuss religion–spirituality by stereotyping the major religious traditions, articulating what each one believes and how they practice. They spend a great deal of time explaining the various religious traditions in terms of history, beliefs, rituals, and practices. They may suggest or imply that members of a particular religious–spiritual group tend to think and behave alike. The challenge with these books is that, of course, not all people who claim to come from the same ethnic, religious, political, gender, or cultural group think and behave alike. In fact, many tensions exist between various branches within each of the religious traditions. Books that focus on describing the religious traditions may fail to help the reader understand the remarkable diversity within each religious community and subcommunity. In terms of my flight analogy, they are flying so low that they may fail to see the bigger picture from higher altitudes. They may not examine the similarities among religious groups and may perhaps focus too much on the religious differences among groups.

APA has published several books on this topic and has graciously published this one. Most of the other APA books are edited volumes in which leading experts from a variety of professional perspectives have written diverse chapters that focus on the scholarship and clinical practice of religiously/spiritually-influenced psychotherapy (Miller, 1999; Richards & Bergin, 2003, 2005; Shafranske & Malony, 1996; Sperry & Shafranske, 2005). They are very useful books that complement rather than compete with this book, which seeks to fill an important gap by offering a single-author volume that, although based on sound research findings, primarily offers religious–spiritual tools taken from diverse religious traditions that are practical for typical clinicians and clients.

Thus, although the other books on religious–spiritual integration into psychological treatment all offer something unique for readers, this book aims to be practical; to give average clinicians in professional practice principles, tools, and perspectives to help them in their work; and to provide evidence of the solid clinical science and practice that support these techniques. This book pulls from the various religious traditions and focuses on their similarities that can then be applied to clinical settings. It offers religious–spiritual tools that have emerged from the great wisdom traditions over millenia and that can be used to supplement the high-quality psychological tools, techniques, and perspectives already used by competent mental health professionals. Ultimately, this book introduces a set of religious–spiritual tools that can be used as clinicians see fit with their clients given the individual needs of both therapist and client. It attempts to speak to the typical mental health professional as well as graduate students in training who evaluate and treat clients regularly and wish to be more thoughtful about integrating religious–spiritual tools and perspectives into their clinical work.

THE PURPOSE OF THIS BOOK

This book is not trying to promote any one religious–spiritual tradition or even ask therapists to be religious–spiritual if they are not so. This book also is not asking therapists to be unscientific or do anything very different from what they might normally do in providing quality mental health services to diverse clients. Also, it is not asking therapists to become experts on all variations on religious–spiritual traditions, and it does not provide a *Reader's Digest* summary of all religions.

The purpose of this book is to add value to the high-quality, state-of-the-art services that the psychologist or other mental health professional is already providing. Its goal is to help professionals use spirituality and wisdom from the religious traditions to benefit their clients, without having to get a degree in theology or religious studies or become a member of the clergy. It offers, I hope, easy-to-understand tools to help clinicians be better clinicians.

INFORMED CONSENT: MY STORY, MY BIASES

The phrase "spiritual but not religious" has become a popular way to describe many people's view of their religious–spiritual experience (Fuller, 2001). Many have rejected formal church structure with particular rules, dogma, decrees, and desire for the submissive acceptance of the faith tradition. Many have recoiled from what they perceive to be the oppressive, outdated, and paternalistic faith traditions of the past and perhaps of their youth.

Somehow, for many, being spiritual is positive, whereas being religious is pathological. In fact, Pargament (2007) reported that psychologists and other contemporary mental health professionals tend to view spirituality among their clients as good and religiousness as bad. The extremely negative press associated with various church scandals such as the priest sexual abuse crisis in the Roman Catholic Church, the financial and sexual misdeeds of prominent church leaders in the evangelical Protestant churches, and the terrorism and violence encouraged by minority elements in the Islamic tradition have all helped to support the point of view that organized religion can be destructive and hypercritical and that one may need to act on one's own to achieve spiritual comfort and direction. It is unclear how many people have abandoned religious traditions because of these issues; however, many of them still seek spiritual engagement and growth—but more on their own terms (McLennan, 2001). Perhaps it is American individualism that has made religion–spirituality become somewhat of a buffet here: Select the buffet items that appeal to one and ignore the rest. However, often those who reject the religious tradition of their youth "throw out the baby with the bathwater" by overgeneralizing their particular experience to the entire religious tradition. Sometimes they cannot see the rich diversity even within their own tradition.

A brief comment on my own personal background may be relevant to provide the reader with informed consent about my perspective and why I am fascinated by religious–spiritual integration in psychotherapy and wish to share some of my interests in this book.

I grew up in a working-class home in Rhode Island during the 1960s and 1970s. My family is Irish and French Canadian Roman Catholic, and the vast majority of the people I knew growing up were working class and either Irish Catholic, French Canadian Catholic, Italian Catholic, or Portuguese Catholic. I jokingly often say that we were all envious of the Italian Catholics because they seemed to have the best food and appeared to have the most fun! I was very involved with church-related activities as a youngster, especially music ministry in the age when Vatican II had just allowed folk-style music to be played at services. I played the piano and sang in "folk Masses" and was the pianist for a traveling Christian musical called *Brand New Day* (which was very similar to the musical *Godspell* but based on the Acts of the Apostles rather than the Gospels) sponsored by a local Catholic parish. For a brief time during high school and college, I was also involved with Protestant youth groups (e.g., Young Life). Although I started my college career at Boston College (a Catholic, Jesuit university) and continued my participation in music ministry, I ended up completing my college career and graduating from Brown University (a secular school in Providence, Rhode Island, where approximately 30%–40% of the student body identified with the Jewish religious tradition). At Brown I also directed and participated in music ministry for the Catholic community. One of my biggest thrills in college was being part of the papal choir when the newly elected Pope John Paul II made his first visit to the United States and presided over a Mass at the Boston Commons in October 1979.

While growing up I struggled to make sense of my faith tradition. I was often troubled by the famous "Irish Catholic guilt," a sense of being sinful and unworthy. The fear of eternal damnation was also very present in my mind, and I would listen intently to the Catholic Mass, read Gospel stories, and talk with friends, relatives, and clergy about the finer aspects of mortal and venial sin as well as paths to salvation. We attended weekly confession on Saturdays, never missed Mass on Sundays or other "holy days of obligation," and found religious themes woven through all that we did and said. I must admit it was all rather intense, and usually not especially pleasant.

I went to the secular University of Kansas for graduate school in clinical psychology and then secular Yale University for a clinical internship and a postdoctoral fellowship in clinical and health psychology. I completed my postdoctoral fellowship under the mentorship of Judith Rodin and Gary Schwartz, two brilliant but very different psychology professors and professionals. During those years, I generally took an "ecclesiastical vacation," being so focused on getting through graduate school and securing my psychologist credentials that I did not continue much participation in religious practices such as attending Mass but did continue daily prayer.

In 1988, I married a Jew from the Reform tradition who grew up in the San Francisco Bay area and was a fellow clinical psychology graduate student with me at the University of Kansas. We met and became fast friends during our first days of graduate school in 1982. After being with her for about 25 years, I have learned a great deal about the Jewish tradition. I currently belong to a Roman Catholic church at both Stanford and Santa Clara universities as well as a Reform Jewish temple. I attend daily Mass at Santa Clara, Sunday Mass at Stanford, and all the major Jewish High Holiday and other events at Temple Beth Am in Los Altos Hills, California. We host Passover, Hanukkah, and other Jewish holidays in my home for family and friends. Over the years, I have returned to being highly engaged in my Catholic faith while remaining active in my wife's tradition. I suppose I have evolved to become more of a liberal Catholic in thinking and theology after years of reading, reflection, ongoing spiritual direction, and other activities along my religious–spiritual journey.

My only child, a 12-year-old son named Zachary, is being raised Jewish and attends Hebrew school, Sunday school, and various temple events and activities. Yet, he has a Jesuit priest as a godfather. His godfather, Sonny Manuel, who is both a priest and a licensed psychologist, gave a lovely homily at Zach's bris! Zach is very active at my university (e.g., being a bat boy for the university baseball team for 4 years) and is very close to many Jesuit priests and faculty, whom he visits frequently.

After starting my career at Stanford University Medical School in psychiatry, I have spent over a decade as a psychology professor at a Jesuit, Catholic university in California (i.e., Santa Clara University). I also developed and direct the Spirituality and Health Institute at the university, which conducts multidisciplinary research on spirituality and health integration. The members of the institute include faculty from Santa Clara University, Stanford University, and the University of California at Berkeley. These professors are from just about all the faith traditions, and some are from no tradition. I spent a recent sabbatical in 2003 at the Graduate Theological Union in Berkeley (often referred to as "Holy Hill"), where I studied systematic theology with an emphasis on Christology. While writing this book during a sabbatical in 2007–2008, I was a student in the pastoral ministries graduate program at Santa Clara University, taking a course on the history of Western spirituality.

I have maintained a small private practice as a licensed psychologist in Menlo Park, California, since the late 1980s. Over the years, the vast majority of my clinical practice has focused on the integration of spirituality, religion, and psychological services (mostly psychological testing, psychotherapy, and consulting) in a variety of ways with several religious groups and traditions. Specifically, many of my clients are members of the clergy who struggle with their vocation or who have sometimes gotten themselves in trouble with their religious superiors or congregants. For example, I evaluate and treat many sex-offending clergy and clergy who have engaged in marital affairs. I also help victims of clergy abuse. In addition, I conduct screening evaluations for those interested in ordained ministry as priests, deacons, nuns, brothers, and others in the Roman Catholic and Episcopal Churches. I serve on several review boards for church groups to help them manage behavioral and psychological issues among their clergy and employees. I also serve on the National Review Board for the United States Council of Catholic Bishops, advising the bishops on issues related to the protection of children and vulnerable others from sexual abuse by clergy and other church employees. I have mostly worked with Christian and Jewish religious groups, clergy, and laypersons.

I am fond of saying that we host many dinner parties with colleagues, friends, and family who are very interested in spirituality, religion, psychology, and health integration. I call these events our "gourmet theological salons." The guests around the table may include my wife's cousin, a rabbi at Stanford University; her partner, a Princeton-trained scholar in early Christianity who specializes in the writings of St. Paul (and who likes to tell a few jokes in Coptic, an ancient language spoken in Egypt until around the 17th century); some Jesuit Roman Catholic priests from Santa Clara University and the University of San Francisco, including several who are also licensed mental health professionals; a neighbor from southern India who is an attorney and a devout Hindu; another neighbor who is a cardiologist and a Mormon; several former clergymen; as well as several other mental health professionals from various religious traditions, and some who maintain no religious identification. With good food, wine, and company, we enjoy some remarkable theological conversations and table fellowship. In fact, several of my previous book projects emerged from conversations at these dinner parties.

Therefore, my own personal religious background is within the Roman Catholic tradition but has been informed by Judaism and several other faith traditions along the way. In my clinical practice, I have found myself integrating spirituality and psychotherapy more and more as the years go by. This background and history informs my research and practice and will likely be evident throughout this book. For example, most of my examples will be from either a Christian or Jewish tradition. Although I have studied other faith traditions, Christian and Jewish language, culture, theology, and clients are what I am familiar with and what I know best. As they say, "Write what you know."

ACKNOWLEDGMENTS

Many people other than the author assist in the completion of a book. Some contribute in a direct way, whereas others help in a more supportive or inspirational manner. I would like to acknowledge the assistance of the many people who worked to make this book idea a reality and who have helped me both directly and indirectly.

First and foremost, I would like to recognize the wonderful people at the American Psychological Association who published this book. Most especially, many thanks go to Susan Reynolds, who invited me to complete this project during a meeting at the Society of Behavioral Medicine Convention in 2006, and Susan Herman, who as development editor demonstrated remarkable skill, dedication, and attention. Many thanks also to Devon Bourexis, production editor, and Ron Teeter, technical editing and design supervisor.

Second, I am grateful for the thoughtful, detailed, and insightful comments of several anonymous reviewers who offered numerous suggestions on ways to improve this book.

Third, I appreciate my colleagues at the Spirituality and Health Institute at Santa Clara University who provided helpful feedback and a sounding board for a variety of spiritual and health topics. Special thanks go to Sonny Manuel, Bo Tep, and Carl Thoresen for reviewing an early draft of the manuscript.

Fourth, I thank Santa Clara University as an institution, which has allowed me many opportunities to pursue my scholarly academic interests and granted me a sabbatical to write this book.

Fifth, I would like to acknowledge the anonymous persons, including many of my clients and colleagues, who are referred to in this book. They have allowed their life experiences to become an instrument for learning for others.

Sixth, I thank the remarkable group of professionals who have contributed to the religion–spirituality research and practice to date. They include Allen Bergin, Jill Bormann, Peter Hill, Harold Koenig, Kevin Masters, Mike McCullough, Mark McMinn, Doug Oman, Kenneth Pargament, Edward Shafranske, Shauna Shapiro, Allen Sherman, Len Sperry, Siang-Yang Tan, Carl Thoresen, Ken Wallston, and Everett Worthington. They have influenced not only the field in positive ways but also my thinking and research and provided inspiration in a collegial spirit.

Seventh, I thank family, friends, and colleagues who have been positive models for my own spiritual journey, most especially Margaret Condon, Dominican Father Patrick LaBelle, Rabbi Janet Marder, Henry McCormick, Gary Schwartz, Carl Thoresen, and Jesuit Fathers Don Gelpi, Steve Privett, Mark Ravizza, Fran Smith, and Mike Zampelli.

Finally, I thank my wife, Lori, and son, Zach, for their love and support while I worked on yet another compelling book project. They are constant reminders that life is sacred and blessed. I am eternally grateful for them.

Spiritual Practices
in Psychotherapy

INTRODUCTION

There is a remarkable amount of interest in the relationship between spirituality and health, and a number of books have appeared in both the professional and popular press. In addition, many of the popular news weeklies, such as *Time* and *Newsweek*, have published cover stories on the topic of spirituality and health. The professional, medical, and psychological communities have responded with a number of conferences, articles, and scholarly activities that have greatly helped move this area of interest forward. Clearly, contemporary interest in religion–spirituality is high among not only the general population but also professionals in all of the mental and physical health disciplines.

Because approximately 96% of Americans believe in God and most consider themselves to be spiritual if not also religious, and because about 40% of all Americans attend religious services on a weekly basis or more (e.g., see Gallup, 2002; Gallup & Lindsay, 1999), there is no question that religion–spirituality is an important aspect of the lives of the majority of people who find their way into a mental health professional's office. Yet most

---

All of the many examples presented in this book are based on actual clinical cases. Names and certain details have been altered to protect client confidentiality.

mental health professionals have little, if any, training on spiritual and religious matters.

Psychologists and professionals in related disciplines are addressing this reality by integrating religion–spirituality into their clinical and counseling practice and other psychological services. Therefore, in this book I focus on issues that have emerged from the study of religion–spirituality in relation to mental health care. For example, how can mental health professionals use the scientific understanding of the connection between spirituality and health—both mental and physical health—to better assist the general population in psychotherapy and other professional psychological services (e.g., consultation, psychological testing)? How can they serve clients with religious–spiritual leanings even if they do not share the same interests or traditions? How can they honor what clients may feel are spiritual truths regarding a sense of purpose, meaning, vocation, forgiveness, and living in community when they may be inclined to frame these motivations in secular terms? How can religious–spiritual practices such as meditation, prayer, and ritual be used to improve psychological functioning? Most of all, how can mental health professionals begin to include clients' religious–spiritual attributes as part of the whole of clients' culture and environment?

DEFINING RELIGION, SPIRITUALITY, AND THE SACRED

Before I go further, it is important to define the terms that are used repeatedly throughout the book. Some people might be confused about the similarities and differences between the words *religion* and *spirituality*. Although there is no universally agreed on definition of these terms, in this book I define *religion* as the organizational and community structure of wisdom traditions that generally include sacred scriptures or religious writings, an articulated doctrine or belief structure that describes the faith community's values and beliefs, and an identified leader or spiritual model to emulate. The major religious traditions of the world are Christianity, Judaism, Buddhism, Hinduism, Islam, Taoism, and Confucianism, with each one having various branches and subbranches. For example, the Christian tradition includes Roman Catholics and various Protestant groups such as Methodists, Presbyterians, and Baptists, whereas the Jewish tradition includes Orthodox, Conservative, Reform, and Reconstructionist. Religion is an organized community and tradition that helps members understand and relate to the sacred through various community and personal rituals, traditions, beliefs, and activities. Some religions are highly centralized and organized (e.g., Roman Catholicism), whereas others are highly decentralized, with little, if any, organization and structure (e.g., Buddhism).

Spirituality, perhaps being much harder to clearly define than *religion*, often is described as being attentive to what is sacred and is connected to a concept, belief, or power greater than oneself. This connection might be to God; religious models such as Jesus, Buddha, or Mohammad; or nature. Pargament (2007) defined spirituality as the search for the sacred. The word *spirituality* comes from the Latin word *spiritus*, which means breath or life force (Hage, 2006). Some define spirituality in relational terms, as involving a transcendent relationship with what they perceive to be sacred or divine (Walsh, 1999). In fact, William James (1902/1936) defined spirituality in relational terms as "the feelings, acts and experiences of individual men in their solitude, as far as they apprehend themselves to stand in relation to whatever they may consider the divine" (p. 32). *Sacred* often refers to what is holy, divine, eternal, or perhaps highly meaningful (Thoresen, 2007). Pargament (2007) defined the sacred as

> concepts of God, the divine, and transcendent reality, as well as other aspects of life that take on divine character and significance by virtue of their association with or representation of divinity . . . at the heart of the sacred lies God, divine beings, or a transcendent reality. (pp. 32–33)

Religion is often defined as part of a well-established spiritual tradition, but many people view themselves as being spiritual without identifying themselves as being religious or associated with any religious tradition or church community. In fact, it is estimated that between 20% and 35% of Americans describe themselves as being "spiritual but not religious" (Fuller, 2001). These people are generally not identified with a particular religious tradition or church yet still experience themselves as spiritual. Whereas many describe themselves as being both religious and spiritual, others describe themselves as being either but not both. Many feel connected to a higher power, to nature, to the sacredness of life, to humanism, and others, but they do not identify with any religious group, community, or faith tradition. Many have been turned off by religious scandals or oppression or resent having self-proclaimed religious leaders tell them what to believe and how to behave. Many have witnessed religious persecution and violence and have rejected organized religion entirely. Others identify with a religious tradition and community but do not consider themselves to be spiritual at all.

WHO SHOULD READ THIS BOOK

This book is based on solid research and the best clinical practice evidence available. Empirical findings and state-of-the-art clinical professionalism are highlighted throughout and many case studies and examples are provided. It was written to be readable, practical, and free of academic jargon and details. Thus, this book should be useful for the typical clinician conducting professional mental health services and for graduate students in various mental health disciplines. This book is meant to give mental health professionals some helpful information and principles they can use to integrate religion–spirituality into their psychological practice in a thoughtful, ethical, and scientifically based manner.

WHAT IS IN THIS BOOK

Integrating religion–spirituality in psychotherapy can take a variety of forms, and the process for accomplishing this is described in a broad way, taking into account clients who are very devout in their beliefs and practices and those who are not. Some books define religion and spirituality so broadly that they lose meaning. Still others focus on spirituality but ignore religion. This book includes both religion and spirituality. Topics such as forgiveness, letting go of anger and resentment, and developing purpose and meaning in life are discussed in addition to more traditional religious–spiritual subjects, such as prayer, meditation, and attending religious services. In chapter 1, I focus on the relationship between religion–spirituality and the psychology field as it is broadly defined. I provide evidence for the notion that although most people are spiritual, religious, or both, most psychologists are not. I also discuss methodological issues and both positive and negative findings related to the effect of religion on health. In chapter 2, I present my list of 13 religious–spiritual tools and provide the definition and philosophical grounding of each one. I offer examples from clinical practice to demonstrate how a religious–spiritual tool might be used with an actual client. In chapter 3, I discuss exactly what to assess while integrating religious–spiritual tools in psychological treatment and how to conduct an assessment, including the use of several instruments that evaluate various dimensions of religion–spirituality. I discuss internal religious–spiritual tools, which can be used for self-improvement, in chapter 4, and in chapter 5, I detail external religious–spiritual tools, which are used in community. Both chapters include plenty of clinical examples. In chapter 6, I focus on ethical issues related to use of religious–spiritual tools in psychological treatment, and I address special issues related to working with seven types of clients, such as clients who are very religious and clients outside of one's religious tradition, in chapter 7. In chapter 8, I explain consultation with religious professionals, an option that is often overlooked among mental health professionals. In chapter 9, I offer best practices in action, including the use of manualized programs and several detailed case studies. Finally, in chapter 10, I suggest next steps for interested readers and where the field may wish to turn its focus in the future.

CONCLUSION

Mental health professionals must always be thoughtful, open, and respectful when examining spiritually integrated psychotherapy. There are many clinical and ethical minefields along the journey. For example, one must always be careful to (a) be respectful of beliefs and traditions different than one's own, (b) practice within one's area of competence and licensure in a professional manner, and (c) enlist the support and expertise of colleagues and other professionals such as clergy as needed. Furthermore, mental health professionals need to be aware of their own beliefs, values, and biases and be careful that all their efforts are based on solid research and state-of-the-art clinical practice to serve the best interests of their clients and others with whom they work.

1

RELIGION–SPIRITUALITY IN THE PRACTICE AND SCIENCE OF PSYCHOLOGY

Why should therapists be at all concerned about religion–spirituality? The vast majority of them were trained to offer high-quality, professional psychological services in a state-of-the-art yet secular manner. If they received essentially no training on this topic during their many years of graduate and postgraduate training, then why should it be of any concern or importance now? Why bother integrating religious–spiritual principles into psychotherapy when one can just refer religious clients to clergy members for these needs? How might integrating psychotherapy with spirituality benefit clients and perhaps even therapists? If they so desire, how can therapists integrate spirituality into their professional practice when they themselves may not be spiritual or religious? These are some of the many important questions often asked among contemporary mental health professionals. I

An outstanding, detailed, and comprehensive review of the topics discussed in the chapter can be found in the *Handbook of Religion and Health* (Koenig, McCullough, & Larson, 2001). Also, please note that the section titled "Mental Health Associations With Spirituality and Religion–Spirituality" in this chapter is based in part on *Faith and Health: Psychological Perspectives* (pp. 240–264), by T. G. Plante and N. Sharma, 2001, New York: Guilford Press. Copyright 2001 by Guilford Press. Adapted with permission.

begin to address these and many more related questions in this chapter and the rest of this book.

MOST AMERICANS ARE RELIGIOUS, SPIRITUAL, OR BOTH

Most people identify with a particular spiritual or religious tradition as well as engage in some kind of religious–spiritual activity on a regular basis with others of like mind (e.g., formalized religious services, religious holiday observances, prayer and meditation groups or sessions, didactic sacred-scripture study groups). High-quality research from a wide variety of reliable and independent sources clearly indicates that religion–spirituality are important parts of most people's lives, with more than 95% of Americans, for example, believing in God and 40% attending religious services at least once per week (e.g., see Gallup, 2002; Gallup & Lindsay, 1999). Furthermore, most people report that religious–spiritual beliefs give them meaning and purpose in life and a framework that helps them cope with the stressors of life (Oman & Thoresen, 2003). In terms of religious affiliations, according to Gallup and Lindsay (1999), most Americans are Christian, with about 85% affiliated with either a Protestant (59%) or a Catholic (26%) denomination. Approximately 2% report being Jewish; Hindu, Muslim, and Buddhists together account for about 3%. Only about 6% of Americans are not affiliated with a religious tradition. The number of Americans who report they are interested in increasing their spiritual growth and development has increased remarkably, from about 50% in the mid-1990s to well over 80% by the beginning of the 21st century (Myers, 2000a). It is clear that religion–spirituality is an important part of most people's lives and that the vast majority of the population is affiliated to some degree with a traditional religious faith community.

These individuals do not check their religiosity or spirituality at the door when they enter the office of a therapist. They may repress or suppress this part of themselves when talking with a therapist or anyone else whom they may perceive to be either not interested in or not supportive of their religious–spiritual traditions, beliefs, or practices, but they are still very much a part of who they are. They are likely to use their religious beliefs, traditions, and community to help them manage their life in health-promoting (and sometimes damaging) ways. Many do not expect to ignore this critical part of their identity when working with a mental health professional.

MOST PSYCHOLOGISTS ARE NOT SPIRITUAL OR RELIGIOUS

Unlike the general population, most psychologists would not describe themselves as being spiritual or religious (Bilgrave & Deluty, 2002; Delaney,

Miller, & Bisono, 2007; D. P. Smith & Orlinsky, 2004). In fact, "relative to the general population, psychologists [are] more than twice as likely to claim no religion, three times more likely to describe religion as unimportant in their lives, and five times more likely to deny belief in God" (Delaney et al., 2007, p. 542). In one seminal study, only approximately 33% of psychologists were affiliated with any religious faith tradition, 72% reported any belief in God or a higher power, and 51% reported that religion is not important to them (Shafranske, 2000). Curiously, more recent research by Delaney et al. (2007) found that 84% of a psychologist sample had a religious preference and 56% were members of some religious congregation—higher but still far less than in the general population. Moreover, half of the psychologists in their study reported that religion was not important in their lives. Remarkably, 68% of all current training directors in clinical psychology internship training programs report that they "*never* foresee religious/spiritual training being offered in their program" (Russell & Yarhouse, 2006, p. 434). This finding is in sharp contrast to the fact that two thirds of medical schools do offer religious–spiritual diversity training (Puchalski, 2004) as well as a model curriculum to share with others (Larson, Lu, & Swyers, 1996).

It is curious that psychologists are so out of step with the general population in this regard. Perhaps the types of people who choose to pursue a career as a psychologist tend to be more secular and less religious or spiritual than the average person seeking their services. Furthermore, most psychologists have received essentially no training in how best to work with religious–spiritual clients or related themes during the course of their professional training. In fact, two thirds of psychologists report that they do not feel competent to integrate religious–spiritual matters into their clinical work (Shafranske & Malony, 1990).

Therefore, a significant disconnection exists between psychologists, who generally are nonreligious and nonspiritual, and their clients, who generally are religious and spiritual and are seeking professional mental health services about how best to live their lives and cope with various stressful and challenging life events. If psychologists generally have neither the training nor the inclination to address religious–spiritual issues in their work, their clients are not likely to bring up these matters in the course of their treatment.

Although many of the most prominent psychology forefathers, such as William James, were keenly interested in the relationship between psychology and religion (e.g., see Allport, 1950; James, 1890/1936, 1902; Jung, 1938), historically most of professional and scientific psychology has avoided the connection between these two fields. For example, Collins (1977) stated, "Psychology has never shown much interest in religion . . . apart from a few classic studies. The topic of religious behavior has been largely ignored by psychological writers" (p. 95). Perhaps many professionals have been influenced by the strong words and perspectives of such leaders in the field as Sigmund Freud, B. F. Skinner, John Watson, and Albert Ellis, who found little, if any, value in the study, practice, or interest in religion (e.g., see Ellis, 1971; Freud, 1927/1961; Watson, 1924/1983). For example, in *Future of an Illusion,* Freud stated that religious views "are illusions, fulfillments of the oldest, strongest and most urgent wishes of mankind" (Freud, 1927/1961, p. 30) and referred to religion as an "obsessional neurosis" (Freud, 1927/1961, p. 43). Curiously, Freud's father was reported to be a highly religious and devout Jew. Psychology has had a long history of being neglectful if not outright antagonistic toward issues related to religion–spirituality, often considering persons who are spiritual or religious deluded, or at least not as psychologically healthy and advanced as they could be (e.g., see Ellis, 1971; Freud, 1927/1961). Although Freud called religious interest "neurotic," Watson referred to religion as a "bulwark of medievalism" (Watson, 1924/1983, p. 1). Freud, Watson, Ellis, Skinner, and other leading figures in psychology did not mince their words. They strongly suggested that religious interest was a sign of pathology and not of health. Those who tended to agree and follow these psychology models tended to go along with their leader's point of view.

In addition, psychology in the 20th century prided itself on being a serious science and perhaps tended to shy away from all things religious or spiritual in an effort to maximize and emphasize the rigorous scientific approach to both research and clinical practice. Psychology has tried over the years to be a "hard science" in the way physics, chemistry, and biology are viewed. Because so much of religion–spirituality addresses issues that are not readily observable or measurable, the field has avoided religious and spiritual constructs in an effort to be taken seriously as a highly rigorous, scientific, and respected discipline (Ellis, 1971; Richards & Bergin, 2005; Watson, 1924/1983). Psychology has had to prove itself to be a serious, scientific, and empirical field, and being more closely aligned with hard science and empiricism helped to develop the acceptance and prestige it needed to succeed as an independent discipline and profession.

These dynamics have not entirely been erased from professional psychology even now. The push to maintain a more scientific and secular profession still dominates much of the professional psychological scene. For example, partially as an effort to more fully embrace the science of psychology, the American Psychological Society was formed in 1988, with many initial members breaking away from the American Psychological Association (APA), which they perceived to be too clinical, too practitioner oriented, and too "soft" science oriented. The recent efforts to embrace empirically supported and manualized treatments (Task Force on Promotion and Dissemination of Psychological Procedures, 1995) as well as more rigorous scientific approaches to mental health services such as psychotherapy are further evidence for the current emphasis on the science of contemporary clinical practice, which often has no room for religious–spiritual matters. Interventions that have some connection to religious–spiritual issues are often secularized to be more acceptable to the more scientific professional community. The emergence of positive psychology constructs such as the importance of forgiveness, gratitude, and compassion (Seligman, Steen, Park, & Peterson, 2005) and the remarkable interest in mindfulness-based stress reduction recently embraced by professional psychology (Kabit-Zinn, 1990, 1994, 2003; Shapiro & Walsh, 2007; R. Walsh & Shapiro, 2006) are excellent examples.

Historically, those psychologists who were religious–spiritual and may have wanted to integrate their faith traditions and spirituality into their professional work generally needed to keep their interests quiet; they certainly would not have professed their religious beliefs during the more vulnerable years of graduate and postgraduate training. In fact, Kenneth Pargament (2007) referred to the "whisper" that psychology professionals interested in religion–spirituality felt compelled to engage in to keep these interests from their colleagues. Academics working in this area often delayed doing so until after tenure or promotion to full professor was awarded and secured (Pargament, 2007). Those merely interested in psychology and spirituality integration, regardless of personal faith beliefs or traditions, often were counseled to leave the field and pursue philosophy or religious studies. The rigorous empirical science of psychology offered no place for religion–spirituality. However, several training programs often associated with evangelical Protestant churches did emerge that freely embraced and nurtured the integration of religion and psychology (e.g., Fuller Theological Seminary; American Psychological Association, 2008).

Most problematic, and perhaps most destructive, is that nonreligious psychologists working with religious or spiritual clients too often interpreted their clients' attachment to religion–spirituality as pathology and delusion— not evidence of a psychologically developed or sophisticated level of functioning (Ellis, 1971; Freud, 1927/1961). This attachment was often viewed as part of their problem and certainly not part of the solution.

"THE TIMES THEY ARE A-CHANGIN' "

This popular line from the Bob Dylan 1960s folk song was not referring to the relationship between religion and psychology, but it could have been. Toward the end of the 20th century and into the 21st century, psychology (as well as science in general) moved to embrace religion–spirituality and began to use rigorous scientific methods, such as double-blind randomized clinical trials, to examine important questions such as the influence of religious–spiritual behaviors and beliefs on both mental and physical health outcomes (Jones, 1994; Koenig, McCullough, & Larson, 2001; Pargament, 1997; Plante & Sharma, 2001; Plante & Thoresen, 2007). Somehow in recent years, integration of spirituality, religion, psychology, and science has been legitimized and has received significant grant funding and both professional and public support (Hage, 2006; Hartz, 2005; Koenig, 1997; Koenig et al., 2001). Many professional organizations, such as the Society of Behavioral Medicine, have developed special interest groups that focus on religion and health integration. Large organizations, such as the John Templeton Foundation, the Lilly Foundation, and the Fetzer Institute, as well as major government granting agencies, such as the National Institutes of Health (NIH), have funded large-scale projects in this area. Much professional as well as popular attention has focused on the physical and mental health benefits of religion–spirituality.

Professional psychological organizations such as APA have also acknowledged and embraced these changes. In fact, the 1999 National Multicultural Conference and Summit sponsored by APA concluded that "spirituality is a necessary condition for a psychology of human existence" and that "people are cultural and spiritual beings" (Sue, Bingham, Porche-Burke, & Vasquez, 1999, p. 1065). During the late 1990s into the 2000s, APA published about a dozen books on psychology and religion, whereas previously they had none available. In fact, APA asked me to write this book. They approached me; I did not approach them. Thus, the relationship between psychology and religion has come a long way. The times they are a-changin' indeed!

Taken together, most of the recent high-quality research in this area supports the connection between faith and health (Koenig et al., 2001; Pargament, 1997; Plante & Sherman, 2001; Plante & Thoresen, 2007; Richards & Bergin, 2005). People who engage in a religious–spiritual tradition tend to be healthier and happier, maintain better habits, and have more social support than those who do not engage in religious–spiritual activities, interests, and beliefs. Although religion certainly can be highly destructive and gets much press attention when it is so, the vast majority of research supports the notion that religion is good for both mental and physical health. In fact, a prestigious NIH panel concluded that "persuasive" evidence exists, on the basis of highly rigorous scientific criteria, that engaging in religious and spiritual activities is associated with lower all-cause mortality, with overall results suggesting a 25% to 30% reduction in risk of death. Remarkably, on average, religious–spiritual people can expect to live about 7 years longer than nonreligious and nonspiritual people (African Americans can expect to live 14 years longer; see W. R. Miller & Thoresen, 2003).

Given these and other research findings, and because the vast majority of Americans (and others around the globe) consider themselves to be spiritual, religious, or both (Gallup & Jones, 2000; Myers, 2000a), many have been demanding that health professionals (including mental health professionals) respect, acknowledge, and integrate religious–spiritual principles into their professional work (Frick, Riedner, Fegg, Hauf, & Borasio, 2006; McNichols & Feldman, 2007; Shafranske, 2001; Sperry & Shafranske, 2005). In fact, two thirds of Americans prefer to work with a mental health professional who holds religious–spiritual beliefs and values when they are seeking services about serious problems (Lehman, 1993). In addition, most psycho-therapy clients (55%) prefer to discuss religious–spiritual issues in therapy (Rose, Westfeld, & Ansley, 2001). Lindgren and Coursey (1995) reported that two thirds of adults with serious mental illness wished to discuss spiritual issues in psychotherapy, but only a fraction felt comfortable doing so). Psychology's new focus on positive psychology also underscores the desire for a more friendly relationship between religion and psychology (Lopez & Snyder, 2003; Seligman et al., 2005; Snyder & Lopez, 2007).

Although both research and clinical practice now support many benefits to the integration of psychology and religion, much research, training, and practice is still vitally needed. In fact, many vocal critics have adamantly called for less (not more) integration, saying that psychology (as well as science and medicine) should steer clear of anything spiritual or religious. Columbia University psychologist Richard Sloan and colleagues are prime examples of those who believe there are many ethical and scientific reasons why psychology should stay far away from anything to do with religion–spirituality. They stated that psychology and science have no business getting involved with religion–spirituality and that to do so is ethically, professionally, and scientifically dangerous (Sloan, Bagiella, & Powell, 1999, 2001). These critics certainly have a point: Religion–spirituality can evoke strong feelings, beliefs, and biases among professionals and the general population. Psychologists with very strong views are not immune to bias, discrimination, and trying to forward a particular agenda that may not be supported by research and clinical practice. Furthermore, it is critically important that psychologists behave in a manner consistent with both the ethical and the legal guidelines of their professional boards and license. They must maintain competence, responsibility, respect, integrity, and so forth, and these important values can be challenged when integrating spirituality, religion, and professional psychological practice. This is especially true because ethical guidelines now include religion among many diversity issues that psychologists must be suitably trained and experienced in when providing professional services. Specifically, APA's (2002) "Ethical Principles of Psychologists and Code of Conduct" (hereinafter Ethics Code) indicates that

> Psychologists are aware of and respect cultural, individual, and role differences, including those based on age, gender, gender identity, race, ethnicity, culture, national origin, religion, sexual orientation, disability, language, and socioeconomic status and consider these factors when working with members of such groups. (p. 1064)

Thus, being "aware of and respect[ful]" of religious issues is now mandated by the Ethics Code (see chap. 6 of this volume for a more detailed discussion of ethical issues).

As discussed earlier, although most people in the general population are religious, spiritual, or both, most psychologists are not. Whereas most clients bring their spiritual and religious beliefs, practices, and traditions into the psychotherapy office, most psychologists do not. Although psychology and religion have often had a tumultuous and antagonistic relationship, the times have changed in recent years such that a rapprochement has occurred. The great religious and spiritual wisdom traditions have had hundreds and thousands of years to reflect on the great issues and conflicts that we struggle with as humans. Perhaps psychology has something to learn from these great traditions. Perhaps there are principles and both religious and spiritual tools that are available to psychologists in their psychotherapeutic work with clients. Fortunately, high-quality research is available to inform psychologists of how best to use the wisdom of religion–spirituality in the practice of contemporary clinical psychology.

In the next section, I highlight the research evidence for the benefits of religion–spirituality with mental health outcomes. The psychology profession cannot suggest integrating spirituality, religion, and psychotherapy unless there is clearly adequate scientific evidence that doing so is a worthwhile endeavor. Although many books and articles on this topic discuss these research findings in detail (e.g., see Koenig et al., 2001; Masters, Spielmans, & Goodson, 2006; Paloutzian & Park, 2005; Plante & Sherman, 2001; Plante & Thoresen, 2007), I highlight the big picture to help readers better understand the empirical support for the relationship between religious–spiritual engagement and mental health outcomes. Once the supporting research evidence is revealed, one can then look at what the religious and spiritual traditions might offer the mental health professional and the tools and strategies to integrate them into contemporary clinical practice if desired and when appropriate.

METHODOLOGICAL ISSUES IN RESEARCH ON RELIGION AND HEALTH

Before reviewing the research support for the association of spiritual–religious engagement with mental health outcomes, a few comments on methodological considerations are necessary. It can often be very challenging to conduct ethically the kinds of true experimental studies that are critically needed to answer important treatment questions in psychology. For example, one simply cannot randomly assign humans to different religious and control groups and then evaluate mental and physical health outcomes over time on the basis of group assignment. One also cannot force humans to engage in randomly assigned religious activities such as prayer, meditation, religious service attendance, and so forth. Therefore, most research in this area tends to be correlational in nature. In other words, it usually focuses on questions that ask whether people who are engaged in particular religious–spiritual practices tend to have better mental and physical health outcomes than others.

As readers know from introductory classes in psychology and statistics, correlation does not imply causation. Therefore, although compelling correlations or associations may exist between religious–spiritual behaviors and positive mental and physical health functioning, those in the psychology profession and those in society as a whole cannot infer that religious–spiritual engagement caused these positive outcomes. Although correlational research is certainly valuable, and often the best that can be hoped for in so many areas of research, the approach has limitations when trying to answer questions on causation. The real issue is whether engaging in religious–spiritual activities and behavior *causes* better mental and physical health. Yet the best one can do more often than not is to examine the relationship or association between religious–spiritual variables and mental and physical health.

However, true experimental methodologies using, for example, randomized double-blind clinical trials, have been used to a limited degree in this area of research during recent years (Masters et al., 2006). For example, a number of distance prayer studies have been conducted to determine whether people might receive mental and physical health benefits if they are prayed for by others who are part of the research study. Although true experimental designs using random assignment to experimental and control conditions do exist in the spirituality, religion, and health research area, these studies are very few when compared with the numerous correlational or quasi-experimental designs typically conducted.

Research from a variety of independent sources suggests that those who are actively engaged in religious–spiritual behavior and practice basically live a healthier lifestyle, and thus they may minimize the many risks associated with the leading causes of death (e.g., see Barbour, 2000; T. D. Hill, Ellison, Burdette, & Musick, 2007; Koenig et al., 2001; Oman & Thoresen, 2005; Powell, Shahabi, & Thoresen, 2003). They tend to have fewer sexual partners and practice safe sex, exercise more, eat better, not smoke cigarettes, drink less alcohol, and avoid illegal drugs; and they are at lower risk of both murder and suicide. Religious–spiritual people simply tend not to engage in the types of health damaging behaviors that place them at higher risk of life-threatening disease or risky behaviors that could kill them. For example, Mormons and conservative Protestant groups such as Seventh-Day Adventists tend to have lower cancer rates (e.g., see Dwyer, Clarke, & Miller, 1990; Koenig et al., 2001; Phillips & Snowden, 1983). These groups tend to avoid many of the common health behaviors that can be so damaging to so many, such as alcohol and drug abuse as well as cigarette smoking (T. D. Hill et al., 2007; Koenig et al., 2001).

In essence, *cleaner living* is associated with lowering the risk of premature death in a variety of ways for a variety of people. Whatever encourages individuals to avoid unhealthful behaviors and engage in healthful behaviors, from wearing seat belts to minimizing their number of sexual partners, all of these factors work together to create a healthier lifestyle and less vulnerability to the many contemporary causes of disease and death. If people engage in these better behaviors because of their religious beliefs and practices or other reasons, positive health outcomes can be expected (T. D. Hill et al., 2007; Hummer, Rogers, Nam, & Ellison, 1999; McCullough, Hoyt, Larson, Koenig, & Thoresen, 2000).

MENTAL HEALTH ASSOCIATIONS WITH RELIGION–SPIRITUALITY

A careful review of the many research studies that have focused on the mental health associations with religious–spiritual involvement clearly indicates that those who are engaged in religious–spiritual activities have better mental health functioning than those who do not (Hackney & Sanders, 2003; Koenig et al., 2001; Marks, 2005; Plante & Sharma, 2001). Research suggests that people who are involved with religious–spiritual activities tend to be less anxious, depressed, and stressed; have a better sense of well-being and self-esteem; and cope better with life stressors. Furthermore, associations suggest they are less likely to experience alcohol and other substance abuse problems, eating disorders, divorce, and unsafe sexual practices, and are less likely to attempt suicide, commit homicide, or engage in other criminal behavior. In a nutshell, religious–spiritual people tend to have better mental health and do not seem to have the kinds of behavioral problems that plague so many people. Because they generally live a healthier lifestyle, get social support, and usually do not engage in unhealthful behavior, they have a higher level of mental health, including mood and general affect control, than do others.

Although it is beyond the scope of this chapter to review all of the research in this area, I do comment on research findings in the major categories of mental health functioning, such as well-being, depression, anxiety, and substance abuse. Before doing so, it is important to differentiate between intrinsic and extrinsic religiosity. *Intrinsic* religiosity refers to personal beliefs, prayer, meditation, and other religious behavior done privately, whereas *extrinsic* religiosity refers to public and often community behaviors, such as attending worship services or participating in social justice projects sponsored by a religious community. It is important to state these differences here because some of the research studies have focused on either intrinsic or extrinsic religiosity and some have examined both.

Well-Being

Well-being is a broad concept that includes general satisfaction with life and sense of peace and comfort with one's place or position in the world. It includes a sense of congruence with expected and achieved goals in life

(Diener, Suh, Lucas, & Smith, 1999; Levin & Taylor, 1998), positive self-esteem (Wilcock et al., 1998), and prosocial values and behaviors (Donahue & Benson, 1995). The vast majority of research studies examining the relationship between religious–spiritual involvement and well-being have found a close association between these constructs (Koenig, 1995; Koenig et al., 2001; Lee & Newberg, 2005; Levin, 1997). For example, in a study using the Santa Clara Strength of Religious Faith Questionnaire, Plante and Boccaccini (1997) found that college students with a strong sense of religious faith tended to have higher levels of self-esteem and adaptive coping, to be more hopeful, and to have less interpersonal sensitivity. Koenig et al. (2001) reviewed 100 studies that examined the relationship between religious–spiritual engagement and well-being and found that 79% showed significant associations between religious–spiritual measures and positive well-being outcomes, such as greater happiness and life satisfaction, better mood, and improved morale. These positive associations occurred at all age levels and for both genders. More recent reviews have found similar results (e.g., see Lee & Newberg, 2005; Marks, 2005). Most of the research in this area was conducted with either Christian or Jewish groups, and studies were cross-sectional rather than longitudinal, thereby measuring research responses at one point in time rather than following people over the course of many years.

Many theories exist about why there appears to be a positive relationship between religious–spiritual engagement and well-being. It may be due to the impact of faith on emotional functioning associated with increased forgiveness and reduced guilt, which may contribute to feelings of well-being (Ellison, 1998; Marks, 2005). Research also indicates that social involvement through religious congregational services and activities likely enhances both prosocial and adaptive behavior and thus may elevate mood, lessen distress, and enhance well-being (Donahue & Benson, 1995). For example, research has shown that church involvement and activities within the African American community have been associated with coping mechanisms that promote a sense of well-being (Blaine & Croker, 1995; Krause, 2003b; Marks, 2005). Most religious organizations function as a source of social support for participants. Educational support is also provided by teaching the spiritual community about ethics, values, and both mental and physical health issues, such as substance abuse, violence prevention, enhancing healthful behaviors, and avoiding unhealthful behaviors—all of which may increase well-being (Donahue & Benson, 1995; Marks, 2005). Religious–spiritual organizations also provide emotional–social support by bringing together networks of people with similar values and interests as well as maintaining connectedness for individuals in the congregational community (Blaine & Croker, 1995; Krause, 2003b). This support may be especially useful for those who live alone or are often isolated from others. Some of the positive effects of religion–spirituality on well-being include increased self-esteem and positive life outlooks as well as social networks that may lessen the detrimental effects of stressful life events (Lee & Newberg, 2005; Levin, 1994, 1997). Overall, engaging in religious–spiritual interests, practices, and behavior tends to be associated with higher levels of peace, calm, and well-being.

Depression and Suicidal Ideation

So many of the clients therapists serve present with perceived stressors that result in various forms of depression. Furthermore, many people who are depressed never seek the services of a mental health professional and thus often suffer without adequate help. Untreated depression can easily lead to numerous additional associated problems, such as substance abuse, child abuse and neglect, suicidal and homicidal behavior, and a host of both psychological and physical illnesses.

Research on the relationship between religious–spiritual engagement and depression indicates that religiosity is usually associated with less depression (Cosar, Kocal, Arikan, & Isik, 1997; Koenig et al., 2001; Marks, 2005; Plante & Sharma, 2001), with most studies in this area focusing on one of three issues: (a) religiosity–spirituality decreasing vulnerability to depression, (b) religion–spirituality as a productive coping strategy for managing depression, and (c) the advantages of religious and spiritual beliefs and practices in treating clinical depression. In all of these research categories, religious–spiritual interests and practices seem to be associated with fewer depressive symptoms. In a review of more than 100 published research studies, including 22 prospective cohort investigations, Koenig et al. (2001) found that religiously and spiritually oriented people were less likely to experience depression or were better able to cope with depression-inducing stressors than were others. However, they did find that Jews were actually at elevated risk of depressive symptoms across a large number of high-quality, well-designed studies. Furthermore, their review found that religious activities within structured faith communities were more closely associated with less depression than was private religious expression. Finally, they found that studies that focused on religious–spiritual practices and behavior were associated with better coping with stressful life events, which may reduce depressive symptoms at least as well as secular psychotherapy. Remarkably, a 10-year longitudinal study (L. Miller, Warner, Wickramaratne, & Weissman, 1997) found that maternal religiosity tended to act as a protective agent against depressive symptoms in children, thus suggesting a generational influence.

As a possible productive coping mechanism, religious–spiritual faith and practices may help the grieving process of those who have experienced a severe loss, who also are at high risk of depression. For example, parents who regularly attended church prior to the death of their infant were less likely to report depressive symptoms over time than those who did not (Thearle, Vance, Najman, Embelton, & Foster, 1995). Religious– spiritual involvement and coping have been associated with less susceptibility to depression among caregivers responsible for terminally ill family members (Harrington, Lackey, & Gates, 1996; Kazanigian, 1997; Mickley, Pargament, Brant, & Hipp, 1998; Reese & Brown, 1997). Mickley et al. (1998) found that caregivers who interpreted their work in terms of positive religious coping tended to display fewer depressive symptoms. Also, the acceptance of death and the decrease of depression after bereavement among older people were closely associated with religious–spiritual beliefs (Hinton, 1999; Koenig, 2007). This association also has been found among terminally ill cancer patients (e.g., see McClain, Rosenfeld, & Breitbart, 2003). Therefore, research suggests spiritual–religious interests and practice are associated with people either avoiding or coping better with depressive symptoms.

One of the most concerning outcomes of depression is suicide. Suicidal ideation and behavior must also be assessed in mental health clients, especially in those who appear to be depressed. A review of all of the research studies that have examined suicidal ideation and behavior and religious–spiritual involvement clearly suggests that religious–spiritual engagement is associated with a lower risk of suicide (Koenig et al., 2001), with 84% of such studies supporting this association. Certainly, religiously oriented persons tend to be less tolerant of suicide as an option and have more moral objections to this behavior (e.g., see Siegrist, 1996). In more recent research, suicidal behavior and ideation were not associated with membership in any particular faith or spiritual tradition but were more likely associated with the degree of involvement with religious–spiritual communities, activities, and practices (Koenig et al., 2001). Contrary to common beliefs based on much older research reports, Roman Catholics, for example, are not at lower risk of suicidal ideation and behavior relative to non–Roman Catholics once level of religious engagement is taken into consideration (Wasserman & Stack, 1993). Thus, research indicates that, in general, a lower probability of suicide among those who actively engage in religious–spiritual traditions, practices, and communities.

Anxiety

So many of the clients with whom we work experience anxiety in all its various forms. From panic attacks to phobias, to general anxiousness, anxiety troubles many people. Furthermore, like depression, anxiety can lead to problematic behaviors that can result in comorbid problems such as substance abuse, sleeping disorders, cardiovascular disease such as hypertension, and a long list of additional mental and physical health troubles.

Religion–spirituality, most especially intrinsic religiosity (e.g., personal prayer, meditation, beliefs, reading) and spiritual practices, have been associated with fewer incidences of anxiety symptoms (Ita, 1995; Kaplan, Marks, & Mertens, 1997; Koenig et al., 2001; Marks, 2005; Shreve-Neiger & Edelstein, 2004). Furthermore, positive mental health outcomes among patients with anxiety have been associated with individuals who are intrinsically religious, individuals who engage in religious–spiritual coping activities, and both religious and nonreligious individuals participating in religion- or spirituality-based treatment approaches (Barr, 1995; Jahangir, 1995). Religious–spiritual engagement seems most closely associated with those who experience serious stressors often associated with dependency, loss of control, and end-of-life concerns (Koenig, 2007; Koenig et al., 2001; McNichols & Feldman, 2007).

Intrinsic religiosity and spiritual practices have been associated with low levels of anxiety in many populations (Lotufo-Neto, 1996; Mickley, Carson, & Soeken, 1995; Richards & Bergin, 2004) and low levels of death anxiety among those who are religious (Clements, 1998; Koenig, 2007; Richards & Bergin, 2004). Intrinsic religiosity also has been found to be negatively associated with neurotic guilt (Richards & Bergin, 2004). In a proposed causal path model, Ita (1995) attributed the negative correlation between age and death anxiety to the increasing importance of religion–spirituality for individuals through the life span.

Religious–spiritual involvement among people experiencing significant stressors has been associated with lower levels of anxiety (Holtz, 1998; Lee & Newberg, 2005). For example, high strength of religious faith was associated with less anxiety among substance abusers (Plante, Yancey, Sherman, Guertin, & Pardini, 1999; Stewart, 2001). Thus, those who are engaged in religious–spiritual practices may experience lower levels of anxiety and cope better with the anxiety they do experience. Furthermore, many of the religious–spiritual practices that people engage in, such as meditation and prayer, are rather similar to the kinds of secular relaxation training techniques mental health professionals offer to their clients. Mindfulness-based stress reduction, for example, has become a very well accepted and productive spiritually based tool to help manage stress and anxiety even among secular populations (e.g., see Shapiro & Walsh, 2007).

Substance Abuse

Substance abuse, such as alcoholism, is also a common problem brought to the attention of mental health professionals by their clients. It is so pervasive that most mental health professionals who evaluate and treat substance abuse ultimately specialize in this area (Norcross, Sayette, & Mayne, 2008) and are often sought after by clients and other professionals alike for this important specialty. Sadly, the Centers for Disease Control and Prevention (CDC; 2000, 2001, 2004) estimated that about 32% of young people who drink are binge drinkers and 15% are heavy drinkers. Furthermore, half of car accidents are alcohol related (CDC, 2000, 2001, 2004). Clearly, substance abuse is a significant problem for many, and this problem too often leads to tragic consequences for the abuser, his or her family, and others in general.

A review of more than 100 research studies that investigated possible links between religiosity–spirituality and substance abuse found that religious–spiritual persons are generally less likely than others to be troubled by substance abuse problems (Koenig et al., 2001; Lee & Newberg, 2005). The more religious–spiritual someone is, the less likely they are to experience substance abuse problems and the better they tend to maintain sobriety if they do. Thus, there is a strong negative correlation between religious–spiritual engagement and substance abuse (Michalak, Trocki, & Bond, 2007). Furthermore, the popular Alcoholics Anonymous (AA) movement is characterized by a very spiritually based 12-step program and ongoing community fellowship. For example, half of the 12 steps of AA specifically refer to God or a higher power (e.g., Step 3: Make a decision to turn our will and our lives over to the care of God as we understand Him; Alcoholics Anonymous World Services, 1977, p. 6).

Numerous research studies have examined the association between religiosity–spirituality and alcoholism, as well as the effectiveness of spiritual interventions in the substance abuse recovery process. As mentioned, a close reading of the popular 12 steps of AA clearly illustrates the spiritual nature of the 12-step program. Research indicates religion in general is likely to play an important role in the decision to use or not use alcohol (Leigh, Bowen, & Marlatt, 2005; Michalak et al., 2007; Rajarathinam & Muthusamy, 1996), whereas intrinsic religiosity is a predictor of low levels of substance use or abuse (Fischer & Richards, 1998). Furthermore, reliable predictors of substance abuse include a feeling of disconnectedness with one's religion (Gillis & Mubbhashar, 1995; Leigh et al., 2005) as well as disconnection with one's specific religious tradition (Peele, 1997). In addition, individuals who are substance users or abusers generally have low levels of religious involvement (Michalak et al., 2007; W. R. Miller, 1998; Stewart, 2001).

Kendler, Gardner, and Prescott (1997) found religiosity to be significantly and negatively associated with substance abuse and a lifetime history of alcoholism. Though religious beliefs influenced a person's tendency to use substances, one's religious devotion or spirituality influenced one's ability to quit or maintain low levels of substance use (Kendler et al., 1997; W. R. Miller, 1998). Similarly, higher levels of religiosity–spirituality among individuals recovering from substance abuse was also associated with enhanced coping, greater resilience to stress, an optimistic life orientation, greater perceived social support, and lower levels of anxiety among inpatient and halfway house substance abusers (Pardini, Plante, & Sherman, 2000). Thus, spiritually and religiously minded persons are less likely to develop substance abuse problems and more likely to cope better with these problems when they do develop.

Other Mental Health Problems

Most of the research on the association between religious–spiritual engagement and mental health has focused on well-being, depression, anxiety, and substance abuse. This focus likely reflects the fact that these are the most typical problems clients experience when they decide to meet with a mental health professional for treatment. However, a variety of studies have focused on other specific mental health problems and disorders that should be at least mentioned here, for example, schizophrenia and other psychotic disorders, personality disorders, and eating disorders.

Schizophrenia and Psychotic Disorders

Overall, religious–spiritual coping styles have been shown to be positively associated with managing schizophrenia (Koenig et al., 2001; Wahass & Kent, 1997). For individuals who have the same religious affiliation as their families, religion can serve as a unifying force for all parties through symbols and traditional rituals that reflect the family's value system (J. Walsh, 1995). For the individual with schizophrenia, religious worship with the family or with a congregation may serve to integrate the person into a community during times when he or she is feeling isolated. For the family, religious worship with the schizophrenic family member may serve as a means of feeling connected with the individual who has lost touch with reality. Thus, a review of the professional literature on schizophrenia and religion finds that religious–spiritual practice can provide a powerful source of hope and comfort for both patients and their families struggling with the challenges of this serious mental illness (Koenig et al., 2001; Ng, 2007). Furthermore, although religious themes and delusions are often found among those with psychotic illnesses, there is no compelling evidence to suggest that religious or spiritually minded persons are at higher risk of developing these psychiatric conditions (Koenig et al., 2001).

Personality Disorders

Most of the research on religious–spiritual involvement and personality disorders tends to focus on borderline personality. In relation to treating patients with borderline personality disorder, Vitz and Mango (1997) discussed the role of psychodynamics and religious aspects of forgiveness, emphasizing how repentance and forgiveness cannot be offered through psychotherapy but rather through religious and morality-based treatment approaches. Marsha Linehan's very popular dialectical behavior therapy (DBT) approach for borderline and other personality disorders and Steven Hayes's acceptance and commitment therapy both include spiritually based interventions such as mindfulness and meditation. (Hayes, 2005; Hayes, Follette, & Linehan, 2004; Linehan, 1993). Other research on personality disorders has had results similar to the research on schizophrenia and borderline personality, suggesting that religious–spiritual engagement can help clients cope with many of the distressing aspects of personality dysfunction (Plante & Sharma, 2001).

Eating Disorders

Religion–spirituality have also been examined with respect to the prevention, etiology, and treatment of eating disorders (e.g., see Jacobs-Pilipski, Winzelberg, Wilfley, Bryson, & Taylor, 2005; Marsden, Karagianni, & Morgan, 2007). In assessing possible causal factors of eating disorders, McCourt and Waller (1996) discussed how religion may have an impact on eating disorders or disturbed eating attitudes. Some religious–spiritual feelings common among individuals with eating disorders include spiritual unworthiness, shame, fear of abandonment by God, and negative perceptions of God (Richards et al., 1997). Spiritual interventions have been found to be helpful with obese, overweight (N. Davis, Clance, & Gailis, 1999), and anorexic individuals (Banks, 1997; Garret, 1996) as well as those at risk of developing an eating disorder (Jacobs-Pilipski et al., 2005). Obese women who attended meetings for Overeaters Anonymous, which focuses on abstinence and spirituality as emphasized in AA, reported success rates that were significantly associated with the importance they attributed to abstinence and spirituality (David et al., 1999).

Overall, research has found that religious–spiritual engagement can be a useful adjunct treatment approach for many who experience major psychopathology. It can also help family members cope with having a loved one with a significant mental health disorder.

Summary of Mental Health Benefits and Some Precautions

From thousands of studies, there is much evidence that religious–spiritual engagement is associated with better mental health and coping. Koenig et al. (2001) and Thoresen (2007) articulated these results, which include the following positive mental health associations: more well-being, happiness, hope, purpose, meaning, self-esteem, marital satisfaction, social support, and coping with grief; less depression, anxiety, suicidal ideation, substance abuse, delinquency, loneliness, and psychotic tendency.

However, it is important to be cautious about these findings. First, as mentioned earlier, the vast majority of these studies used correlational research methodologies. Thus, religious–spiritual engagement may be associated with improved mental health outcomes, but whether they cause them is unknown. A host of other variables may mediate the relationship between religious–spiritual involvement and positive mental health functioning. Certainly these other variables are often controlled in high-quality research, and a number of studies have successfully accounted for many of them. Yet, until true experimental designs are conducted with random assignment to control and experimental conditions, research results must be viewed very carefully.

Second, as in many areas of research, negative findings are often never published. Many studies have been successfully completed only to remain unpublished because expected findings did not surface. It is unclear how many high-quality research studies in this area have been conducted only to be forever lost or forgotten in a file cabinet somewhere. Finally, the vast majority of research studies have used self-report measures that have potential bias and demand characteristics favorable to religious–spiritual influences and beliefs. Of course, most studies are cross-sectional in nature as well. This further precludes clear and convincing support for the relationship between religious–spiritual involvement and mental health functioning. However, even with these precautions, one cannot ignore the vast majority of studies that suggest a positive relationship exists between religious–spiritual engagement and positive mental health functioning. The jury may still be out, but it seems to be leaning in one direction.

NEGATIVE OUTCOMES IN RELIGION–HEALTH STUDIES

As with most things, there is a downside to religion–spirituality that should not be ignored. Religious involvement can be highly destructive to self, others, and the community (Altemeyer, 1988; Kernberg, 2003; Pargament, 1997, 2007; Trenholm, Trent, & Compton, 1998). The events of 9/11 are an excellent example. Tragically, religion has been used to wage war, oppress women, murder people who do not share the same religious beliefs and practices, and instill guilt, depression, and anxiety in many. Furthermore, those who do not belong to the dominant religion in their community often experience prejudice, hardships, stress, and a variety of obstacles that are harmful to their well-being (e.g., see Walls & Williams, 2004). Also, religious leaders can use their power, influence, and control over their congregations for abusive purposes (e.g., see Plante, 2003; Plante & Aldridge, 2005).

Religiosity is also associated with harmful health practices such as rejection of much-needed medical and psychiatric care, with devastating consequences (Pargament, 1997, 2007). For example, research has found that religious African American women may delay seeking medical help for breast cancer, relying instead on religious coping behavior such as prayer (Mitchell, Lannin, Mathews, & Swanson, 2002). In addition, a judging and wrathful image of God relative to a more loving and forgiving notion of God has been associated with many psychological and physical health problems, including problems coping with HIV/AIDS (Kremer & Ironson, 2007). Religion can support and enflame in-group/out-group conflicts as well (Kernberg, 2003).

Pargament (1997, 2007) articulated a comprehensive theory that religious coping can be both helpful and hurtful to self and others. For example, he suggested that negative religious coping can include discontent with one's religious tradition and with God; negative religious reframing such that God is wrathful, judging, and punishing; and maladaptive or destructive religious rituals and practices in response to significant stress. Therefore, although religious–spiritual engagement appears to be generally associated with positive mental health outcomes, research also clearly suggests it can also be associated with negative mental and physical health outcomes. It can be both highly productive and highly destructive.

CONCLUSION

Psychology has evolved and matured as a discipline to be able to use rigorous scientific inquiry and practice with state-of-the-art methodological and statistical techniques to address topics such as religion–spirituality. Psychology no longer needs to prove itself worthy as an independent discipline, as it did in the early 20th century. Psychology as a discipline perhaps is less fearful of research topics that some might consider harder to observe and measure. Clients are more demanding of being treated as a whole person, and that includes addressing diversity issues such as religious traditions and perspectives. Thus, being respectful and attentive to religious–spiritual diversity and its implications for mental and physical health care is important today. Psychology and related fields have become more embracing than rejecting of religious–spiritual issues in recent years. Because the most recent version of the APA Ethics Code (2002) clearly mandates that psychologists be respectful and mindful of cultural diversity that includes religious traditions and beliefs, psychologists can no longer just ignore or pathologize clients' religious–spiritual issues and concerns.

Much of psychotherapy and many of the psychological services provided by contemporary mental health professionals are about developing more productive and healthy strategies to live life and to cope with the variety of stressful challenges that inevitably occur. Psychotherapy often highlights issues pertaining to meaning, purpose, lifestyle choices, and philosophy-of-life questions and deals with highly upsetting life circumstances and problems such as grief, loss, relationship conflicts, and disappointments. It helps people manage their lives in a more thoughtful, health promoting, and productive manner, given the strengths and weaknesses of the client and his or her life circumstances. Because religion–spirituality has been offering wise advice on these issues, concerns, and topics for thousands of years, maybe mental health professionals can learn something from the collective wisdom of these traditions and then, when appropriate and desired, incorporate useful principles into their contemporary work.

Overall, compelling high-quality research clearly supports the many mental, physical, and community health associations for those who engage in religious–spiritual activities. It may be likely that religious–spiritual people generally lead lifestyles that are more health promoting and less health damaging than those who are not religious or spiritual. The former also generally have a social support system through their church or religious community involvement. They may have a productive mechanism to cope with troubles through both intrinsic (e.g., personal prayer, meditation) and extrinsic (e.g., attending church services) religious– spiritual behaviors. Finally, charitable behaviors and an emphasis on ethics motivated by religious–spiritual beliefs, customs, and traditions certainly help make the world a better place by helping those who are marginalized, poor, or living with great need.

However, there is also evidence of religious involvement contributing to either personal problems, such as anxiety, panic, and obsessive–compulsive symptoms, or community problems, such as terrorism and various forms of abuse, oppression, violence, and hatred. For most normal and reasonable expressions of religious–spiritual practice, positive mental and physical health benefits may be expected for most people. Therefore, it is reasonable for mental health professionals to expect that religious–spiritual activities and engagement might be useful to include in an overall psychotherapy treatment package.

Further research is always needed, and it is important to state that the vast majority of research in this area is correlational, cross-sectional, and based on self-report data. Thus, a full examination of possible long-term effects of religious and spiritual engagement on physical and mental health outcomes is still clearly needed. In the final chapter of this book, I discuss in more detail future research directions that may better help bridge the gap between correlational and experimental studies.

In the next chapter, I introduce a variety of tools that have emerged from all of the major religious and spiritual traditions that can be added to the therapist's toolbox to supplement the services already offered to clients. Professionals can use (or not use) these tools as they see fit.

2

THIRTEEN TOOLS FROM RELIGIOUS–SPIRITUAL THOUGHT: DEFINITIONS AND PHILOSOPHICAL GROUNDING

This chapter highlights the most useful tools in all of the major religious and spiritual traditions to apply to the types of problems frequently seen by mental health professionals. These tools are available for therapists to use according to client needs.

Although therapists who use these tools do not have to be similar to their clients in terms of their religious–spiritual beliefs, traditions, and interests, they likely do need to be respectful and open to religious–spiritual interventions to maintain integrity and genuineness in their work. For example, encouraging a client to pray, meditate, or become active in his or her church should be done with sincerity. If the therapist thinks these activities are a waste of time or foolish, the client is likely to sense this contradiction. Therefore, although religious–spiritual tools are available to therapists, they should use only those tools they truly believe might be helpful—and, of course, they should not be forced on anyone.

Therapists may be mindful of these tools without specifically teaching clients how to use them. For example, a therapist may encourage clients to meditate or pray yet not teach them how to do it, especially if they are not qualified to do so. Just as therapists must know when to encourage clients to consider using psychotropic medication without actually prescribing the medication themselves, they may encourage clients to use religious–spiritual tools without actually teaching how to use them. Of course, if therapists have adequate training and experience with a tool, it may be appropriate for them to teach clients directly.

A PHILOSOPHICAL PERSPECTIVE: COMMON QUESTIONS OF FAITH

Few people in recent years have contributed more to the discussion and scholarship of the similarities of the religious traditions than Huston Smith. Professor H. Smith is a well-known theologian who has been on the faculty at University of California at Berkeley, Massachusetts Institute of Technology, Washington University, Syracuse University, and elsewhere, and he is probably best known for being prominently featured in the Bill Moyers PBS special on world religions. In his classic book *The World's Religions*, H. Smith (1991) clearly articulated an ancient view that the world's great religions are more similar than different, and he referred to the Hindu contention that the "various religions are but different languages through which God speaks to the human heart" (p. 73). He quoted Ris-Veda (4000 BC), an ancient and well-known Hindu sage, stating that "truth is one; sages call it by different names" (p. 73).

H. Smith (1991) provided an illustration of how to understand the world's religions that I believe can be very helpful to use with psychotherapy patients and ourselves. It is a metaphor that can be used time and time again to help better understand the positive similarities of the world's religions that offers hope for interfaith relationships and understanding. He stated,

> It is possible to climb life's mountain from any side, when the top is reached the trails converge. At base, in the foothills of theology, ritual, and organizational structure, the religions are distinct. Differences in culture, history, geography, and collective temperament all make for diverse starting points. (p. 73)

He then explained that as one moves higher and higher toward the top of the mountain, the world's religious traditions become one path seeking truth, stating, "But beyond these differences, the same goal beckons" (p. 73).

H. Smith (1991) quoted Sri Ramakrishna, a famous 19th-century Hindu religious teacher:

> God has made different religions to suit different aspirations, times, and countries. All doctrines are only so many paths; but a path is by no means God Himself. In deed, one can reach God if one follows any of the paths with whole-hearted devotion. One may eat a cake with icing either straight or sideways. It all taste sweet either way. (p. 74)

Thus, H. Smith and others have articulated that, at their best and most thoughtful, the various religious traditions converge and ultimately say much of the same thing with different languages, customs, and traditions. Religion–spirituality at its best is certainly not what one sees in the daily newspapers or on television. However, the best examples of religion–spirituality never make it to newspapers or television. Kindness toward others, caring and providing for those who are less fortunate, feeling peace and solace through prayer and meditation, being part of something more important and bigger than oneself, and coping better with the life's stressors through particular beliefs and understandings about the world and beyond never make headline news. Yet, this is what psychologists must focus on to integrate the religious traditions and spirituality into psychotherapy and health care and benefit from what the religious traditions have to offer. Psychologists must constantly climb higher on the metaphorical mountain in order to not get lost, confused, or stuck on some of the trails that are at lower elevations. Tragically, so many people involved with religion–spirituality can climb only a modest amount of the mountain, perhaps never seeing some of the beauty and views from the higher elevations.

Another step in the right direction is from the very popular contemporary writer on religion, Karen Armstrong (e.g., see Armstrong, 1993, 2000, 2006). Armstrong is a former Catholic nun who has written a series of scholarly yet readable books that have well articulated what people can learn from the world's religions and what they offer at their best. She concluded that all of the major contemporary religious traditions, such as Islam, Judaism, Christianity, Hinduism, Buddhism, Confucianism, and Greek philosophical rationalism, emerged in the 9th century BC during the Axial age in four different regions of the civilized world. All of them grappled with similar issues and often came to similar conclusions about religious, ethical, and social views, including that "the spirit of compassion . . . lies at the core of all our traditions" (Armstrong, 2006, p. 476). However, she readily acknowledged that all of the religious traditions have "fallen prey to exclusivity, cruelty, superstition, and even atrocity. But at their core, the Axial faiths share an ideal of sympathy, respect, and universal concern" (Armstrong, 2006, p. 466). The Golden Rule, or treating others as you would like to be treated, is the main point and is well articulated in the sacred texts of all of the religious traditions (Armstrong, 2006; Pargament, 2007). In fact, Armstrong stated that the Axial sages concluded that "religion *was* the Golden Rule" (Armstrong, 2006, p. 468). Armstrong's books and writings have received a great deal of contemporary acclaim and readership and well articulate that the best religion can offer is universal love, compassion, and respect for all.

It is important to mention that although Huston Smith, Karen Armstrong, and others have highlighted the similarities among the religious traditions, religions are not necessarily all the same. They do involve different traditions, rituals, beliefs, sacred scriptures, and so forth. However, they all attempt to answer similar questions about how to live, communicate with the divine or sacred, and behave in harmony with nature and with others. They offer similar principles and tools for living. It is helpful for therapists to respect their differences and similarities and attempt to use the best the traditions have to offer to help their clients in treatment.

In addition to the influential writers on comparative religions mentioned earlier, a variety of psychologists have also offered thoughtful insights into the relationship among psychology, religion, and spirituality. William James, Abraham Maslow, Carl Rogers, Frances Vaughn, and others have thoughtfully contributed to this understanding and perhaps have laid the foundation for recent emphasis on high-quality research and clinical practice in spirituality, religion, and psychotherapy integration (e.g., see James, 1936; Maslow, 1964; Rogers, 1980; Vaughn, 1995). These authors have attempted to integrate spirituality, religion, and psychotherapy in a manner that is open to how religious–spiritual traditions, beliefs, and practices can be put to good use in the psychotherapeutic process.

INTERNAL AND EXTERNAL BENEFITS OF TENDING THE SPIRIT

Psychotherapy and other mental health services may consider what the religious traditions might have to offer the therapist. At the top of the mountain, where the traditions converge, there are a number of highly desirable and useful principles and values. These include a focus on the sacredness of life and of the world, ethical behavior toward others, prayer and meditation, community and service involvement, and love and respect for all. It is difficult to argue with these values, principles, and goals. Most of these values and interests among the great religious traditions can be helpful to many regardless of their particular religious tradition or affiliation, even if one has no interest in any religious tradition or belief. It is also important to mention that some nonreligious perspectives, such as secular humanism, also would likely endorse these values and principles.

Much of the available research and practice guidelines that can be helpful to mental health professionals regarding religion–spirituality can be best categorized in terms of internal, or intrinsic, and external, or extrinsic, benefits (see discussion about intrinsic and extrinsic benefits in chap. 1). *Internal benefits* are benefits for the self, making one a better and more adjusted person, such as meditation, prayer, a sense of vocation and calling in life, being present in the moment, acceptance of self (and others) even with faults, maintaining ethical values and behavior, and feeling part of something greater than oneself. *External benefits* involve advantages that are extrinsic to the self that benefit the community, such as forgiveness, putting others first, volunteerism and charity, ritual and community involvement, social justice for all, and use of spiritual models to teach others how to live well and cope better with the stressors of life. Each of these internal and external benefits are introduced and discussed in more detail in the next section. Think of these religious–spiritual benefits as tools in your toolbox that are available to use in psychotherapy and in life. I introduce the religious–spiritual tools here and provide a brief clinical example or two of their use in psychotherapy. Of course, this outline of religious–spiritual tools is not cast in stone or an exhaustive list but includes a reasonable and useful selection commonly found within the major religious–spiritual traditions. In subsequent chapters I discuss how to actually use these tools in psychotherapeutic interventions and provide more in-depth clinical examples.

THIRTEEN TOOLS FOR YOUR PSYCHOTHERAPEUTIC TOOLBOX

1. Prayer
2. Meditation
3. Meaning, purpose, and calling in life
4. Bibliotherapy
5. Attending community services and rituals
6. Volunteerism and charity
7. Ethical values and behavior
8. Forgiveness, gratitude, and kindness
9. Social justice
10. Learning from spiritual models
11. Acceptance of self and others (even with faults)
12. Being part of something larger than oneself
13. Appreciating the sacredness of life

Prayer

Research results from a variety of sources support the benefits of regular prayer. Prayer can be defined in a number of ways, but it is essentially understood as being a conversation with the sacred. Ameling (2000) defined prayer as "a simple act of turning our minds and heart to the sacred" (p. 42). All of the religious traditions encourage prayer, but they differ in style and technique. Some traditions highlight ritualistic prayer that includes memorized statements to the divine, whereas others encourage more spontaneous conversations with God. Regardless of the tradition, prayer is an opportunity to communicate with the sacred and divine. Prayer has been found to result in a variety of benefits, including improved psychological functioning, a sense of well-being and meaning, and improved stress reduction and coping (Krause, 2003a, 2004; Masters, 2007). Consider this example of how prayer can enhance health:

Marco has always had some trouble sleeping at night, and his internal medicine doctor suggested a visit to the sleep clinic because she was concerned that Marco was becoming overly reliant on prescription sleep medications. Through his work with a psychologist at the sleep clinic, Marco tries to incorporate all of the sleep hygiene techniques into his lifestyle, such as avoiding caffeine and alcohol and ensuring that his bedtime rituals and experiences are relaxing. As an active Catholic, he finds that repeated reciting of the Our Father and Hail Mary prayers is especially helpful for falling asleep and getting back to sleep after he wakes up in the middle of the night. He reports, "Saying these prayers just relaxes and focuses me so much, and I feel calm and even watched over by God. I suppose it also helps keep my mind off other things that keep me up at night."

Meditation

High-quality research from a variety of sources has clearly demonstrated the many mental and physical health benefits of regular meditation (Shapiro & Walsh, 2007; R. Walsh & Shapiro, 2006). All of the religious traditions offer contemplative and meditative practices and techniques (Goleman, 1988; R. Walsh, 1999). For example, the Jewish tradition offers Hassidic and Kabalistic *dillug* and *tzeruf* approaches, Islam offers Sufism's *zikr* approach, and the Hindu and Taoist traditions offer yogas.

An excellent example of what the religious–spiritual traditions might offer others, even outside of the particular religious tradition that the principles came from, is mindfulness meditation. Mindfulness meditation has become very popular in psychology and health care, with numerous workshops, seminars, books, and articles highlighting how it can offer many physical and mental health benefits (Hayes, 2005; Shapiro & Walsh, 2007; R. Walsh & Shapiro, 2006). Although all of the religious traditions offer strategies and techniques for meditation, mindfulness meditation is most closely associated with the Buddhist tradition and is the technique that has been the most successful in being integrated into secular mental and physical health care. Psychologists such as Jon Kabat-Zinn, from the University of Massachusetts Medical Center, have helped to popularize this form of meditation and secularize it in a way that is acceptable to both professionals and clients alike regardless of religious tradition or involvement (e.g., see Kabat-Zinn, 1990). It is an excellent example of how a particularly worthy religion-based technique can be used to help others in a way that is understandable and acceptable to people even if they have no particular religious–spiritual affiliation. Generally, people do not seem to care that mindfulness meditation has its roots in Buddhism. What they learn is that they can use the principles and techniques of this form of meditation to lower stress, improve their psychological and physical health, and ultimately improve their quality of life. The remarkable success of mindfulness meditation in psychology and health care can be used as an excellent model for other useful religious–spiritual techniques and principles from a variety of different faith traditions.

Although mindfulness meditation has received the most press and acceptance among the medical and psychological community, other styles of meditation can be incorporated into psychotherapy with equal success. The Buddhist tradition also offers transcendental meditation (TM), which was especially popular in the United States during the 1960s and 1970s (Shapiro & Walsh, 2007), and the Christian tradition offers many types of meditative approaches, such as the spiritual exercises of St. Ignatius and the popular centering prayer from the Franciscan and Benedictine traditions. In fact, the common meditative principles of focused attention, being present in the moment, and taking the time and space to meditate regularly can be found in all of the different meditative approaches both between and within religious–spiritual traditions. The specific benefits of meditative practices include stress reduction, acceptance of self and others, improved coping, improved cognition, enhanced interpersonal relationships, and many physical benefits (Andresen, 2000; Hayes, 2005; Kabat-Zinn, 1990, 1994, 2003; Linehan, 1993; Shapiro & Walsh, 2007; R. Walsh, 1999). Consider the following case example:

> Isaac describes himself as a classic Type A personality. He is a biology professor and started psychotherapy when his wife felt that he was pushing himself and his kids too hard to be high achievers. He jokes that he comes "from a very high-achieving Jewish family where the fetus doesn't become a viable human being until he graduates from medical or law school." A friend encourages him to get involved with a local Zen center, and over time, he finds his involvement there helps him better manage his Type A style. He claims,
>
> > Participating in meditation sessions and other Zen center activities has especially helped me to live in the moment. Rather than always thinking about what's next or either the past or the future, I am better able to be present. My wife and children really see the difference in me as well.

Meaning, Purpose, and Calling in Life

All of the religious traditions offer at least some answers to the question of what one should do with one's life and provide directions for finding more meaning and purpose. Religion–spirituality provides a framework to develop a better sense of mission in life, including what career to pursue and how to live with meaning and direction (Dreher & Plante, 2007). The following is an example of a religious tradition giving meaning to one's life:

> Delilah is a born-again Christian and attends a local Baptist church. As a teenager, she had troubles with drug abuse and ultimately became homeless. After becoming a Christian through the influence of an inner city missionary program, she stopped her drug use, earned her GED, and ulti-

mately completed a social work degree. Before earning her degree, she volunteered at a large urban homeless shelter for women and children, and now she works there full time. She reports that she feels like she's on a mission to live the Gospel message of feeding the hungry and providing help for "the least of my brothers and sisters." She feels compelled to "give back since [she has] been there." She says, "I love my job and feel that I'm helping God by taking the Gospel message seriously and doing my part to make a better world for those in need."

Bibliotherapy

Mental health professionals have used bibliotherapy for decades (Norcross, 2006), encouraging their clients to read self-help literature and both fiction and nonfiction to supplement their treatment. These materials might be used to inform clients of the diagnosis, treatment, or issues they face in psychotherapy or to give them motivation. For example, reading stories about how others managed their stressors successfully might provide a model as well as inspiration for clients to cope more productively with their challenges.

The religious–spiritual traditions and church communities also tend to encourage their members to read the Bible and other sacred and common literature to improve their spiritual lives. Bible studies, sacred scripture commentaries, and biographies of great religious leaders, saints, prophets, and others all help interested readers to grow and deepen their faith and understanding of their religious–spiritual traditions. Therapists can use these religious–spiritual readings to augment psychotherapy with many clients, as in the following example:

> Aldo struggles with anxiety and guilt about religious–spiritual matters. He admits that he tends to get very anxious about the afterlife and struggles to understand his Baptist beliefs and sermons from his church pastor. Aldo mentions to his therapist that he heard Karen Armstrong on National Public Radio talking about one of her new books on religion and that he is interested in learning more about various religions. With encouragement from his therapist, Aldo begins reading about the history of religion with the assistance of several of Armstrong's popular books. Over time, Aldo feels he develops a more informed and thoughtful understanding of his religious tradition, which results in less anxiety and distress for him. He says, "I guess a whole new way of understanding opened up to me by reading Armstrong's books. It helped put my faith tradition and beliefs in better perspective in ways that I never learned from my pastor or church community."

Attending Community Services and Rituals

Much research has highlighted the mental and physical health benefits of community social support and the need for ritual and structure in life (e.g., see Berkman & Syme, 1979). Religious communities all encourage regular ritual activities that are usually done in the context of a group of community members who share similar values, beliefs, and traditions. Regular church attendance, Bible studies, and holiday celebrations with family and faith communities all provide rich opportunities for social connection, support, and networking. Furthermore, social support can combat loneliness and isolation. Consider the following case example:

> Kira is a college student attending a Catholic university. Every day at noon she goes to Mass. It is an important ritual of her day and helps her cope with the stressors of being a college student and managing exams, papers, relationships, and career uncertainties. Kira says,
>
>> I feel weird if I don't go. It is sort of like brushing your teeth each morning and night. You just do it without even thinking about it. It calms me, relaxes me, and helps me feel more at peace and clearheaded. There is something about the ritual and seeing a community of students, faculty, and staff every day coming together for Mass that makes me feel connected and at peace.

Volunteerism and Charity

All of the religious traditions encourage charitable works and volunteerism to help make the world a better place for all. Research also suggests volunteer activities are associated with positive mental and physical health outcomes, including mortality risk reduced by as much as 40% (Oman & Thoresen, 2003). Religion provides a reason and organizational structure to support community engagement that most especially focuses on helping those in greatest need, such as those who are poor. Furthermore, volunteerism makes volunteers feel an enhanced sense of meaning, purpose, and value that can also help put their own troubles and concerns into better perspective. In a recent study in my laboratory, my colleagues and I found that college students participating in an alternative spring break that involved an immersion project with a poor and marginalized group returned with a better sense of vocation and scored higher on coping ability than students who did not participate in the program (Mills, Bersamina, & Plante, 2007; Plante, Lackey, & Hwang, in press). Clearly, when people help others they also help themselves, as shown in this example.

> Arjun is a retired auto mechanic who never married and has no siblings or children; his parents are deceased. He feels isolated and depressed. Because he lives frugally, he has extra money that he uses to support charitable organizations. He says, "I do it for me. It feels great to know that my money is helping others and that if it wasn't for my money, more people would suffer." He volunteers at several community nonprofit agencies, saying,

It gets me out of the house, and I always feel so much better after I have helped others in some way. Gee, I feel selfish that my donations and my volunteerism probably do more for me than for the people I'm trying to serve.

Ethical Values and Behavior

All of the religious traditions offer suggestions on ethical ways to live. Some, such as the Jewish tradition, have highly detailed writings that very specifically offer a way to decide how one should manage ethical issues and conflicts. Living more ethically, with or without religious involvement, is likely to have many positive psychotherapeutic benefits (Plante, 2004). Examining the ethical principles for psychologists as well as other mental health professionals highlights many of the very same ethical principles that are offered around the various religious traditions. These include respect, responsibility, integrity, competence, and concern (Plante, 2004). Both professional mental health practice and religious wisdom encourage people to be concerned for others, be honest and maintain integrity, be respectful to everyone and to life, and so forth (Koocher & Keith-Speigal, 2008). Ethics is discussed in more detail in a later chapter, but for now I emphasize that ethical living is an important way that the religious traditions frame strategies for how people should live their lives. Consider this example:

> Francisco prides himself on living ethically. Although he does not consider himself especially religious, he credits his upbringing in his nonaffiliated Christian church and his involvement with Boy Scouts as a youth living in the inner city as having been highly influential in helping him value ethics. Francisco seeks therapy because of job stress. He feels that the job he currently has in a local roofing company is "sleazy," stating that his boss and coworkers "don't break the law but sure get close to it in their activities." He reports that he does not want to work for such an unethical company but likes his work, and it pays enough for him to provide well for his family. He reports, "I'm grateful to have a moral and ethical compass. So many people I interact with at my company really don't."

Forgiveness, Gratitude, and Kindness

Religion–spirituality at its best fosters helpful qualities such as forgiveness, gratitude, love, kindness, and compassion. For example, research has demonstrated the many benefits of forgiveness (Koenig et al., 2001; Worthington, Berry, & Parrott, 2001). Religious traditions at their best highlight the importance of forgiveness and redemption and their benefits. One benefit of forgiveness is that it is an important foil to anger and bitterness; letting go of these feelings from real or perceived slights from others, and of transgressions of all sorts, can have many positive mental and physical effects (Worthington et al., 2001). Gratitude is the ability to be thankful for what one has and the ability to appreciate daily events and experiences (Langston, 1994). It involves "counting your blessings" and is encouraged within all of the major religious traditions (Armstrong, 2006). Research has indicated that those who experience more gratitude tend to sleep better, are more optimistic, are more energetic, and maintain better interpersonal relationships (e.g., see Emmons & McCullough, 2003). Finally, all of the major religious traditions encourage love, kindness, and compassion, which also have numerous mental and physical health benefits (Snyder & Lopez, 2007), as shown in the following examples:

> Henry works as a short-order cook in an inner city deli. He greets each day by saying, "Thank you God for giving me another day." He generally flows with whatever happens to him, joking, "I suppose I keep my expectations low. If I'm alive, it's a good day. Everything else is icing on the cake." Henry generally gets strength from his religious–spiritual life, often focusing on forgiving others, treating everyone with loving kindness, and being grateful for whatever he has or gets. He attributes this way of being to a loving relationship he has with God and doing a great deal of reading on the various religious traditions. When he finds himself getting upset about something, he reminds himself to "let go and let God."

> Fatima used to have chronic tension headaches and experienced much stress in dealing with her dysfunctional parents and siblings as well as her high-stress job in a bakery. She says that after having several children she learned that "it isn't about me anymore." Somehow, she found this attitude freeing and now finds herself putting her children and community first. Some in the neighborhood joke that she is the "Mother Teresa of the neighborhood." She organizes meals for sick neighbors and is involved with many school and community events. She states that one advantage of working in the bakery is that her hours allow her to be available in the afternoons. She claims, "If I don't focus on myself but focus on others, somehow I feel more at peace and less stressed out. It is curious how it works that way."

Social Justice

All of the religious traditions encourage social justice activities to help those in need and make the world more humane and just. These activities often spill into the political and secular environment. For example, activists who support a living wage, fair trade, and immigration rights, and those who try to put pressure on communities that exploit children or vulnerable others often engage in these social justice activities for religious–spiritual reasons. Social justice activities help people to become less self-focused and nurture a more productive perspective on life. Often it is more difficult to feel stressed by the daily hassles of contemporary life when confronted with the significant problems of poverty, oppression, and violence experienced by so many in the world. Consider this example:

> Genevieve is a caseworker for child protective services. She feels strongly that her faith has led her to do what she can to help abused and battered children and their families. Although she grew up Catholic, she became a Baptist after a born-again experience during her teen years. She has tried a variety of evangelical churches and currently attends a Seventh-Day Adventist church that she really enjoys. She reports that her faith underscores social justice issues and feels that she should use her skills and talents to do what she can to help abused children. Unlike most people she works with, who leave after a few years, she proudly states that she has worked in this area for 25 years and reports, "I could never do it without my faith and conviction that this is where God wants me to be."

Learning From Spiritual Models

Religious–spiritual models provide followers with important exemplars to imitate (Oman & Thoresen, 2003, 2007). The popular question "What would Jesus do?" is an excellent example. Religious models such as Jesus, Buddha, Mohammad, and Moses as well as more contemporary models such as Gandhi, Mother Teresa, Billy Graham, Martin Luther King Jr., and many other little-known models across the globe provide a blueprint for how to live life in a better way. Research has clearly demonstrated that observational learning is a powerful way to learn new skills and behaviors (Bandura, 1986, 2003); role models who demonstrate productive ways to live can motivate and inspire others to "go and do likewise" (Luke 10:37; Spohn, 2000). These models are found in all faith traditions and help followers to have a clearer path toward a better functioning life. Here is an example of the benefits of having such a model:

> Gerard was very close to his maternal grandfather, who was a mentor and model for him. He says he cannot help but model his behavior and way of being in the world after his grandfather, James. He says,
>
> > It's funny. He's been dead now for about 15 years and yet he feels very much alive to me. I can see how I model so much of how I am in the world from him. He was a wonderful guy and was so due to his faith and religious involvement. I suppose he lives on through me.

Sadly, religious–spiritual role models can also be damaging. When a religious– spiritual model engages in highly negative, unethical, immoral, or illegal behavior, he or she can negate the more positive role models within the faith tradition. Sexual abuse by priests in the Roman Catholic Church is a good example (Allen, 2004; Plante, 2003). The abusive behavior of a few priests, representing 4% of the total (John Jay College, 2004), has resulted in negative evaluations of many of the 96% of priests who have not violated children and negative views of the Roman Catholic Church as a whole (Plante, 2003).

Acceptance of Self and Others (Even With Faults)

Many religious–spiritual traditions offer suggestions about the acceptance of self and others. Even those that focus on the sinfulness of humans offer strategies for redemption and acceptance from others as well as from the divine. So much of psychotherapy focuses on helping people accept what they cannot change and change what they can to improve quality of life for themselves and those with whom they interact. The well-known Serenity Prayer perfectly articulates what secular psychotherapy works so hard to accomplish. It states, "God, give us grace to accept with serenity the things that cannot be changed, courage to change the things that should be changed, and the wisdom to distinguish the one from the other" (Niebuhr, 1987, p. 251). Consider the following example of the benefits of spiritual acceptance:

> Elly seeks psychotherapy primarily for anger management issues at both home and work. She finds herself being chronically disappointed and upset with others who do not meet her high expectations for performance and behavior. Although she reports that she has always been this way, she is concerned that these issues have transferred to her relationship with her son. Her high expectations for his behavior at home, school, sports, Boy Scouts, and other activities have caused much conflict. Over time in therapy, Elly has worked hard to live the Serenity Prayer of accepting the things she cannot change, change the things that she can, and have the insight to know the difference. She jokes, "I've never been very religious or spiritual, but I can't believe that the Serenity Prayer has become such an important part of my life. It just makes sense."

Being Part of Something Larger Than Oneself

Religion–spirituality clearly articulates ways that we as people are part of something larger and greater than our individual lives, needs, and desires. Religion provides a way of thinking about what came before us and what might come after us. It puts each person in context with the greater natural, and sometimes supernatural, world. It is clearly important for us to feel part of something bigger than ourselves (Pargament, 2007), and some fulfill this need in nonreligious communities and activities such as the military, sports teams, companies, or universities. Being part of something bigger than ourselves can help us better cope with the stressors and challenges of life. Here is an example:

Gertie comes from a Reform Jewish background and does not experience herself as being spiritual or religious. However, she attends all of the High Holiday events (i.e., services, lectures) and loves the sense of community, music, prayers, and the grandness of it all. Gertie says she feels connected to something bigger and more important than herself. She says, "Being part of a family of Jews dating back thousands of years makes me feel less isolated as well. Somehow it gives me peace."

Appreciating the Sacredness of Life

All of the religious traditions highlight the notion that life is sacred, with many suggesting that the divine lives within all of us (Pargament, 2007). This notion that everyone is important, sacred, and a "child of God" has important implications for how we interact with others. The religious–spiritual traditions suggest that if everyone is sacred, then everyone should be treated with respect, kindness, love, and compassion. Certainly, this notion that everyone is sacred has not always been supported or highlighted, as when members of religious groups have lashed out at others in violence.

Therapists can well use this religious–spiritual notion of sacredness to support their psychotherapeutic work and to encourage their clients to find ways to improve their interpersonal relationships and develop a more helpful way of viewing themselves, as shown in the following example:

> Ashanti feels depressed and has had thoughts of suicide. She also struggles with alcohol problems and has a history of using methamphetamines. Her self-esteem is very low, and she wonders whether life is worth living. Ashanti's therapist discusses with her the notion that all life, including her own, is sacred. Ashanti's religious background supports this view, and she well remembers a sermon she attended recently entitled, "God Doesn't Make Junk." Ashanti's therapist works with her on the implications of seeing herself as sacred and a child of God consistent with Ashanti's religious beliefs and tradition. After a number of months of comprehensive treatment, Ashanti's mood improves, and she reports that this notion of sacredness is useful to her progress. She says, "I got so down on myself, but if God lives in me and made me, who am I to hurt myself and thus insult God? What a slap in the face that would be to God."

ETHICAL AND CULTURAL CONSIDERATIONS

Several ethical precautions should be noted before embarking on the integration of religion–spirituality into contemporary psychotherapy. Although some of these common ethical issues are introduced here, they are discussed in greater detail in a later chapter on ethical issues (see chap. 6). First, it is critical to stay within one's areas of competence. Psychologists generally are not theologians or trained clergy and must be careful not to overstep their bounds. Therapists who are spiritual, religious, or both may wish to use their beliefs in the service of their psychotherapeutic work, and although that may be a reasonable desire, it can be professionally dangerous when therapists practice outside of their areas of expertise or promote their religious spiritual views during client sessions. It is critical that therapists perform their professional duties in a manner that is consistent with their training and experience and follow both ethical guidelines of competence and legal requirements to stay within the limits of what their license allows. This point cannot be emphasized too strongly. Although it is natural and expected that therapists who benefit from their particular brand of religious–spiritual beliefs and practices may wish to integrate those perspectives into their work, they must be careful not to impose them on their clients or practice outside their area of competence. Ongoing training and consultation may help them avoid this temptation.

Second, mental health professionals must be careful to avoid potential dual relationships, especially when their clients are members of their own faith tradition and perhaps part of the same faith community. Patient referrals often come from people mental health professionals know, and someone who knows a therapist from his or her faith community and related activities might want to receive professional services from someone who shares not only their religious beliefs but also a similar religious community experience. Unforeseen dual relationships and conflicts can easily emerge this way. This is not to say that there may not be very good reasons to professionally work with members of the same faith tradition community. One must be sensitive to potential exploitive dual relationships and unforeseen consequences that can emerge when working with fellow spiritual community members.

Finally, mental health professionals must avoid potential bias and prejudice by not promoting one faith tradition or belief system over another. Therapists, just like the general population, may have certain positive or negative beliefs or impressions about persons from particular religious–spiritual traditions. They may enjoy people of like mind or similar religious background but maintain stereotypes about those from religious traditions they only hear about in the news. For example, many religious traditions get a lot of negative press, and it would be easy for therapists to maintain stereotypic views of people from traditions they are not very familiar with. Mental health professionals must be attentive to the rich diversity of beliefs and practices even within each particular religious–spiritual tradition and avoid bias or stereotyping others. This is especially true for mental health professionals who have very little, if any, contact with members of particular religious groups in either their professional or their personal lives.

Perhaps several examples might illustrate this point. Women from an Islamic background may wear traditional head coverings. Therapists might maintain stereotypic beliefs about these clients, especially since Islamic fundamentalist views and extreme violent behavior such as terrorism have received so much publicity in recent years. Someone who knows little about Islam might assume all Muslims are terrorists, or at least sympathetic to terrorists. Clients from a Roman Catholic tradition may be seen as being anti-abortion, antihomosexual, and anti-intellectual on the basis of negative media stories about the Roman Catholic Church. From the daily news reports, the average person might assume Catholics are interested in only abortion, divorce, homosexuality, and pedophile priests. Evangelical Christians may also be victims of stereotypes perpetrated by negative media attention and might be perceived as Bible-quoting, anti-intellectual fundamentalists who are trying to convert others at all times. Psychologists and other mental health professionals may be highly educated and scientifically minded, with many years of graduate and postgraduate education, yet still stereotype and feel put off by those who embrace a religious tradition or faith community that differs from their own.

It is important to mention that many religious–spiritual affiliations, beliefs, and practices are part of or a by-product of important cultural differences. Many religious–spiritual customs are thus steeped in ethnic and geographical diversity. For example, Roman Catholics from Eastern Europe may have many different religious traditions, practices, and perspectives relative to Roman Catholics from Latin America, who may also differ from those in parts of Africa. Jews from Israel and the Mediterranean region often experience their religious faith and tradition differently from Jews from Eastern Europe or the United States. The traditions, rituals, and perspectives of Buddhists from parts of Asia may be different from those of Buddhists in North America. Although this point may seem obvious, it is important to mention that both subtle and not so subtle cultural, ethnic, geographic, and political differences all can be woven into the religious experience, beliefs, and customs of all of the major religious–spiritual traditions. In fact, some religious–spiritual beliefs, rituals, and practices may have originated within an ethnic and cultural community before being adopted by a particular religious or cultural tradition. Mental health professionals must be sensitive to these cultural issues and differences in order to offer high-quality professional services (Wasserman & Stack, 1993). Furthermore, psychologists' professional ethics demand that they be culturally sensitive and competent in their work (American Psychological Association, 2002, 2003). Thus, mental health professionals must be mindful of the cultural influences that are often intimately woven into particular religious–spiritual expressions.

Perhaps a few examples will be helpful. Recent media attention has focused on the plight of Muslim women in Afghanistan, Africa, and the Middle East, who often are denied educational, medical, and other freedoms; cannot leave their home without a male relative; and are sometimes subjected to female circumcision and honor killings. These customs are rooted in ethnic and cultural traditions and are not strictly religious practices (Armstrong, 2000). Over time, these practices have come to be equated by many with the Muslim religious tradition, yet they did not originate with Islam and are generally not found in other parts of the world where Muslims live, such as the United States and Indonesia. This is an example of cultural, historical, ethnic, and geographical influences that merged with a particular religious tradition in particular regions of the world.

Another example is how Christians celebrate Christmas and Easter in much of the world. Many of the traditions associated with these holidays (e.g., Christmas tree, Easter eggs and bunnies, special foods) and the dates they are celebrated have their origins in pagan and other life-cycle celebrations that Christians adopted and incorporated into their religious holidays long after they were well established (Armstrong, 2000). Some customs and expectations associated with these holidays vary by culture, ethnicity, and region.

Thus, mental health professionals must be mindful of the intersection of cultural, ethnic, geographic, and religious traditions among their clients. Although they cannot be expected to become experts on all aspects of these influences, they must be sensitive and thoughtful about them in their work with clients.

CONCLUSION

Some of the tools of religion–spirituality are found at the bottom of the metaphorical mountain described earlier in the chapter. For example, religious rituals unique to particular traditions can be powerful ways to manage stress, cope with trauma, and celebrate holidays and life's transitions of birth, death, marriage, coming of age, and so forth. The Catholic Mass, the High Holiday services, baptisms, bat mitzvahs, confirmations, religious pilgrimages, special prayers, and foods consumed all provide something very important for members of a faith community. To those outside the religious community, many of these practices may appear odd and perhaps even distasteful. Further up the metaphorical mountain, there are a variety of religious–spiritual tools that are much more similar across the traditions, such as ethics, social justice and charitable works, and a sense of the sacredness of life. Mindfulness meditation and some of the programs described in chapter 9 are good examples of spiritual principles and techniques that can be used regardless of religious–spiritual tradition and are thus found higher on the metaphorical mountain.

Overall, the religious–spiritual traditions, at their best, offer many tools to improve psychological, physical, interpersonal, and community functioning. Regardless of one's religious–spiritual interests, or lack thereof, the great wisdom traditions have had thousands of years to fine-tune their strategies for living. Although psychology as an independent discipline has been conducting research and practice for only about 100 years, the great religious communities have reflected on life and offered suggestions for much longer. Rather than ignore what these traditions offer, psychology should embrace them in a way that makes sense for contemporary professional practice. In this chapter, I identified the religious–spiritual tools that can be used by therapists. In subsequent chapters, I focus on how to actually use these tools in clinical practice. However, before discussing how to use religious–spiritual tools in psychotherapy, it is important to understand assessment and evaluation issues in spiritually integrated psychotherapy. That is the topic of the next chapter.

3

ASSESSMENT ISSUES

Maribel has been in psychotherapy for about 3 months, working on marital conflicts. Her psychologist, Dr. A, never asks about religious–spiritual matters, but one day he happens to see her at a local supermarket parking lot driving off in a car that has several Christian bumper stickers, such as "What Would Jesus Do?" and "Got Jesus?" Dr. A had assumed Maribel was Jewish because of her last name and because she had once mentioned picking up her son at Hebrew school. When Dr. A mentions seeing her car at the supermarket, Maribel breaks down in tears and starts talking about the interfaith conflicts she and her husband began experiencing after having children. She states, "Before kids, it just wasn't an issue. He is Jewish, and I'm Christian, but once the kids came along, religion became more important to both of us, and conflicts developed once we had to decide on religious education for them." Dr. A wonders how he could have missed this important issue during several months of therapy.

Mary has been in therapy for several weeks, discussing her feelings of depression about the loss of her father. She wears a crucifix around her neck, and her therapist, Dr. B, assumes she is Catholic and religiously minded. Dr. B suggests she consider talking with her priest about the loss of her father for some religious comfort, and Mary states she is not religious at all, and certainly not Catholic. Dr. B apologizes, explaining that because she wears a crucifix and her name is Mary, he assumed that she was Catholic. Mary says, "Oh no, I wear this because it belonged to my great grandmother and it's a family heirloom. I really don't think of it as a religious object—more as a piece of jewelry that connects me to my great grandmother, who was an important member of our family because she was the first one to come to America. Plus, I'm named after her."

Aseem is receiving biofeedback services from Dr. C for low back pain. Once Dr. C hooks him up to the equipment and starts to take baseline measures, she becomes alarmed because Aseem's heart rate is only 38 beats per minute. Dr. C is worried that he may have a medical problem and asks Aseem whether he knows why his heart rate is so low. Aseem assumes it is because of mindfulness meditation, which he does regularly; in fact, he was meditating as he was being hooked up to the biofeedback equipment.

The cases of Maribel, Mary, and Aseem are not atypical. Too often, mental health professionals do not conduct any type of assessment of the role of religion–spirituality among their clients. At most, they may ask about religious affiliation on an intake questionnaire or perhaps make some assumptions on the basis of the patient's name, appearance, or behavior. For example, if one wears a crucifix, a therapist may assume the client is Catholic, or if one enters therapy with a star of David around his or her neck, a therapist may assume the client is Jewish. Mental health professionals may assess or discuss religious–spiritual influences only when the client brings up these issues. Yet, as mentioned earlier, religious–spiritual issues can easily be part of the clinical problem or part of the solution to many issues typically addressed in psychotherapy, and certainly could and perhaps should be assessed by the clinician.

How do mental health professionals best evaluate the role of religious–spiritual issues in their clinical work? What observational, interviewing, and assessment instruments are most helpful? What aspects of religious–spiritual influences are most productive to evaluate? How might this information be helpful in treatment planning? In this chapter, I discuss the assessment and evaluation approaches available when examining religious–spiritual influences in psychotherapy. Therapists cannot hope to use religious–spiritual tools unless they have a solid assessment of how these interventions might or might not help a particular client. Different clients and clinical situations may call for different approaches. In this chapter I focus on clinical observations, clinical interviewing, and various pencil-and-paper surveys that can assist mental health professionals to better understand the role religion–spirituality plays in the life of the client as well as providing some way to help determine how religious–spiritual integration and interventions might be suitable in psychotherapy.

WHAT THERAPISTS ARE TRYING TO ASSESS

An appropriate assessment can help mental health professionals develop a better sense of the religious–spiritual influences on their clients as well as provide a better understanding of how religious–spiritual tools may or may not be helpful in their work with particular clients. Broadly understanding something about a client's religious affiliation, beliefs, and engagement in a religious community helps to start the assessment process. However, religious–spiritual assessment is much more complex than asking clients what their religious affiliation (if any) might be and whether they go to services regularly. A number of important religious–spiritual elements might be part of an assessment. Richards and Bergin (1997, 2005) articulated nine categories of information that could be useful to evaluate during assessment. It is important to mention, however, that clinicians must decide which of these nine categories are to be evaluated and to what depth; these decisions depend on both the level of religious–spiritual history and engagement of the client and the nature of the problem for which they are seeking help. For example, clients who have no religious affiliation or history of religion in their lives, who have not really thought about a metaphysical worldview, and who are seeking help for an issue that has little to do with religious–spiritual themes may require only a very brief assessment of these categories, which might stop after the first few categories are addressed. Perhaps at minimum clinicians should ask clients whether they have a particular religious–spiritual affiliation and whether they would like it considered in their treatment. Clients who have a rich religious history or are more devout may need a more detailed assessment that evaluates all nine categories in depth. Furthermore, particular clinical concerns might be especially appropriate for religious–spiritual assessment, such as death, dying, and sudden loss.

A list of the categories and short descriptions of each one are provided, followed by a few brief clinical examples to illustrate them.

1. Metaphysical worldview
2. Religious affiliation
3. Religious orthodoxy
4. Religious problem-solving style
5. Spiritual identity
6. God image
7. Value–lifestyle congruence
8. Doctrinal knowledge
9. Religious and spiritual health and maturity

Metaphysical worldview refers to the various beliefs one holds about the universe and one's place in it. These beliefs might include a belief in God or some kind of divine or supreme being and whether that being generally is loving and benevolent, judging and malevolent, or a combination of the two. The metaphysical worldview might address issues such as determinism and free will, whether humans are basically good or evil, and the purpose and meaning (if any) of their lives and the earth. One's worldview is likely to directly relate to how one acts toward and feels about others and oneself. On the one hand, if one has the worldview that we are all created by God and have an element of the divine within us, then he or she is likely to believe that all humans are sacred and should be treated in a loving and respectful manner. On the other hand, if one has the worldview that there is no God or divine being and no purpose or meaning to life other than what one gives it, that person is likely to view relationships with others very differently. Those who have the worldview that humans are predestined to a particular apocalyptic outcome, as outlined in the book of Revelations at the end of the Christian New Testament, may live their lives in accordance with that belief, such as waiting for the second coming of Jesus or the Rapture, in which believers are suddenly called up to heaven. The worldview that one's religious community is the only one acceptable to God and that all others are cursed by God will likely play an important role in that person's relationships with nonmembers of his or her faith community. Perhaps a couple of examples will demonstrate this notion:

> Jake is an engineer who prides himself on being a scientist. Although he is actively engaged in his Reform Jewish temple and participates in many activities that support the Jewish community and Israel, he considers himself an atheist. He values the intellectual rigor of scripture study and fellowship with others who share his ethnic and cultural background but does not value personal acts of devotion or religious beliefs. He sees his religion as more of an ethnic and cultural experience than a religious one; his worldview is that religious beliefs are based on scientific and intellectual ignorance and that "once you die, it's just lights out."

> Peter believes that somehow all things will work out according to God's plan. He feels that even if he cannot begin to understand why tragic things happen to good people for no apparent reason, God has a plan and that he has to learn to just accept that in the end God knows what He is doing. Peter gets great comfort and solace in this worldview, and it helps him cope with various stressors in life.

Religious affiliation includes any particular membership or identification with a faith tradition, such as Judaism, Catholicism, Islam, and Methodism. It also includes particular affiliations within each religious tradition. For example, individuals who are affiliated with the Reform Movement within the Jewish tradition are likely to experience their version of Judaism very differently from those who identify with the Orthodox branch. Those who identify with the Roman Catholic Church from the Irish Catholic perspective may experience their faith differently from those who are Roman Catholic from Mexico. Persons who are Sunni Muslim likely experience their faith differently from those who are Shiite Muslim. All of the faith traditions have liberal, conservative, and fundamentalist branches as well. Furthermore, ethnic, racial, and regional differences may interact with religious tradition and faith communities in ways that create highly unique religious–spiritual experiences for various subgroups. Thus, in addition to general faith tradition or religious affiliation, an understanding of which subculture or branch of the tradition can be informative and important to assess.

> Jake identifies himself as Jewish from the Reform tradition. He finds those who are Orthodox rather odd and feels he has nothing in common with Jews from that branch. He does not keep kosher but attends the High Holiday services and enjoys them a great deal. He is proud to be affiliated with his Jewish community and enjoys the intellectual rigor and support of Israel that it provides. However, he thinks the strict dietary and other laws observed by the Orthodox branch of his religious tradition are "very weird."

> Peter is Catholic but has attended services within various Protestant denominations.

Religious orthodoxy refers to how closely the client adheres to the various beliefs, expectations, and behaviors associated with their particular faith tradition and branch within that tradition. For example, whereas some Jews eat only kosher foods and attend weekly Sabbath services, others do not. Whereas some Catholics attend Mass each Sunday and attend all holy days of obligation, others do not. Whereas some try to both understand and believe the doctrine of their faith tradition, others choose what to support as their conscience dictates. For example, whereas the official Roman Catholic position on birth control forbids use of artificial contraception (e.g., condoms), many Catholics who disagree with this position use artificial birth control and still identify themselves as Catholic. Some Christians believe in the physical bodily resurrection of Jesus, whereas others do not, regardless of official Church teachings and doctrine. Some Jews strictly follow Sabbath laws, and others choose which (if any) to follow.

> Jake does not keep kosher, nor does he attend regular Sabbath services. However, he goes to great lengths to attend all High Holiday celebrations, regular Torah and Talmud study classes, and other events at his temple.

> Peter says he has "faith that seeks understanding" and that his conscience is informed by his Bible study, church service attendance, prayer, and "God's grace," and that no one, not even Church officials, have the "corner on the truth." Therefore, he describes himself as not being very orthodox in his beliefs except for what he considers basic fundamental principles of Christianity and says he is "open to new ways of thinking and believing" as he learns more about his faith and the perspectives of contemporary religious scholars.

Religious problem-solving style refers to how one uses a faith tradition to solve problems and cope with stress. Some use their religious tradition in health promoting ways, and others use it in health damaging ways. For example, some turn to prayer, meditation, and religious rituals to help better manage the troubles they experience. They may pray for the welfare of their loved ones and the world in general, ask God for favors, or use religious sayings, scripture, or music to cope with uncomfortable medical or dental procedures, for example. They may find their religious tradition provides solace during stressful times. They may believe they will see their loved ones in the afterlife, and thus the loss of a loved one may feel temporary rather than eternal. However, others may use their religious beliefs and rituals to justify harming or hating others. For example, they may deal with stress or problems in living by becoming more orthodox, exclusionary, and rejecting of others who do not share their views. Also, they may work to kill, harm, or withhold freedoms from those who do not share their beliefs and traditions.

> Melissa copes with the stressors of life by praying, asking friends and family to pray for her well-being, and lighting candles at her Catholic church. She says, "God won't give me more than I can handle," and that gives her solace during times of stress. She also remembers the suffering of Jesus on the cross, which helps her better manage her own daily hassles and concerns.

> Marilyn does not describe herself as very spiritual, but she uses religious problem solving by being very active in her Jewish temple. She considers herself very engaged in her religious community and gives practical support to community members, including cooking for those who are ill, donating money to various Jewish causes, and trying to help out where possible. When she needs support, she immediately turns to her temple friends and rabbis for help.

> Cal copes with stress by becoming more conservative and restricting in his beliefs and practices. He believes he is being punished by God when bad things happen to him and worries that his religious rituals may not appease God. He also becomes more rejecting of others who do not share his faith beliefs, which creates further isolation and rejection from others.

Spiritual identity refers to one's view of his or her relationship to the sacred or divine. For example, some individuals experience themselves as sinners who constantly need forgiveness and reconciliation from God. Others view themselves as having a more neutral or benign relationship with the sacred. Some may believe they are primarily a spiritual being encased in flesh, whereas others see themselves as only flesh and blood, without any particular spiritual identity. Some believe their spiritual soul is immortal and others do not.

> Peter sees himself as a spiritual being encased in flesh for his time on earth. He sees himself (and others) as sacred yet believes his sinful desires sometimes make him choose to behave in ways that displease God, such as eating too much, lusting after material possessions and attractive women, and not having more charity for others.

Jake does not see himself as spiritual at all despite being very active in his religious community.

God image refers to how one views the divine or God. Is God primarily loving and compassionate or critical and judgmental? Is God personified as a father with a long, flowing beard or as a divine life force or spirit without any particular shape, size, or gender? Is God personal or impersonal—active in one's daily lives or remote? Does God micromanage events or the behavior of others, or is God separate from daily occurrences?

> Melissa views God as an old man with white flowing hair and a beard. She admits this may not be the real image of God, but she has it in her mind while she engages in prayer or attends religious services. She claims it helps her in prayer to have some kind of real person–like image in mind. She tends to believe God micromanages people's lives, sometimes granting favors and sometimes allowing bad things to happen for an unknown purpose.

> Peter views God as an eternal life force without human-like appearance and describes him as something beyond knowing or understanding that propels life. He does not believe God micromanages people's lives.

Value–lifestyle congruence refers to lifestyle choices that may or may not be consistent with religious values and practices. For example, someone might highly value social justice and caring for those who are the poor and marginalized of society because of his or her religious beliefs yet never donate to charity or volunteer to help those in need. Someone might highly value commitment to his or her faith tradition yet never go to religious services. Someone may believe in mercy toward others and forgiveness for transgressions yet treat family members, coworkers, or subordinates very differently. Value lifestyle congruence thus examines how religious–spiritual beliefs correspond to actual behavior and lifestyle choices.

> Peter feels a bit guilty that he highly values charity and missionary work but is too self-centered and afraid to actually do much of this work himself. He relieves some of his guilt by donating to various Church missionary and charitable organizations, but in his heart feels that God expects more from him and others to help those who are less fortunate.

> Melissa takes very seriously her religious value of helping others. She seems always willing to assist stressed neighbors and friends, and sometimes people take advantage of her helpfulness. Melissa says God calls us all to be loving to all and that she must do her part to do God's work. Her husband, Chris, admires her ability to live her values but admits to feeling frustrated when people exploit her goodness.

Doctrinal knowledge is one's understanding of the theology and belief structure of his or her religious tradition. It refers to how well one understands exactly what one's religious tradition affirms in terms of beliefs and behaviors. Many people who are engaged in a faith community do not always understand or appreciate its official doctrine or are perhaps misled by it.

> Peter is remarkable in his knowledge of Church doctrine. Although he is not a member of the clergy, he has read a great deal and has taken classes to help him understand exactly what his Church believes and supports.

> Melissa struggles with her religious beliefs and doctrinal knowledge. She tends to take the Bible literally and has trouble understanding her Church's view on some very challenging scriptures that discuss harming homosexuals, slaves being obedient to their masters, women being subservient to their husbands, and so forth. She struggles with what the Bible seems to state and what her Church supports.

Religious and spiritual health and maturity refers to how high on the metaphorical mountain discussed in chapter 2 the client is regarding his or her religious beliefs, understanding, and practices. It also includes how thoughtful, reflective, and knowledgeable the client appears to be on his or her religious–spiritual journey.

> Lee used to be a fundamentalist Christian engaged in an evangelical church community. However, her interest in theology has led her to take more and more courses and to read more about various religious traditions. Over the years, she has concluded that theology is much more complex than she used to believe and that there are many paths to religious–spiritual enlightenment other than her own. Curiously, she has developed more love, compassion, and empathy for others as her beliefs and knowledge have increased, and she feels she is a better Christian now than she was when she was more of a fundamentalist.

> Cal believes only his small religious sect has the truth and will obtain eternal life. He believes all those not associated with his church are doomed. He tries to convert friends, family, and coworkers to his point of view, which they uniformly reject, and several times has been fired from a job because of his evangelizing.

Whereas Lee climbed higher on the metaphorical mountain, Cal did not.

These assessment categories offered by Richards and Bergin (1997, 2005) provide a helpful framework in which to assess the role of religious–spiritual factors in the lives of clients. It is a handy way to organize clinical observations, interviewing, and other assessment tools.

HOW THERAPISTS ASSESS RELIGION–SPIRITUALITY

Now that I have commented on what to assess, I must address how to assess. In general, therapists use intake forms, clinical observations, clinical interviewing, and self-report pencil-and-paper questionnaires to assess religious–spiritual influences on their clients. Which method or methods to use depends on the needs of the client and professional. Some clinicians may generally use interview and observational approaches and never feel the need to use self-report questionnaires. Others might wish to use questionnaires within a packet of materials that clients complete prior to the start of treatment. Clinicians may wish to use what makes the most sense for their clients and the nature of their clinical practice.

In the next few sections, I comment on intake forms and then clinical observations that may help clinicians better assess religious–spiritual issues in therapy. Then, I discuss clinical interview issues and pencil-and-paper assessment instruments that can be used to evaluate religious–spiritual dimensions. I also provide actual questionnaires for your review and possible use in the Appendix at the end of this book.

Intake Forms

Most mental health professionals use some type of intake form or brief demographic questionnaire in their clinical practice. It may be productive for therapists to include in them several basic questions that assess religious–spiritual factors. For example, asking about religious affiliation (if any) as well as the branch within the affiliation (e.g., conservative, liberal) is a starting point. Furthermore, a question about how important religious–spiritual issues and community are to the client might also be worth including on any intake form. An example suitable for editing is provided in Figure 3.1.

Clinical Observations

In many subtle and not so subtle ways clients communicate the role religion–spirituality plays in their lives. Just as a wedding ring communicates that someone is not available to others for marriage, a star of David, head scarf, crucifix, cross, turban, or yarmulke all communicate something about religious–spiritual identification and engagement. Some of these signs are subtle (e.g., a small cross on a necklace); others are prominent (e.g., the robes of a Christian or Buddhist monk; the habit of a nun; the long beard, side curls, and black garments of a Hassidic Jew; the black suit and white Roman collar of a Roman Catholic priest). Yet, not everyone who wears an external sign of religion is devout. In fact, some may see religious adornments as being nothing more than a fashion statement. For example, in recent years some Hollywood celebrities have worn a particular red wristband that represents the Jewish mystical tradition of Kabala as a fashion statement. In fact, someone may wear a cross around his or her neck yet not identify with Christian beliefs or practices. Hip-hop and rap artists sometimes wear a very large cross on their outfits even if they do not especially identify with Christian values, beliefs, or practices. Religious symbols may or may not reflect actual religious engagement. However, religious–spiritual jew-

1. Religious–spiritual affiliation (if any):

2. Branch or subgroup of religious affiliation (if any):

3. How often do you attend religious services?

   (a) *never*   (b) *major events or holidays only*   (c) *monthly*

   (d) *weekly*   (e) *multiple times per week*

4. How important are spiritual matters to you?

   (a) *not important*   (b) *slightly important*

   (c) *moderately important* (d) *extremely important*

5. How important are religious issues to you?

   (a) *not important*   (b) *slightly important*

   (c) *moderately important* (d) *extremely important*

6. How important are religious–spiritual issues for you when you are confronted

   with stressful life events?

   (a) *not important*   (b) *slightly important*

   (c) *moderately important* (d) *extremely important*

If you wish to do so, please elaborate on any of these items in the space provided:

_____

_____

_____

_____

_____

Figure 3.1. Examples of intake questions pertaining to religious affiliation.

elry, clothing, books, bumper stickers, and other items may be an invitation to ask about the role of spirituality and religion in their lives.

Clinical observations naturally go well beyond jewelry, clothing, and bumper stickers. The language, manner of speech, and ways that clients interact with their loved ones and the mental health professional also are clues about the role of religion–spirituality in their lives. For example, many Christians pepper their speech with phrases such as "if the Lord is willing" or "Praise be to God." Others state they feel "blessed" or that someone is a "brother [or sister] in Christ." They may also use Bible quotes or scriptural references in their speech and storytelling and be very uncomfortable with swearing or using the name of God or Jesus in a disrespectful way. Some Jews may sprinkle their language with Yiddish words and phrases. Of course, it would be inappropriate to suggest that all Christians and Jews behave this way, and it is critical not to stereotype these or other groups. These examples are provided as observational data that suggest how religious–spiritual identification and beliefs could unfold in the office of a mental health professional.

It is important for therapists to fine-tune their observational skills of religious–spiritual behaviors in their clients as well. Religious backgrounds, traditions, and behaviors are often very much part of a cultural tradition and are often closely intertwined with ethnic, racial, and even tribal influences. For example, although I grew up in an Irish and French Canadian Roman Catholic environment in Rhode Island, others who grew up in an Italian Roman Catholic background in the same community had traditions and ways of interacting different from my own. The foods, traditions, and language of many Jews in America are greatly influenced by Eastern European cultural roots. Therefore, although people may or may not report that they are influenced by religious–spiritual traditions, they may be influenced by cultural, geographical, ethnic, and racial differences that are often closely aligned with particular religious–spiritual backgrounds. A therapist cannot expect to be an expert on all variations of religious, spiritual, and cultural traditions and influences, but he or she can work to be more open to these influences, which often are very subtle yet important in clinical work. Perhaps a clinical case example can be of help to better understand some of these influences.

> Oscar is Jewish and married to Marie, who comes from an Irish Catholic background. Oscar and Marie often have disagreements about interactions with their in-laws. Oscar wants to include his parents in many of the intimate details of family life, whereas Marie does not. After several ongoing conversations with their psychologist, they conclude that part of their conflict and challenge is that cultural differences exist between how Jewish and Irish Catholic families interact and communicate. Their experience growing up and with others who come from their religious tradition is that Jewish families are more likely to talk about intimate family details, confront and argue with each other, and want to know details about family interactions, whereas Irish families are more likely

not to talk about these matters nor confront family members about the types of topics Oscar feels comfortable discussing with his family. Having examined their conflict through the lens of cultural and religious differences, Oscar and Marie experience less discomfort and anger with each other and more collaboratively work on their cultural and religiously influenced differences.

On the surface, Oscar and Marie's conflict about what to discuss or not discuss among family members may appear to be unrelated to religious–spiritual differences. Yet, on reflection, they concluded with their therapist that their conflict was influenced by cultural and religious differences, which provided them with an ultimately more useful framework for working on their differences. They also learned not to take these differences so personally and to understand them within their cultural context. Furthermore, their therapist encouraged each of them to read some books about their culture and that of their spouse to develop a better appreciation of these differences.

Clinical Interviewing

Interviewing clients specifically about the role that religion–spirituality plays in their lives can be very fruitful. Having a better understanding of both the positive and possibly negative ways that religion–spirituality has influenced their lives and the role it can play now is important in working on many issues clients bring to a therapist. One approach that is easy to use and remember is called *FICA* (Pulchalski & Rommer, 2001). It represents four key words: *faith* (i.e., What is your faith tradition, if any?), *importance* (i.e., How important is your faith to you?), *church* (i.e., What is your church or faith community, if any?), and *address* (i.e., How would you like me to address these issues in your care?). These simple questions can also provide a springboard for further questions and discussion as needed.

In addition, a variety of specific interview questions can help the clinician get the religious–spiritual "lay of the land." Although hardly an exhaustive list, the following 10 questions address some of the major categories discussed earlier and also offer a basis for additional questions and discussion. They include the following:

1. Do your faith, spiritual traditions, religious community, beliefs, and practices help you in your life? If so, how?
2. Do your faith, spiritual traditions, religious community, beliefs, and practices hinder you? If so, how?
3. How were religious–spiritual issues discussed or experienced within your family while you were growing up? Did you experience this as a positive, negative, or mixed bag?
4. Did anyone act as a religious–spiritual model in your life when you were growing up? If so, how?

5. Have you been stressed by religious–spiritual beliefs, practices, or experiences? If so, how?
6. What, if any, religious–spiritual practices do you participate in now? How do they help or hinder you?
7. Do you regularly attend religious–spiritual services? What are they like for you?
8. Are you or have you been engaged in volunteer or charitable activities associated with religious–spiritual beliefs, practices, and community? If so, which ones, and what has the experience been like for you?
9. What do you find sacred in life? Has this always been true, or has it changed over the years?
10. What moments in your life made you feel especially close to the sacred, and what moments did you feel furthest away from the sacred?

The purpose of these and other questions is to better assess the role religion–spirituality plays in the life of the client and determine how it may serve as a helpful ally or perhaps foe during the course of psychological treatment. I provide the following example (with Peter's responses) to illustrate the use of these 10 questions (note that follow-up questions were added to respond to the answers provided):

1. Do your faith, spiritual traditions, religious community, beliefs, and practices help you in your life? If so, how?
   It gives me meaning, purpose, and a sense of peace. I'm a pretty nervous guy by default, and somehow my faith gives me solace, joy, and peace.
Follow-up question: So do you find that your faith is primarily a way to help you cope with anxiety?
   Well, it certainly does that for sure. But I think it also gives me a sense of meaning and comfort even when I'm not stressed or anxious about anything.
2. Do your faith, spiritual traditions, religious community, beliefs, and practices hinder you? If so, how?
   I suppose at times. Sometimes I worry about the afterlife and whether I will experience heaven, hell, or something else. I suppose if it were clear that once you die it's "lights out" with no possibility of hell, then I would rest a bit easier.
Follow-up question: So if you knew there is no heaven or hell or any other kind of consciousness after death, you would be more at peace?
   Yes, I would say so. I suppose if we just didn't experience anything after death then that would be better than worrying about hell or something else that might be awful.

3. How were religious–spiritual issues discussed or experienced within your family while you were growing up? Did you experience this as a positive, negative, or mixed bag?

It was most definitely a mixed bag. There were wonderful moments and awful moments in my life associated with my religious tradition. I had a lot of religious guilt that I have worked very hard to cope with over the years.

Follow-up question: Can you give an example of an awful moment and a wonderful moment?

Sure. I remember once as a young child, probably about 8 years old, being so upset that I was going to hell that my mother took me to see the priest about it. I really was upset, and the whole idea of eternal damnation was pretty awful to ponder as a kid. I remember him being very comforting and telling me that there was no way I could do anything at my age to even have the remote possibility of eternal damnation. I felt better after that for a while at least. However, it still haunted me and perhaps still does, at least to some extent. A wonderful moment was being involved with some youth groups as a kid and having some wonderful experiences at retreats and other church-related events where I felt I was on cloud nine. It was transformative and memorable.

4. Did anyone act as a religious–spiritual model in your life when you were growing up? If so, how?

I think my grandfather. He was very religious and very kind. His faith meant a lot to him, and he was a great model of a gentle, kind, and loving soul.

Follow-up question: How do you model him today?

Well, I pray daily as he did. I try to be very friendly and loving and to see everyone as a child of God, which he really did well. He attended daily Mass, which I do as well. I think we are a lot alike actually.

5. Have you been stressed by religious–spiritual beliefs, practices, or experiences? If so, how?

Sure. I think fear of death and hell bother me. I suppose it just is in my DNA. It does upset me at times, and I try to cope with it as best as I can.

Follow-up question: You mentioned this was stressful for you as a child. How does it trouble you now?

I suppose every now and then (especially when you can't sleep in the middle of the night) it bothers me. Also, sometimes when I'm fearful about something, such as flying in planes after the September 11th terrorist attacks, it troubles me. I try to just put myself in God's hands and pray about it, which makes me feel a bit better.

6. What, if any, religious–spiritual practices do you participate in now? How do they help or hinder you?

I go to weekly and daily services. I pray each day. I say prayers when I'm driving, hanging around, and so forth. I listen to religious music in the car during my commute. I think it all helps me and gives me peace.

Follow-up question: Do they hinder you in any way?

Not really. Other than the time commitment to attend services and pray. I guess that might be it.

7. Do you regularly attend religious–spiritual services? What are they like for you?

Yes, indeed. I attend daily services as well as on Sunday. Somehow it is always a time for reflection and contemplation. It relaxes me. Sometimes I let my mind wander and don't pay attention to the service, but overall it just is a time for contemplation and prayer. I like it and feel uncomfortable when I can't go.

Follow-up question: Any downside?

Well, I suppose sometimes the services are boring or I don't agree with the point the sermon is trying to make. Not much really.

8. Are you or have you been engaged in volunteer or charitable activities associated with religious–spiritual beliefs, practices, and community? If so, which ones, and what has the experience been like for you?

I suppose I try mostly to be kind, gracious, and loving to everyone I interact with, and that stems from my faith. I feel guilty that I don't do more charity work, however.

Follow-up: Can you say more about the guilt you experience?

Well, the Gospel says you should sell all of your possessions and give them to the poor and follow Jesus. This Gospel passage has always troubled me. I just can't do that. I know others can't either, with few exceptions, but it still bothers me. I feel like I am not doing nearly enough for others.

9. What do you find sacred in life? Has this always been true, or has it changed over the years?

Gee, I guess I find everything sacred. I believe that God is in all things, and thus everything living is sacred.

Follow-up question: Any changes over the years in this view?

It gets more and more salient for me. I think I see the sacredness in everyone more and more as I get older and see God's presence in life.

10. What moments in your life made you feel especially close to the sacred, and what moments did you feel the furthest away from the sacred?

Hmm, lots I suppose. The birth of my child, my wedding day, an interaction with someone who needs a loving or kind word. It all makes me feel in touch with the sacred. I suppose I feel far from the sacred when I'm watching some of the junk you see on TV.

These questions provide a window into Peter's religious–spiritual life that potentially can be used in his treatment planning. Again, they are far from being an exhaustive list, but perhaps they are a solid place to start.

Assessment Instruments

A wide range of instruments now exists that clinicians can use to better understand the role that religion–spirituality plays in clients' lives. There are many to choose from—too many to discuss in detail here. In this section, I focus on instruments that are reliable, valid, and useful to the clinician; are generally easy to use, score, and administer; and take little time to complete. Most professionals want to get adequate information from their assessment questionnaires but are also very sensitive to the length, complexity, and possible costs of these instruments. Unfortunately, too often test developers use lengthy instruments that might be appropriate in laboratory and research environments but are usually impractical in clinical settings. Before using an assessment instrument, several factors should be considered. First, regardless of the title of the instrument, it should be a valid measure of the construct or variable in question. Second, the professional must have a clear view of exactly what information he or she wants to get by administering the assessment questionnaire. For example, is the professional primarily interested in assessing religious–spiritual beliefs, practices, or behaviors—or all of the above? Is the professional interested in religious coping or how the client uses his or her religious–spiritual tradition and practices to cope with stressful life events? Is the professional interested in assessing internal or intrinsic spirituality, external or extrinsic spirituality, or both? Finally, are the measures used appropriate to the client population of interest? For example, some measures were designed for Christians and others can be used with anyone. Some measures assume the respondent is religious to begin with and others do not. Of course, questionnaires also must be available in a language understandable to the client. These types of issues should be carefully considered before choosing an assessment instrument.

Several researchers (e.g., see P. C. Hill, Kopp, & Bollinger, 2007; Tsang & McCullough, 2003) have argued that a general and dispositional measure of religiousness can be productive to use in clinical settings. They cite that various elements of religion–spirituality, such as attendance at church services, prayer, meditation, and so forth, are often closely intercorrelated and that general religiousness accounts for many religious–spiritual behaviors, practices, and beliefs. Several reliable, valid, useful, and brief questionnaires offer a measure of general religiousness. Additionally, some scales focus on particular aspects of spirituality and religiousness, such as mysticism, religious motivation, religious behaviors, and the use of religion and spirituality as a coping strategy for medical or psychological stressors. In the next section, I briefly introduce and describe some of the most common and useful measures available. All selected have demonstrated adequate reliability and validity and are brief and easy to use, score, administer, and interpret. As appropriate, I provide the actual measures in the Appendix at the end of this book.

Primary Selected Measures

Brief Multidimensional Measure of Religiousness/Spirituality. The Fetzer Institute's (1999) Brief Multidimensional Measure of Religiousness/Spirituality is a multidimensional measure of religiousness and spirituality that can be useful in both clinical and research settings. The scale emerged from meetings with prominent social and medical scientists over a series of conferences. It assesses a wide range of religious–spiritual dimensions, including denominational affiliation, organizational religiousness, private and public religious practices, religious coping and social support, moral values, time and money donated to religious causes and organizations, spiritual experiences, and self-reported measures of religious–spiritual activities and interests. Much research has been conducted using this scale, and it has been shown to be reliable and valid (Fetzer Institute, 1999; Koenig et al., 2001; Underwood, 2006).

Santa Clara Strength of Religious Faith Questionnaire. The Santa Clara Strength of Religious Faith Questionnaire (SCSORF; Plante & Boccaccini, 1997; Plante, Vallaeys, Sherman, & Wallston, 2002) is a 10-item (or 5-item brief version) instrument designed to assess general religiousness in any faith tradition as well as lack of involvement in religious–spiritual behaviors or traditions (e.g., "My faith impacts many of my decisions"). This is important because many scales were developed for specific religious traditions (e.g., Christian) or assume the person taking the questionnaire is already engaged with a faith tradition (Plante & Boccaccini, 1997). In a variety of research studies, the SCSORF has demonstrated high internal consistency, test–retest reliability, and excellent convergent and divergent validity among diverse psychiatric, medical, student, and general populations (P. C. Hill et al., 2007; Pardini, Plante, Sherman, & Stump, 2000; Plante & Boccaccini, 1997; Sherman et al., 1999, 2001).

Duke University Religious Index. The Duke University Religious Index (DUREL; Koenig, Meador, & Parkerson, 1997) is a 5-item measure developed to assess three dimensions of religious engagement: organizational or public religious expression (e.g., church attendance), private religious expression (e.g., prayer, meditation), and intrinsic religiosity (e.g., incorporation of religious convictions into one's daily life). The DUREL was developed primarily for a medical population, and much of the research on the scale has been conducted in health care environments (Koenig et al., 1997). The DUREL has demonstrated adequate reliability and validity in various clinical and general population settings (Sherman et al., 2001).

Religious Commitment Inventory—10. The Religious Commitment Inventory—10 (Worthington et al., 2003), a 10-item questionnaire originally part of a 20-item Religious Values Scale (Worthington, 1989), measures how committed the respondent is to his or her religious beliefs, and practices. It demonstrates adequate reliability and validity (Wade & Worthington, 2006; Worthington et al., 2003).

RCOPE. The RCOPE (Pargament, Koenig, & Perez, 2000) is a 105-item questionnaire that provides information on 17 factor-derived religious coping strategies (e.g., benevolent religious reappraisal, seeking spiritual support, religious purification/forgiveness) and has adequate reliability and validity (Pargament et al., 2000). Of course, the length of the questionnaire may be problematic in most clinical settings, and thus a 14-item version is available: the Brief RCOPE (Pargament, Smith, Koenig, & Perez, 1998). The Brief RCOPE yields two global dimensions: positive religious coping (i.e., movement toward religious resources in response to stress) and negative religious coping (i.e., conflict or movement away from religious resources during stress).

CONCLUSION

Before therapists can potentially integrate religious–spiritual principles into psychotherapy and other psychotherapeutic endeavors, they must assess the religious–spiritual lay of the land with their clients. Religious–spiritual influences may be helpful to understand before attempting any type of integration approach. For some clients, religious–spiritual influences not only can help therapists better understand their concerns but also can be used as an avenue for healthy behavioral change. For others, religious–spiritual influences have been part of their problem, leading to troubles in living. For still others, religious–spiritual issues are mostly irrelevant to the reason they sought professional mental health services. At least some minimal assessment can help the clinician to determine how (if at all) religious–spiritual factors might be used in better understanding and treating clients. Various interview and pencil-and-paper assessment measures as well as high-quality clinical interviewing and observation can all be enlisted to better evaluate the religious–spiritual influences and dimensions for each client. Clinicians must individually decide for themselves and their clients how and when to evaluate religious–spiritual dimensions and influences among their clients. I hope this chapter provides a framework and tools to do so.

This brings me to the issue of how to use religious–spiritual tools in psychotherapy, which is the focus of the next several chapters.

4

INTERNAL RELIGIOUS–
SPIRITUAL TOOLS

Dr. A is treating a client who is angry about her husband's marital affair. Although her husband has apologized in what appears to be a sincere manner and has broken off the relationship, the client is having trouble forgiving him. Because the couple report they are devout Christians from an evangelical tradition, Dr. A wonders whether their religious perspectives and faith tradition can be enlisted to improve their marital crisis.

Dr. B is treating a man who has a variety of stress-related psychological and physical conditions, and he suggests several relaxation strategies to enhance coping. He heard a lot about mindfulness-based stress reduction at a recent convention and wonders whether this approach might help his client.

Dr. C treats a devout Orthodox Jew who experiences depression. She quickly learns how important the client's religious tradition and culture are to his life and lifestyle and wonders whether his tradition can somehow be used to help him better cope with his depression. Dr. C asks the client whether he thinks a coordinated treatment approach that includes ongoing consultation with his rabbi would be more helpful than therapy alone.

Drs. A, B, and C are treating clients who may benefit from treatment that uses religious–spiritual tools. How should they proceed?

As mentioned in earlier chapters, being aware of and having access to these religious–spiritual tools does not require the clinician to be an expert with them. For example, it is important for clinicians to understand that prayer and meditation may be very helpful to their clients, but that does not mean that clinicians must be able to teach clients how to pray or meditate. They may instead refer appropriate clients to other professionals for instruction.. Being aware of and comfortable with religious–spiritual tools as well as knowing their potential benefits is the goal.

One helpful way to categorize religious–spiritual tools in psychotherapy is whether they focus on spiritual development internal to the client, such a prayer and meditation, or on involvement with others, such as community service (see earlier chapters for additional information about internal and external tools). Some tools can be easily applied to both internal and external areas, such as the acceptance of self and others (even with faults) as well as the sense that one is part of something larger than oneself. Perhaps none of these religious–spiritual approaches is completely orthogonal in nature. For example, prayer and meditation can be very private and personal experiences, but they also can occur within the context of a religious community, church ritual, or liturgical celebration. One can be forgiving with others as well as forgiving of oneself. For the ease of discussion here, I separate the religious–spiritual tools into internal and external categories. Each technique along with some research support was briefly discussed in earlier chapters, and thus in this and subsequent chapters, I describe the application of these approaches. How to actually use the tools, along with brief illustrative examples, is what clinicians most likely will find useful. In this chapter I focus on internal tools (see chap. 5 for a discussion about external and other tools).

Before discussing the use of religious–spiritual tools in psychotherapy, it is important to mention three issues: (a) the need for therapists to maintain spiritual mindedness in their work, (b) the distinction between implicit and explicit religious–spiritual interventions, and (c) problems clinicians may bring to the psychotherapy when integrating religious–spiritual tools.

SPIRITUALLY AND PSYCHOLOGICALLY MINDED SERVICES

Before discussing how to use the tools of religion–spirituality in psychotherapy, it is important to mention the need to maintain a spiritually and psychologically informed mind-set when working with clients (McMinn, Aikins, & Lish, 2003; McMinn, Chaddock, Edwards, Lim, & Campbell, 1998; Pargament, 2007). Mental health professionals and psychology students in training are well aware of the need to develop and maintain a psychological approach and mind-set in working with clients. Part of what graduate and postgraduate training accomplish is the development of a psychological mind-set. Psychologists and other mental health professionals use the principles of psychology and behavior as a lens for viewing the world and of understanding human feelings, behavior, relationships, and conflicts.

A spiritual mind-set includes being aware of and thoughtful about religious–spiritual influences and developing an openness to the religious–spiritual dimensions of clients. It involves the development of a spiritually and religiously informed lens to better understand and interact with clients that supplements the psychological lens therapists have already developed and feel comfortable using. Therapists may or may not consider themselves religious–spiritual yet still be mindful of the religious–spiritual influences and perspectives of their clients. They could also remind themselves of the sacredness of others, which may help them treat all clients with added or enhanced respect and graciousness. Viewing everyone as sacred (with or without religious–spiritual perspectives) elevates our view of others, which one hopes will lead to better clinical services.

Pargament (2007) discussed specific qualities that therapists should strive toward in developing and maintaining a spiritual orientation or mind-set as they work with clients. These include the attitude that although religious–spiritual qualities in clients can be the source of clinical problems and resistance to possible solutions they also may provide a variety of resources and a cultural and community context for possible clinical solutions. Also, therapists, to be effective, must maintain a degree of spiritual literacy, knowledge, competence, openness, tolerance, self-awareness, and authenticity in religiously–spiritually integrated psychotherapeutic services. Having a spiritual orientation entails seeing psychotherapy as having a spiritual dimension even if discussions about religious–spiritual issues are not a focus in treatment and knowing that psychological interventions can enhance spiritual development, and spirituality can enhance psychological interventions. Overall, Pargament suggested that a manner that is thoughtful, respectful, responsible, and open is required to integrate religious–spiritual matters into psychotherapeutic services.

IMPLICIT AND EXPLICIT APPROACHES TO PSYCHOTHERAPY

Another important distinction that should be mentioned before reviewing religious–spiritual tools is the concept of implicit and explicit approaches to religiously–spiritually integrated psychotherapy (Tan, 1996, 2003, 2007). An *implicit* approach refers to more covert, quiet, and subtle religiously–spiritually informed interventions and approaches to psychotherapy. It might include privately praying for the well-being of clients, participating in a brief mindfulness-based meditation prior to seeing clients, encouraging clients to accept themselves and others without any particular religious–spiritual reference, and so forth. An *explicit* approach is more overt and direct, and it specifically uses religious–spiritual interventions in psychotherapy. It might include praying with a client during a treatment session, encouraging a client to read particular sacred scriptures or other religious readings between sessions, referrals to particular clergy or church groups, and so forth. Some of the religious–spiritual approaches can be used in either an implicit or an explicit manner. For example, a therapist might pray for the well-being of a client without discussing it with him or her and engage in joint prayer during a therapy session, thus using both implicit and explicit prayer interventions with the same client.

PROBLEMS CLINICIANS MAY BRING TO PSYCHOTHERAPY WHEN INTEGRATING RELIGIOUS–SPIRITUAL TOOLS

Pargament (2007) discussed problematic attitudes mental health professionals may bring to psychotherapy when integrating religious–spiritual tools: "spiritual bias, spiritual myopia, spiritual timidity, spiritual overenthusiasm, spiritual cockiness, and intolerance of ambiguity" (p. 333).

Spiritual bias occurs when clinicians maintain stereotyped and often negative views of religious–spiritual concepts and people. This is especially true when the clinicians have few, if any, interactions with people from religious–spiritual traditions different from their own or perhaps feel uneasy with those who are different than themselves. For example, clinicians may assume their Muslim clients are sympathetic toward Muslim terrorists or that their Jewish clients are wealthy, smart, and always eat kosher foods. However, spiritual bias may also include favoring religious practices that clinicians feel comfortable with or to which they can relate.

Spiritual myopia refers to viewing religious–spiritual issues, conflicts, and interventions in a narrow, focused, and undifferentiated manner. For example, clinicians may believe their Catholic clients will never consider the use of birth control or that their Buddhist clients will never eat meat under any circumstances. They may also believe that particular interventions are always helpful, such as prayer or meditation, for all concerns. Whereas spiritual bias highlights stereotypes and, often, prejudice, spiritual myopia underscores spiritual tunnel vision.

Spiritual timidity refers to the notion that clinicians should avoid any conversation involving religious–spiritual matters unless the client explicitly requests to talk about these issues in treatment. Curiously, many therapists appear to feel much more comfortable talking about intimate sexual matters with their clients than they do about religious–spiritual matters. For example, clinicians may quickly refer clients to clergy or elsewhere when they bring up these topics in treatment. Thus, they may refuse to engage clients in religious–spiritual dialogue.

Spiritual overenthusiasm occurs when clinicians see religious–spiritual roots to all client problems and insist that their clients discuss these matters regardless of their diagnosis or the issues they bring to psychological treatment. This is similar to the adage that "if your only tool is a hammer, you'll see nails everywhere." Some clinicians may be so convinced that religious–spiritual conflicts and issues are at the core of psychological and behavioral problems in their clients that they insist their clients work on their religious–spiritual development regardless of the reasons they sought treatment.

Spiritual cockiness refers to overconfidence that clinicians may exude about religious–spiritual matters, overestimating their level of competence to provide spiritually–religiously integrated mental health services. These professionals lack the humility necessary when attempting to use religious–spiritual tools in psychotherapy.

Finally, *intolerance of ambiguity* refers to the black-and-white thinking clinicians may engage in when using religious–spiritual tools in psychotherapy, focusing on simple interventions for complex issues. For example, a clinician may insist that prayer or meditation will stop anxiety or phobic reactions in their religious client or that enhancing their belief in God or Jesus will solve all of their psychological distress.

It is critical that mental health professionals maintain a spirit of humility and thoughtfulness as they use the religious–spiritual tools described in this and subsequent chapters. They certainly must follow ethical guidelines, staying within their area of competence and maintaining responsibility, respect, integrity, and concern for the welfare of their clients (American Psychological Association, 2002, Plante, 2004). And they must do their best to avoid the problems described in this section.

TOOLS FOR NURTURING INDIVIDUAL SPIRITUAL GROWTH

The following are examples of internal religious–spiritual tools: prayer; meditation (including mindfulness); meaning, purpose, and calling in life; and bibliotherapy.

Prayer

Prayer can be defined as an ongoing conversation with the sacred. William James (1902/1936) defined it as an "inward communication or conversation with the power recognized as divine" (p. 454). All of the theistic world religions and many nontheistic traditions advocate prayer. However, the type and style of prayer vary not only among religious–spiritual traditions but within them. Gallup polls suggest most people pray regularly; in fact, they have found that 90% of Americans report they pray, 97% believe prayer is heard, and 86% believe prayer makes them better people (Gallup & Jones, 2000; Gallup

& Lindsay, 1999). Research also indicates that prayer can be very helpful in enhancing psychological functioning as well as coping with various life stressors (e.g., see Dossey, 1993; McCollough, 1995; Richards & Bergin, 2005). Dossey (1993) suggested that prayer may work because of placebo effects, biopsychosocial relationships associated with mind–body connections, or divine or transcendent healing interventions.

Also, prayers can be individually tailored to the specific needs of each person or others at any given time. As my wife jokingly states, prayer seems to include two types that can be defined as "Please, God; Please, God; Please, God!" and "Thank you, God; Thank you, God; Thank you, God!" Regardless of faith tradition and beliefs, people ask for divine favor during crises and other times of great need and thank God when they get something they badly want. Actually, prayer may include petitions (i.e., asking for intervention for oneself), intercessions (i.e., asking for intervention on behalf of others), confessions (i.e., admitting wrongdoing and seeking forgiveness), adoration (i.e., offering praise), thanksgiving (i.e., offering gratitude), meditation (i.e., seeking solace and peace), or rituals (i.e., participating in prayer services; McCullough & Larson, 1999; Richards & Bergin, 2005).

For some, prayer can be an ongoing conversation with God or other sacred figure such as Jesus. Prayer can be as conversational as talking with a close friend or relative. For others, or at different times, prayer is more formalized and structured, including very specific words and phrases that are read or recited in a ritualized manner. An example is reciting the Our Father, often referred to as The Lord's Prayer, in the Christian tradition. Catholics might use prayers such as the Hail Mary and the Prayer of St. Francis. Jews might recite the Schma (i.e., "Hear, O Israel: The Lord is our God, the Lord is One!") or particular prayers during events such as when Shabbat lights are lit or over challah bread before a meal.

Mental health professionals may wish to inquire about the role (if any) of prayer in the lives of their clients and encourage those who pray to find ways to make it work better for them as they deal with whatever psychological and behavioral issues they are working on in therapy. Because more than 90% of Americans report they pray regularly (Gallup & Jones, 2000), the odds are very high that clients who seek mental health services are using prayer in their lives, and this interest and behavior can be enlisted to help them better manage and cope with their psychological, behavioral, and relational concerns. For those who pray and believe in the power of prayer, research and practice suggest it can be an excellent way to cope with stressors and can help both psychological and physical functioning (Pargament, 2007; Richards & Bergin, 2005; Tan, 2003, 2007).

Generally, mental health professionals do not pray with their patients because of such issues as professional boundaries, personal discomfort, and professional expectations for behavior (Frame, 2003; Jones, Watson, & Wolfram, 1992; Richards & Bergin, 2005). They also generally do not teach their clients particular prayers or how to pray, for similar reasons. However, mental health professionals, depending on their religious experiences and identifications, may pray for their patients privately or encourage their clients to use prayer to help manage their concerns when appropriate (Frame, 2003).

Tan (2003, 2007) encouraged therapists to pray directly with their clients in an explicit manner, assuming that the therapist and client share similar religious beliefs and traditions, informed consent has been secured, and prayer is not clinically contraindicated, such as when patient prayer behavior is part of a thought disorder or an obsessive–compulsive disorder. He offered a particular seven-step approach to prayer for inner healing that might be especially useful with Christian clients and therapists (Tan, 2003, 2007). It begins with a prayer for healing and proceeds with a brief relaxation technique; focused attention on the problem, conflict, or issue the client has brought to therapy; additional prayer, religious music, or imagery; and a debriefing discussion. Other religiously–spiritually based manualized psychotherapeutic interventions use explicit prayer in their approach with Christian clients and therapists (e.g., see Rye & Pargament, 2003; Worthington, 2004). Consider the following case example:

> Lucy has an anxiety disorder and experiences periodic panic attacks. She is especially phobic about doctor visits, blood draws, and injections and therefore tends to avoid scheduling much-needed doctor appointments and lab visits. She is a devout Roman Catholic and reports that she prays regularly. In therapy, she agrees to use prayer to help her better cope with her fear of doctor visits and medical procedures. She says the rosary while waiting in the doctor's office for her scheduled appointment and quietly recites the Hail Mary prayer on her way to the doctor's office and lab visits. She quietly sings a version of the Our Father when she has blood draws or any injections. Lucy reports,
>
>> Somehow prayer takes the edge off my anxiety. While I don't feel completely relaxed or comfortable, it helps me get through the experience better, and I'm grateful for it. Without prayer, I likely would find an excuse not to go to the doctor or have any medical procedures at all.
>
> However, Lucy sometimes uses prayer to ask favors of God, and then if her prayers are not answered in a way she desires, her faith is challenged, and she gets angry with God and herself. In this way, her prayer life can be destructive and problematic for her at times. For example, a close relative of Lucy's had heart disease and then suddenly died of a heart attack. She began praying for his well-being when he was diagnosed and then got angry with God when he died, stating, "It isn't fair! His wife and kids need him, and I can't believe God took him now. Why didn't he grant our prayer request? We even had lots of priest friends praying for him, too."

Lucy found a way to use prayer to help her better manage her anxiety and acknowledged that prayer is just one tool of many she might be able to use to deal more effectively with issues that create emotional and relational conflicts and stress in her life. However, her prayer life at times was destructive and caused her stress when she felt her prayers were not answered in a manner that suited her wishes. The therapist worked with Lucy in finding ways to use prayer that are healthy for her (such as coping with anxiety) and encouraged her to consider consulting her priest when she is upset about prayers not being answered as she desired. Furthermore, the therapist worked with Lucy to have an appreciation for all of the factors that contribute to heart disease, including genetic background and lifestyle factors. Her relative who died from a heart attack had a strong family history of heart disease, smoked cigarettes throughout his life, maintained a high-fat diet, and avoided exercise. Her therapist discussed with Lucy the notion that we cannot micromanage God, ignoring our own contributions to our health and well-being and expecting God to grant whatever we want whenever we want it. The therapist also encouraged Lucy to discuss her feelings of disappointment, grief, and loss both in individual therapy and in a local support group with others who have lost loved ones.

Meditation

Like prayer, meditation has many forms. Each of the religious–spiritual traditions, as well as denominations within each tradition, offers various types of meditation practices. Also like prayer, meditation has been found to enhance psychological health and well-being and improve physical functioning (Baer, 2003; Marlatt & Kristeller, 1999; Shapiro & Walsh, 2007). In the psychological and medical communities, mindfulness meditation has received the most clinical and research attention (Baer, 2003; Germer, Siegel, & Fulton, 2005). The work of Jon Kabat-Zinn (1990, 2003) and other health care professionals who have brought meditation techniques into mainstream health care services has greatly assisted both physical and mental health clinicians in better understanding the potential benefits of meditation (Bormann et al., 2006; Bormann & Oman, 2007; J. P. Miller, 1994). Mindfulness techniques are briefly discussed in the next section. For now, I focus on meditation in general and provide a few examples that might not be familiar to mental health professionals.

Meditation is thought to comprise three general categories: concentrative, mindfulness, and transcendental (Hartz, 2005; Marlatt & Kristeller, 1999). *Concentrative* meditation is reflective contemplation that involves "concentrated practice" (W. R. Miller, 1999, p. 3) and focused attention (Goleman, 1988). Concentration is usually enhanced by focused attention on an external object, such as a candle or religious–spiritual figure, or on something internal, such as one's breath (Marlatt & Kristeller, 1999). The goal of *mindfulness* meditation, perhaps the most popular type in both mental and physical health care settings, is to develop a detached way of noticing but not judging or manipulating one's experience (Shapiro & Walsh, 2007). Buddhists value detachment because they believe when people try to make permanent what is impermanent (which includes much of life), they will become frustrated, stressed, and ultimately dissatisfied. *Transcendental* meditation uses a mantra, such as a Sanskrit or religious term or phrase, to help focus one's attention (Hartz, 2005). All of the meditation styles involve concentration and focused attention, a retreat from distracting stimuli, muscle relaxation, and so forth, but each have different elements or perspectives that are emphasized.

Curiously, in contemporary times, meditation is generally associated with the Eastern religious–spiritual traditions, such as Buddhism, or spiritual traditions that are not associated with any particular religious tradition. Perhaps much of the popularity of mindfulness-based stress reduction in health care and other environments is because of the secularization of meditation to appeal to diverse religious and nonreligious populations. This secularization is especially important when meditation is offered and encouraged in government and other nonreligious institutions, such as public hospitals and schools. However, all of the religious traditions, including the more theistic ones such as Judaism, Christianity, and Islam, have a long history of meditation based on principles and techniques similar to those of the more popular and secularized meditative practices. For a variety of reasons, the meditative practices of these well-known theistic traditions have not received the attention and perhaps acceptance in contemporary mental and physical health care as those associated with Eastern traditions.

Research has consistently demonstrated the psychological and physical benefits of meditation (Baer, 2003; Benson, 1996; Bormann et al., 2006; Borysenko & Borysenko, 1994; Kabat-Zinn, 2003; Marlatt & Kristeller, 1999; J. Miller, Fletcher, & Kabat-Zinn, 1995; Shapiro, Schwartz, & Bonner, 1998). Benson, for example, suggested that meditation helps to promote the relaxation response and that when relaxation is associated with one's religious–spiritual convictions, it further enhances relaxation, leading to greater psychological and physical health benefits. In fact, recent empirical research has offered support for Benson's suggestion (Wachholtz, 2005; Wachholtz & Pargament, 2005; Wachholtz & Pearce, 2007). These studies randomized participants into meditative practices that involved secular mantra phrases (e.g., "I am happy") or religiously based mantra phrases (e.g., "God is peace") and found better results for spiritual meditative approaches than for secular approaches among college students and patients who experience headache, cardiac symptoms, and chronic pain.

One excellent example of a meditative technique used with psychotherapy is mantra, or holy name repetition (Bormann et al., 2006; Bormann & Oman, 2007). A *mantra* is a short phrase or a few key words associated with one's understanding of the sacred. Mantras are found in all religious–spiritual traditions and might include the name within a religious tradition for God or perhaps a brief quote from sacred scripture. Examples include "Heal me, Jesus" in the Christian tradition, "Hare Krishna" in the Hindu tradition, and "Om mani padme hum" in the Buddhist tradition, among many others. Ongoing repetition of a mantra throughout the day is recommended for spiritual comfort and inspiration as well as for coping with stress. In fact, research confirms that ongoing use of a mantra is associated with feelings of self-efficacy, confidence, and peace (Bormann et al., 2006; Bormann & Oman, 2007; Oman & Driskill, 2003) and with better coping with stress, enhanced spiritual well-being, and improved physical wellness, such as lower blood pressure (Bormann et al., 2006). Bormann et al. (2005) successfully used mantra training as an adjunct treatment with combat veterans who have posttraumatic stress disorder, patients with HIV, and health care workers experiencing job stress (see also Bormann et al., 2006). Clients can be encouraged to choose a mantra that feels most comfortable for them. Many other forms of meditation exist besides mindfulness and use of the mantra. For example, centering prayer is a popular contemporary contemplative Christian approach that has been used in both religious and secular communities for centuries. It became more widely known and practiced among Christian groups in the 1960s and 1970s through the influence and writings of Thomas Merton and Thomas Keating, both Trappist monks (e.g., see Keating, 1981; Keating, Pennington, & Clarke, 1978; Merton, 1969, 1973). It is used to develop relaxation, peace, solace, a closer relationship with God, and *hesychia* (i.e., inner silence). Methods vary, but all tend to follow four general steps:

1. Choosing a word or phrase that connects one to the sacred and divine within (e.g., in the Christian tradition, *Jesus, Abba,* or *Mary*).
2. Sitting in a comfortable position with eyes closed in order to be focused and avoid potential distractions.
3. Returning to the sacred word regularly, especially when distracted.
4. Remaining in silence with eyes closed for several minutes following the meditative prayer period.

The particular prayers and words used vary but often include the repeated use of the Jesus Prayer (i.e., "Lord Jesus Christ, Son of God, have mercy on me" or the briefer version, "Lord Jesus, have mercy"). Centering prayer has many similarities to the Eastern meditative processes but is focused on Christian beliefs and values and therefore may be more appropriate for Christians.

Therapists may wish to suggest meditation for their clients when it is appropriate and consistent the client's religious–spiritual tradition. Consider the following example:

Shana identifies with the Buddhist tradition and uses "Om mani padme hum" as her mantra. She reports that she especially finds herself using the mantra during her long and frustrating commute to work and that it somehow makes the commute less stressful and more relaxing. Shana says, "I'm a pretty Type A personality, and I've always hated my commute. Since I've become more involved with Buddhist traditions, including meditation, the commute doesn't feel quite as bad." However, Shana's involvement with meditation has caused some conflict in her marriage. She likes to attend meditation workshops and retreats on a regular basis and is actively involved with a local Zen center. Her husband, who appreciates the benefits of meditation but is not as actively involved with it as his wife, thinks Shana spends too much time and money on these activities. Now that they have several children, he thinks she should cut back on her involvement, and during an argument, he said it had become "a self-indulgent and time-consuming hobby." Shana thinks her meditation activities give her the peace, solace, and stress reduction that she vitally needs.

Shana found a mantra that is suitable for her, and she used it to cope more effectively with her stressors. She learned to use her mantra and meditative techniques in a variety of ways to reduce stress in both her personal and her professional life. However, her engagement with meditation activities also caused stress in her relationship with her husband. Shana's therapist encouraged her to continue to use meditative practices but said she may wish to consider them in the context of her family. Couples counseling was suggested so that Shana and her husband might come to some resolutions about how they spend their time as a family and manage the activities and responsibilities of their growing children. They used a variety of problem-solving approaches to outline their needs and desires, and over time negotiated a plan they could both live with. Shana and her husband also worked out a schedule and secured support from local family members.

Meaning, Purpose, and Calling in Life

Many people seek the services of mental health professionals in an effort to find more meaning and purpose in life (Delaney et al., 2007; Dreher & Plante, 2007). Although clients often articulate concerns about depression, lack of energy, feelings of disconnection from others, among other symptoms, these issues often, at their root, are concerns closely connected with a lack of meaning, purpose, direction, vocation, and calling in life. Many people find their religious–spiritual beliefs, traditions, and community help to frame these existential issues in a way that provides some direction as well as solace and peace of mind.

Dreher and Plante (2007) integrated positive psychology and spirituality principles with a proposed *calling protocol* that can be used in psychotherapy. It uses principles from the spiritual exercises of St. Ignatius (Mottola,

1964) to help clients develop a better sense of calling and purpose in their lives.

The calling protocol highlights the four Ds: discovery, detachment, discernment, and direction. *Discovery* refers to developing a better understanding of personal strengths. The positive psychology literature refers to these as "signature strengths" (Seligman, 2002; Seligman & Csikszentmihalyi, 2000; Seligman, Steen, Park, & Peterson, 2005). Therapists can help clients think about, define, and appreciate their particular gifts or strengths, And getting a firm understanding of them can then be used to determine how they can best be used to improve the client's sense of meaning and purpose and quality of life. For example, social skills, the ability to counsel others, musical talents, and organizational skills are just a few examples of strengths that can be used to improve quality of life and help find one's calling. It is important to have a realistic understanding of gifts to maximize the odds that they will be used effectively.

Detachment refers to working to move away from problematic and sometimes debilitating behaviors, thoughts, and attitudes that prevent individuals from appreciating and nurturing their gifts. These behaviors and tendencies include consumerism, greed, workaholism, alcoholism, dysfunctional relationships, low self-esteem, fear, anxiety, and a variety of other damaging behavior patterns that distract clients from their calling and prevent them from using and nurturing the talents defined during the discovery phase. Mindfulness meditation, for example, discussed in the previous section, can be used to help the client become more detached from these psychological and behavioral obstacles.

Discernment refers to thinking through how clients can best live their lives and use their gifts to experience consolation (e.g., peace, solace, joy) rather than desolation (e.g., depression, anxiety). The process of discernment is much of what psychotherapy can offer clients looking to secure more meaning, purpose, and sense of calling in their lives. Discernment helps clients better appreciate how their gifts can be used productively and realistically in a way that gives them comfort and peace.

Direction refers to developing a vocational path to live a more meaningful and purposeful life. Direction is the action plan that emerges when the discernment process is complete. Spiritual direction within many religious traditions has used variations on these four steps to help individuals develop more purpose, meaning, and sense of calling in life. These strategies can also be used with psychotherapy clients. Certainly the four Ds are not unique. Therapists without any interest or training in religious–spiritual matters have likely been using some variation on these themes with their clients for years. Perhaps what is unique is the integration of a spiritual mind-set, in this example, within the Jesuit and Roman Catholic tradition, to help psychotherapy clients find a way to better achieve a sense of calling, meaning, and purpose in their lives. Consider the following example:

Kali is a nurse in a large community hospital. She works primarily with patients with HIV/AIDS. She states that she has done much frontline work as a nurse with those who often were poor and marginalized even before they contracted HIV/AIDS. Over the years, she finds herself being touched by their life stories and the way many of these patients have managed their illness. She reconnects with her local Episcopal church, participating in a variety of social ministries in her city. After much thought and reflection, she decides to receive psychotherapy to better understand how she might find additional purpose and meaning to her life by entering the church diaconate training program. She says,

> While I have found a great deal of satisfaction working with patients, somehow I feel called to be able to do more by being both a nurse and a deacon. I think I could better blend my medical skills with spiritual skills in this way.

She hopes psychotherapy will help her better understand her gifts and possible calling in a neutral environment. Her therapist discusses the 4 Ds and how they work together to help her discern her next steps.

In this example, Kali found more meaning, purpose, and sense of calling in her life by working with a therapist who helped her work through the calling protocol, integrating spiritual and psychological mind-sets and perspectives to find a path that is more suitable for her. In the discovery phase, the therapist encouraged Kali to ask others who know her well in both her personal and her professional life to articulate her strengths and weaknesses and to give her honest corrective feedback for her to better understand what her gifts might actually be. The therapist also suggested she take vocational testing with the assistance of human resource professionals who might help her to more objectively evaluate her skills and weaknesses. During the detachment phase, the therapist encouraged Kali to participate in several guided imagery exercises to visualize herself in various work and career roles and to discuss her reactions to these experiences. Kali participated in guided imagery exercises that also asked her to visualize herself in various volunteer activities with emotional detachment and to observe herself as though she were watching a movie or television show. During the discernment phase, the therapist requested that Kali talk with clergy, spiritual directors, deacons, human resource consultants, and others to learn more about how her skills and interests might fit in various positions and vocational activities. She was asked to shadow or observe others in their positions to better determine whether particular activities felt suitable for her. During the direction phase, Kali decided to apply to the diaconate and go through the rigorous evaluation and application process. She also learned what additional training and experiences she would need to move forward with her goals.

Bibliotherapy

Bibliotherapy has been used in psychotherapy for decades (Norcross, 2006). Asking clients to read books that can help them better understand themselves, others, symptoms, diagnoses, or other issues they are struggling with has long been a useful tool for therapists. Religious–spiritual readings can also be added to the bibliotherapy toolbox for therapists. Reading sacred texts such as the Bible, Torah, or Koran, as well as the many commentaries written on them, can help clients in psychotherapy. Eastern religious traditions may include, for example, the Sruti and Smriti within the Hindu tradition or the Tripitaka in the Buddhist tradition. Furthermore, many self-help books that integrate spiritual and psychological principles are available as well. Many are listed in the Additional Resources section of this volume. However, the lists and suggestions in this book are certainly not exhaustive. More and more books are published regularly that can be used in spiritually–religiously informed bibliotherapy.

Richards and Bergin (2005) offered several helpful principles to consider when using spiritual bibliotherapy with clients. They suggested that the therapist be careful to recommend texts that are consistent with the client's religious–spiritual belief system and to avoid imposing the therapist's preferred spiritual readings that may not be consistent with the faith traditions of their clients. They further suggested that therapists be careful to stay within their area of competence by avoiding appearing as a religious–spiritual authority or by interpreting sacred texts for clients. Instead, therapists should be ready to refer patients to members of the clergy or other experts to help them answer questions about the meaning of sacred writings.

In addition to sacred scripture such as the Bible or Koran, Exhibit 4.1 contains a list of books that might be of interest to clients experiencing a variety of religious–spiritual concerns in psychotherapy. A more complete list of books (as well as other resources in bibliotherapy, such as Web sites and professional organizations offering free or low-cost materials) can be found in the Additional Resources section of this volume. A case example is as follows:

> Rondall struggles with his faith and religious teachings. He was brought up in an evangelical Christian home but stopped believing in church teachings during college. After he majored in engineering and received a master's degree in computer engineering, he embarked on a career as a software engineer. He thinks science does not support many of the things he was taught in church. His wife is a believing Christian from a similar background, and his struggles with his faith have caused conflict in their marriage. After discussing these matters in depth, he and his wife begin to read books by Huston Smith, John Spong, and others who present modern, nonfundamentalist Christian perspectives. They both find the books helpful and enroll in courses offered by a local theological seminary. Rondall says, "After [having] read several of these books, we [find]

EXHIBIT 4.1
Examples of Helpful Books for Bibliotherapy

Armstrong, K. (1993). *A history of God: The 4,000 year quest of Judaism, Christianity, and Islam.* New York: Gramercy.

Armstrong, K. (2000). *The battle for God: Fundamentalism in Judaism, Christianity, and Islam.* New York: HarperCollins.

Armstrong, K. (2006). *The great transformation: The beginning of our religious traditions.* New York: Anchor Books.

Benson, H. (1996). *Timeless healing: The power and biology of belief.* New York: Scribner.

Dossey, L. (1993). *Healing words: The power of prayer and the practice of medicine.* San Francisco: HarperCollins.

Easwaran, E. (1991). *Meditation: A simple eight-point program for translating spiritual ideals into daily life.* Tomales, CA: Nilgiri Press.

Fuller, R. C. (2001). *Spiritual but not religious.* New York: Oxford University Press.

Goleman, D. (1988). *The meditation mind.* Los Angeles: Tarcher.

Heschel, A. J. (1986). *The wisdom of Heschel.* New York: Farrar, Straus, & Giroux.

Kabat-Zinn, J. (1990). *Full catastrophe living.* New York: Delacourte Press.

Keating, T. (1981). *The heart of the world: An introduction to contemplative Christianity.* New York: Crossroad Publishing.

Koenig, H. G. (1997). *Is religion good for your health? The effects of religion on physical and mental health.* Binghamton, NY: Haworth Pastoral Press.

Luks, A. (1993). *The healing power of doing good.* New York: Ballantine Books.

McLennan, S. (2001). *Finding your religion: When the faith you grew up with has lost its meaning.* San Francisco: HarperSanFrancisco.

Merton, T. (1969). *The climate of monastic prayer.* Kalamazoo, MI: Cistercian.

Merton, T. (1973). *Contemplation in a world of action.* Garden City, NY: Image Books.

Myers, D. (2000). *The American paradox: Spiritual hunger in a land of plenty.* New Haven, CT: Yale University Press.

Plante, T. G. (2004). *Do the right thing: Living ethically in an unethical world.* Oakland, CA: New Harbinger.

Plante, T. G., & Thoresen, C. E. (Eds.). (2007). *Spirit, science and health: How the spiritual mind fuels the physical wellness.* Westport, CT: Praeger/Greenwood.

Smith, H. (1991). *The world's religions: Our great wisdom traditions.* San Francisco: HarperSanFrancisco.

Spong, J. S. (2001). *Why Christianity must change or die: A bishop speaks to believers in exile.* San Francisco: HarperCollins.

Spong, J. S. (2005). *The sins of scripture: Exposing the Bible's text of hate to reveal the God of love.* San Francisco: HarperCollins.

Walsh, R. (1999). *Essential spirituality: The seven central practices.* New York: Wiley.

ourselves hungry for more knowledge and information and actually [find] ourselves getting along much better. We seem to be on a productive track both spiritually and in our marital relationship."

Rondall and his wife enjoy learning more about religion, but some of their new perspectives conflict with those of their friends and family, who maintain more fundamentalist views. Sadly, they feel rejected by some of their friends and family, some of whom think they might be jeopardizing their eternal salvation.

Rondall found a way to integrate spiritually based bibliotherapy into his work with a therapist to achieve psychological, behavioral, and relationship gains. However, there were losses as well. Their readings led Rondall and his wife in theological directions that conflicted with the views of some family and friends, which contributed to several estranged relationships. The couple were pleased that they were more open minded and better informed but felt bad that several important relationships were perhaps lost in the process. The therapist worked with Rondall on the notion that any behavior or cognitive changes may result in both good and not so good outcomes, and they worked toward accepting the possibility that changes in thinking will change some relationships.

USING INTERNAL TOOLS IN INTEGRATION: A CASE EXAMPLE

The following case illustrates how several internal religious–spiritual tools can be integrated into therapy at once.

> Alma is a 32-year-old Latina originally from Mexico City who moved to the United States with her family when she was very young. Over the years, Alma developed an alcohol problem and received several citations for driving under the influence. She has been in a local chemical dependency treatment program associated with a community mental health clinic and now attends AA. She is married with no children and works in a hair salon.
>
> Alma, who is Catholic but attends church sporadically, repeats the Hail Mary prayer throughout the day to help her cope with stress. She feels connected to Mary and is proud that the Our Lady of Guadalupe vision occurred near where she grew up outside of Mexico City. When she is tempted to drink and is vulnerable at family events, parties, or after work with coworkers, she prays the Hail Mary and asks for help to avoid alcohol.
>
> Alma meditates using the rosary and also says the Jesus Prayer. She tries mindfulness-based stress reduction, which was discussed in her chemical dependency rehabilitation program, but does not find it useful. On reflection, she says it leaves her feeling empty because in her view it is not very religion centered. Also, she says she sometimes goes to her local church and meditates in front of the Our Lady of Guadalupe statue, which she finds comforting.
>
> Alma tries to find more meaning and calling in life, although she is greatly distressed that she is unable to have a child. In fact, she reports that her drinking problems seemed to get worse after having a miscarriage a number of years ago. She says family is very important in her culture and tradition and that several of her sisters now have large families. She is worried that she will not be able to have children and needs to think of a way to maximize vocation and meaning in her life, which might not involve having her own family. Using the calling protocol, Alma looks into teaching preschool or elementary school. She also looks into adopting but worries that her alcoholism and DUI record will make it difficult to be accepted as a good applicant for adoption.

Alma enjoys reading about the lives of the saints, especially the ones who struggled with personal demons and bad habits. Her therapist and she discuss a reading list that might give her inspiration and motivation to overcome some of her difficulties by learning about how others have done so.

Alma used several internal religious–spiritual tools with some success. These tools supplemented her chemical dependency treatment and improved its effectiveness.

CONCLUSION

Internal religious–spiritual tools such as prayer; meditation; meaning, purpose, and calling in life; and bibliotherapy can be integrated into psychotherapy to help clients achieve enhanced benefits. Mental health professionals are not required to become experts on prayer, meditation, vocational discernment, and bibliotherapy to help their clients benefit from these tools. Resources are available to help clients and therapists learn more about these tools, and consulting with other professionals, such as clergy, librarians, meditation centers, and churches, can be used to maximize the chances that clients will benefit from them.

In general, the internal religious–spiritual tools discussed in this chapter assist clients without any direct involvement with others. In the next chapter, I focus on external and other religious–spiritual tools that generally involve other people or other ways of viewing and interacting with one's community.

5

EXTERNAL AND OTHER RELIGIOUS–SPIRITUAL TOOLS

Tyrone tries to see the sacredness in everyone because he believes God dwells in all. He has tried to develop this perspective especially toward people with whom he has trouble interacting, such as his boss, several coworkers, and his brother. Tyrone says,

> Somehow I get along better with people, even those who drive me nuts, when I try to remind myself that God dwells in everyone. Since I've nurtured this way of thinking, I've noticed that my relationships have improved and those that can't really improve don't bother me quite so much.

Fiona volunteers at a local church-sponsored soup kitchen. She has a history of being depressed, lonely, and isolated. She also has a history of drug and alcohol abuse. Her pastor and counselor suggested that volunteer work might help her mood. Fiona tried volunteering during the holidays and found it surprisingly gratifying. She works at the soup kitchen several times each week. She says,

> I know it sounds trite, but I get more out of it than I give. I feel connected to the folks there and feel that the least I can do is be of some help a few times per week. Since working at the soup kitchen,

I feel less depressed and lonely, and I feel connected to many of the regulars there.

Noah attended Friday night Shabbat services after the September 11th terrorist attacks and has been attending ever since. Although not especially religious, he says he feels connected to his culture and religion by going to services. He reports,

> I feel part of something bigger than myself and something eternal when I go to services. The rituals, the language, the people all somehow make me feel more at peace and more grounded. I find that it helped me cope with the terror of September 11th, and I suppose it has helped me cope with life stressors ever since.

Tyrone, Fiona, and Noah have all found a way to use religious–spiritual engagement in community and with others in ways that have helped them cope with the various stressors they experience.

TOOLS FOR NURTURING EXTERNAL ENGAGEMENT AND ACCEPTANCE

In addition to the internal tools discussed in chapter 4, external tools can not only help clients in psychotherapy but also make the community a better place. In the sections that follow, I present a variety of external tools for consideration.

External Religious–Spiritual Tools

The common denominator with external religious–spiritual tools is that they focus on interactions or relations with others. These tools are often used both within and outside the religious–spiritual tradition and community and can be used not only to improve the well-being and functioning of psychotherapy clients but also to enhance their relationships with others. The following are examples of external tools: (a) attending community services and rituals; (b) volunteerism and charity; (c) ethical values and behavior; (d) forgiveness, gratitude, and kindness; (e) social justice; and (f) learning from spiritual models.

Attending Community Services and Rituals

Well known for his research and practice in relaxation and stress management in general, Herbert Benson (1996) stated that religious services "are full of potentially therapeutic elements—music, aesthetic surroundings, familiar rituals, prayer and contemplation, distraction from everyday tensions, the opportunity for socializing and fellowship, and education" (p. 176). Religious services and communities are a ready-made structure to help clients reap psychological and social benefits on a regular basis and at little or no cost.

Research clearly indicates social support can be effective in enhancing both mental and physical health (e.g., see Kulik & Mahler, 1989; Stroebe & Stroebe, 1996; Sugisawa, Shibata, Hougham, Sugihara, & Liang, 2002). Religious–spiritual communities and all faith traditions offer a ready-made social support system for members. They provide a forum and structure for people with at least some similar background, beliefs, and traditions to come together in community on a regular basis. Many of these groups offer not only regular religious services and liturgical celebrations but also various support groups (e.g., for divorce, unemployment, addictions), social justice activities (e.g., food pantries, demonstrations, political action committees), lecture series, and numerous other social activities to support, nurture, inspire, and improve their members. Most of these services and activities are free to church members and their guests. Furthermore, many church groups offer support services to the sick and older people in their community as well as to those struggling with life transitions such as the loss of a loved one, a new baby, or divorce. In fact, many church organizations offer services specifically targeted to community members experiencing mental health problems such as depression, anxiety, and so forth (Walters & Neugeboren, 1995).

Religious–spiritual communities provide a social networking opportunity that can be helpful to clients in numerous direct and indirect ways. When people come together on a regular basis with common interests and beliefs, friendships, business contacts, and other supportive relationships can develop and be nurtured over time. This can be especially useful in a society that has become more and more fragmented and whose members are increasingly isolated from each other. Too often secular social contacts and networks come and go and thus are generally not stable or reliable in contemporary culture. This is especially true in the highly mobile society of the United States, in which people often live in communities far from where they grew up or attended school and move often. However, religious–spiritual organizations and communities usually remain available, consistent, and stable and can be found even in remote locations. Religious communities also provide structured services and rituals that can be very helpful in the psychotherapeutic process. Funerals, baptisms, weddings, confession, and services of various kinds can all help people cope, manage, and punctuate life events, transitions, and important life moments. People seem to need rituals and ceremonies in their lives, and religious organizations provide plenty to choose from on a regular basis.

Of course it is important to mention that clients should not be encouraged to join religious–spiritual organizations or attend activities sponsored by these groups solely to make friends and business contacts. The social opportunities are added value to participating in religious–spiritual organizations, and clients may be encouraged to take advantage of them in addition to enjoying the religious–spiritual benefits they may achieve through these groups. Consider the following example:

> Pilar has felt lonely and isolated ever since she began her new job in a city thousands of miles away from her family and most of her friends. Although she grew up in the Episcopal tradition, she stopped being involved with any religious community after she went away to college. She would like to get married and start a family soon, saying, "My biological clock is ticking, and I worry that if I don't find a suitable partner soon, the odds of me being able to have children will decrease a great deal." Pilar has been unsatisfied with meeting potential dates in her small company, at local clubs and bars, or at fitness clubs. Although she does not consider herself to be particularly religious and does not identify with a particular faith tradition, she loves the values and "big picture" perspective that religion can provide. Her discussions with her therapist lead to the suggestion that she consider participating in some of the activities sponsored by the local Presbyterian church. The church is well known for welcoming people of many faith traditions and offers a successful singles group and a social-networking program. Pilar attends services at the church and later joins one of the singles groups. She reports that she likes the people in the group and that they generally share her values, ethics, and life perspectives. Over time, she begins to date a young man in the group and eventually marries him.
>
> However, once married, she experiences her new husband, Jack, as being "much more religious than I am." Pilar states that Jack never misses church on Sunday mornings, likes to participate in several of the church ministries, and in her view, gives too much of his time and money to the church. Pilar adds, "He's not a 'holy roller' but, gee, sometimes I really would like to sleep in on Sunday morning."

Pilar found a way to use religious ritual and community to help her cope with stress and feel connected to others. Furthermore, she found a marital partner through her church who shared her values and interests. However, once married, she noticed that she and her husband differed in their level of religious commitment and engagement, which created some distress for her. Over time, her therapist worked with her and her husband to help them accommodate each other's level of religious involvement. For example, Jack agreed to attend some religious services and activities without Pilar. He also agreed to donate to church missions from his own salary rather than from funds he and Pilar shared. Pilar agreed to engage in some of the church activities that she found most rewarding and interesting, including some of the social activities. Pilar and Jack compromised to develop a level of engagement with their church that was more agreeable to both of them.

Volunteerism and Charity

One of the remarkable paradoxes in life is that when we give to others, we seem to get much in return. Volunteerism and charitable works are critical parts of most religious organizations. Social justice activities—operating a soup kitchen; giving aid to victims of war, poverty, oppression, and disease; supporting those who are hospitalized, have new infants, or are grieving— are a large part of the mission of most religious communities. Research on volunteerism has demonstrated both its psychological and its physical benefits (Benson, 1996; Levin, 1994; Luks, 1993; Oman & Thoresen, 2005). Volunteerism helps people to feel they are contributing something important to others, distracts them from their own life stressors, and provides a helpful and productive perspective on life that few other activities can provide. Religious organizations are ready-made groups to help those interested in volunteering to do so. They supply the infrastructure, manpower, and support to make volunteering easy and efficient. They also often provide opportunities for volunteers to reflect on their experiences through a religious–spiritual lens.

Of course, some people should not volunteer if they have personality or other psychiatric disorders that might cause them to harm others. Furthermore, some people volunteer so much that they are chronically stressed and have little energy for themselves or for their own families and other personal responsibilities. However, in general, research and practice clearly show many benefits to ongoing charitable and volunteer activities, and religious organizations are well equipped to provide clients with these opportunities in a structured, organized, meaningful, and thoughtful manner. Pargament (1997) and Richards and Bergin (2005) articulated a number of benefits from volunteerism, including many unforeseen positive consequences, such as helping people minimize self-preoccupation and self-centeredness; learn to be more loving and giving; gain a sense of meaning, purpose, and belonging; and connect their religious values and beliefs with social actions. Furthermore, volunteers also provide the much-needed manpower to help others, making a better world for many. The following is a case example:

> Lola is having a tumultuous experience as a teenager. She experiments with drugs and alcohol, engages in a variety of sexual experiences, and is oppositional at school and home. Sadly, she is date raped by a 24-year-old man she meets at a local park while she is high. Because Lola is only 14 years old, police and the local child protection agency get involved with the case. Her family is actively involved in a local Christian church. During the holidays, her church's youth group works at a local soup kitchen for people who are homeless. Lola participates in the project and feels needed and wanted by the staff. After the holidays, she continues to volunteer on her own and feels committed to her work there. Her parents believe her work at the soup kitchen helps her focus her energies on something important and outside of herself. Furthermore, Lola states,
>
> > I know that if I don't find a way to do well in school and control myself better I could end up homeless myself. It helps me with my recovery, and I have an idea where my behavior can take me if I don't turn things around for good.

However, Lola's parents worry about the influence of some of the homeless clients from the shelter. Several have a criminal record and long history of substance abuse, and a few have been flirtatious with Lola. Lola asks her parents whether she can invite several of the clients home with her for their Easter celebrations. Lola's parents are concerned about whether Lola will maintain appropriate boundaries, and although they believe her volunteer activities are productive and healthy, they worry that she might make poor choices with some of the clients at the shelter.

Lola found a way to engage in volunteerism that resulted in improved psychological, behavioral, and relational functioning, perhaps getting more out of the experience than she had anticipated. However, some conflicts emerged when Lola's parents felt that several of the clients at the shelter may not be a good influence on her. In family therapy, Lola and her parents discussed their concerns, and the therapist talked with them about strategies for managing appropriate boundaries with homeless clients. The therapist also encouraged the family to talk with the director of the shelter about their concerns to determine what advice and policies the organization maintains regarding interactions with clients both in and outside of the shelter environment. They also worked out a buddy system in which Lola was paired with a more mature female volunteer who enjoyed watching out for Lola when she worked at the shelter.

Ethical Values and Behavior

Ethical values and behavior help to answer the age-old question "How ought we live?" All of the religious–spiritual traditions offer principles for living. The American Psychological Association's (2002) Ethics Code and those of other mental health organizations (e.g., see American Association for Marriage and Family Therapy, 2001; National Association of Social Workers, 1999) also provide guidance by describing values and principles for professional behavior. Religious traditions and moral philosophy have provided thousands of years of wisdom on ethical principles for living (Armstrong, 2006; Rachels & Rachels, 2007), and these principles can be used in various ways to help clients answer questions about how one ought to live (Plante, 2004).

Too often mental health professionals who do not have much experience with or knowledge about religion and philosophy (especially moral philosophy) assume the ethical principles for psychologists and other mental health professionals originated in professional mental health disciplines. In fact, principles such as avoiding exploitive dual relationships, including sexual misbehavior with patients, and maintaining confidentiality are well articulated in the Hippocratic Oath, written several thousand years ago (Von Staden, 1996). Most of the ethical principles mental health professionals endorse can be found in ancient documents, including religious–spiritual texts (Rachels & Rachels, 2007).

Regardless of the religious tradition, sacred texts such as the Hebrew Bible, the Christian New Testament, and the Muslim Koran often emphasize ethical and religious principles for living, such as maintaining integrity, responsibility, respect, and concern for others. The command to treat others with respect is mentioned in many ancient religious texts. For example, the Talmud asks, "Have you dealt honorably with your fellow man?" (Talmud Shabbat 31a) and also commands, "Respect one another" (Eleazar ben Azariah, Talmud). Concern for others and social responsibility also are repeatedly mentioned in these documents. For example, "If the community is in trouble, a person must not say, 'I will go home, and eat and drink, and my soul will be at peace.' A person must share in the concerns of the community" (Talmud Ta'anit). Issues regarding integrity are also discussed in biblical passages such as "The Lord detests lying lips, but he delights in men who are truthful" (Proverbs 12:22). Justice and mercy are repeatedly mentioned as well. One of my favorite biblical verses is "and what does the Lord require of me, but to do justly, and to love mercy, and to walk humbly with my God?" (Micah 6:8).

In the Christian New Testament, concern for others is a frequent theme in all of the gospels as well as the writings of St. Paul. For example, chapter 5 of the Gospel of Matthew reports that Jesus said, "Love your enemies and pray for those who persecute you." The chapter ends with Jesus commanding, "Be compassionate as your heavenly father is compassionate." Another example states that people should "share with those in need" (Ephesians 4:28). Respect toward others is highlighted in many Biblical references, such as "Be devoted to one another in brotherly love. Honor one another above yourselves" (Romans 12:10). Thus, ethical principles for living are well articulated in these religious texts. Although I have provided examples from the Jewish and Christian traditions here, they certainly exist in all of the religious traditions.

Clients likely have their own ethical principles that they try to follow, and it can be productive for therapists to assess what ethical principles are most important to them. For example, many try to adhere to the Golden Rule: "Do unto others as you would like them to do unto you." There is much wisdom and common sense to the Golden Rule regardless of one's religious tradition. In fact, all of the major religious traditions throughout much of history have concluded that the Golden Rule is one of the most important principles to live by (Armstrong, 2006). Many people value being honest. Others believe the divine (however defined) lives within everyone and thus believe all people are important and sacred. If one believes that the divine (or perhaps God or God's spirit) lives within all people, then one is likely to strive to interact with everyone in a more respectful, loving, and kind manner.

Determining the ethical principles most important to each client provides a baseline from which to work. For example, if clients report it is very important for them to be honest, psychotherapy could be directed toward enhancing honesty in them. If clients report that helping others is an important ethical principle for them, then that virtue could be emphasized during treatment.

One way to use the wisdom of all of the various approaches to ethics in an easy-to-remember structure is the RRICC model. Discussed in greater detail in chapter 6, the RRICC model refers to the following five ethical values: respect, responsibility, integrity, competence, and concern for others. Many of the challenges clients face in psychotherapy can be discussed using one or more of these ethical principles for living. There is nothing magical about these five principles, and clients may have other ethical principles or values that they find more useful or ring truer for them. For example, values such as civility, courage, generosity, moderation, loyalty, self-reliance, prudence, and patience might appeal to certain clients. The RRICC model is at least a place to start discussions of living ethically that is often useful to many people from various faith traditions. If clients agree that living according to these five values is important for them, they can discuss their efforts in treatment through this particular ethical lens. A case example is as follows:

> Ken prides himself on being a person of integrity. He feels he is a "stand up" guy who is honest in his business and personal dealings. He is an active member of the local Presbyterian church, and his family has been active in this church for several generations. However, during a work-related team-building event held offsite, he has a sexual encounter with his secretary after several days of team-building activities. Ken's wife finds out about the sexual liaison and confronts him. The couple experience a marital crisis and enter couples counseling. Ken struggles with the conflict between his perception of himself as a man of integrity and his behavior that was inconsistent with his view of himself. He identifies other ethical principles that can be used in his treatment: being responsible for his actions and being both respectful and concerned for the welfare of his wife and others affected by his sexual misbehavior (e.g., his secretary, her husband). He uses these ethical guidelines to respond to this crisis, make amends, and move forward.
>
> However, Ken passes on to his wife a non-life-threatening sexually transmitted disease that he had contracted during his encounter. His wife is furious and finds it very difficult to forgive him. Furthermore, at his wife's insistence, he encourages his secretary to leave his work group so that they will not have to work with each other any longer, which she does.

In this example, ethical principles and values consistent with the RRICC model were used to enhance the psychotherapy. Ken embraced the ethical principles of integrity, concern, respect, and responsibility to best cope with his marital infidelity. However, ethical challenges emerged when he felt forced to ask his secretary to leave his work group at the insistence of his wife. In addition, Ken's wife had a lot of difficulty forgiving him for his infidelity and for giving her a sexually transmitted disease. Ken stated, "I've made a mess of things, and ethical principles have helped me manage the mess but they don't make everything right. They just can't."

The language and principles of ethics, including very specific values articulated in the RRICC model, are used in therapy to help these clients best manage the stress and conflict in their lives. Therapists can help clients to discern what ethical principles and values matter to them most and then to find ways to incorporate them into their lives. As Ken stated in this case example, the ethical principles do not make everything right. Trying to solve one ethical problem (e.g., making things better with his wife) can result in other ethical challenges (e.g., asking his secretary to leave the work group). The ethical principles can help guide behavior but may create a situation in which one must decide among several less than perfect outcomes.

Forgiveness, Gratitude, and Kindness

Although one might not know it by reading the newspapers, nearly all religious–spiritual traditions (at their best) emphasize the need to approach others (and oneself) with forgiveness, gratitude, and kindness (Armstrong, 2006). Religiously inspired conflicts, intolerance, and warfare are highlighted in the news on a daily basis, but what these news stories fail to report are the more positive contributions of religion–spirituality in interpersonal and intergroup relationships. Forgiveness, gratitude, and kindness are often religiously inspired ways of being in the world that can be very useful to clients. Helping clients see the benefits of being forgiving, grateful, and kind with others while nurturing these qualities in themselves and those around them can be very productive for mental health functioning. Furthermore, compelling research in positive psychology has demonstrated the benefits of these qualities for psychological well-being and interpersonal relationships (Seligman, 2002; Seligman & Csikszentmihalyi, 2000; Seligman, Steen, Park, & Peterson, 2005).

Research suggests that encouraging forgiveness is actually one of the spiritual interventions most frequently used by therapists (e.g., see DiBlasio, 1992; Richards & Bergin, 2005) and that forgiveness is an effective way to minimize anger and promote both psychological and physical health and healing (McCullough, Pargament, & Thoresen, 2000; Worthington et al., 2001; Worthington, Sandage, & Berry, 2000; Worthington & Wade, 1999). Although encouraging clients to work toward forgiveness of self and others does not depend on religious–spiritual practices or traditions, the religious–spiritual aspects of forgiveness may give clients added inspiration.

What exactly is meant by *forgiveness*? A variety of definitions have been used. Enright, Freedman, and Rique (1998) suggested that forgiveness is a "willingness to abandon one's right to resentment, negative judgment, and indifferent behavior toward one who unjustly hurt us, while fostering the undeserved qualities of compassion, generosity, and even love toward him or her" (cited in McCullough, Pargament, & Thoresen, 2000, p. 8). Hartz (2005) suggested that the critical ingredient in forgiveness is letting go of anger and reducing negative thoughts and feelings about self and others. Forgiveness is also understood as being part of a continuum (Hartz, 2005) rather than being either all or nothing. On one end of the spectrum is no forgiveness, which perhaps embraces the anger one feels about another person perceived have committed an injustice. On the other end of continuum is complete forgiveness, which results in no negative thoughts or feelings toward the person who committed the injustice. Perhaps it is unrealistic to assume that clients will reach the complete forgiveness end of the spectrum for all experiences of injustice. However, they may be able to see the wisdom in working toward forgiveness of both self and others to achieve greater peace of mind and comfort.

One useful model of forgiveness used in psychotherapy is the REACH model, offered by Worthington and colleagues (i.e., Worthington, 2004; Worthington et al., 2000; Worthington & Scherer, 2004). REACH is a five-step process: recalling the hurt, empathizing with the perpetrator, being altruistic, committing to forgiveness, and holding on to forgiveness during doubts. Worthington suggested forgiveness is a religious–spiritual calling and necessary to stop the resentment victims find ultimately so destructive to their psychological functioning and healing. His model has been used in not only traditional psychotherapy situations but also war-torn areas of the world, such as Bosnia and Africa. Perhaps some of the most challenging aspects of forgiveness using the REACH model is the effort to develop empathy toward the perpetrator, to understand the behavior through his or her point of view, and to behave in an altruistic fashion. The five-step process is a stage model, in which each principle is discussed and worked on before moving to the next stage.

Of course, forgiveness and reconciliation is an ongoing process, and it is important to be aware and warned that premature forgiveness may expose a victim to more abuse. For example, a battered spouse might feel that he or she should forgive the abusing spouse out of religious conviction but in doing so may continue to expose him- or herself to potentially fatal violence. In addition, after thoughtful reflection, some clients may choose not to forgive others who they believe have harmed them. It is important for therapists to be respectful of their clients' decisions and not insist on forgiveness. Thus, the principle of forgiveness must be used in ways that help clients let go of anger and cope with relational stressors in a way that is health promoting, productive, and safe, with therapists being mindful of the clients' choice to forgive or not forgive on their own timetable.

The principles regarding forgiveness can also be applied to gratitude and kindness. One can approach others and life in general with these qualities without the influence of religious–spiritual directives or traditions. However, this way of being in the world is enhanced and highlighted by religious–spiritual teachings and traditions. Furthermore, as with forgiveness, one must be thoughtful about encouraging gratitude and kindness with clients who may put themselves in danger without duly considering how to incorporate these principles into their lives. Approaching others with a spirit of loving kindness and compassion and approaching life with a spirit of gratitude can be effective ways to enhance psychological functioning and interpersonal relationships, but they must be tempered with realism to avoid destructive or unsafe behavior patterns. Consider this example:

> Linda is struggling with her son and daughter-in-law. She has very high expectations for their behavior and generally feels they should be perfect in her eyes. For example, Linda is angry with her son and daughter-in-law for not sending her a birthday card for her 60th birthday. However, her son hosted a party, gave a nice gift, and planned on taking Linda out to dinner and a musical performance in celebration of her special birthday. Linda discusses how negligent her son was by not sending a card. After several sessions, Linda agrees it is important for her to be grateful for what she has and that she is expecting too much from her son and daughter-in-law. As an engaged Christian, she discusses the need for forgiveness and gratitude and understands the need for her to be more loving and kind regardless of how her son and daughter-in-law managed their lives and her birthday celebration. However, Linda continues to be challenged by her lack of forgiveness and inability to be grateful on a regular basis. Sometimes she says, "But I don't want to forgive and be grateful. Sometimes I just want to tell them off, and I don't care what they think when I do so." Her therapist has worked with her many times to remind her of the benefits of forgiveness and gratefulness as well as the consequences of her actions. Each time, Linda states how important these goals are for her but that it is so challenging for her to follow through with them, especially when she is in "the heat of the moment." Regular reminders, ongoing consultation, and additional spiritual practices such as prayer, meditation, and looking toward spiritual models have helped her improve. However, setbacks occur frequently.
>
> Linda also has trouble with alcohol, and often when she has a few drinks she tells her son and daughter-in-law how she really feels about them. Several encounters escalate into name calling, yelling, and hurt feelings.

Linda tried to incorporate a spirit of forgiveness, gratitude, and kindness into her life, with positive results. She worked to forgive her son and daughter-in-law and be grateful for what she has with them and also asked her son and daughter-in-law to forgive her for her angry outbursts, especially when she drank. Linda agreed to get help for her alcohol problem through a specialty clinic and Alcoholics Anonymous (AA). She worked toward both asking for forgiveness from and offering forgiveness to others. Although she continued to struggle with her sobriety, she worked hard to make amends and be grateful for what she has.

Social Justice

All religious traditions emphasize social justice in their effort to make the world a better place. Activities might include helping those who are poor and marginalized, charitable works, and influencing institutions to be more just to others. Religious groups are often at the forefront of social justice issues, advocating for the vulnerable among us, such as those who are less fortunate and/or cannot defend themselves. Religious institutions also frequently spearhead disaster relief efforts, food drives, and other community interventions.

Participants in these social justice causes have an opportunity to not only help others in need but also find inspiration, meaning, purpose, and compassion for others (Plante, Lackey, & Hwang, in press). In fact, research has found that engaging in social justice activities reduces perceived stress and enhances coping (Mills et al., 2007). Perhaps being attentive to the needs of those who are struggling helps clients keep their problems in better perspective and remain grateful for their lives (Mills et al., 2007; Plante et al., in press). One's own stressors often do not seem so bad when compared with the problems of those who are in greatest need.

Psychotherapy clients may also receive additional benefits regarding psychological well-being by supporting social justice causes that interest them: (a) added meaning and purpose in their lives, (b) a supportive community with common values and goals, and (c) distraction from their own life stressors. Justice activities also can help clients channel their attention and energy into a productive, healthy, satisfying, and worthwhile direction.

It is important to note, however, that social justice efforts can also create a situation in which harm is done to others. Efforts on the part of some religious groups to make the world a better place can greatly harm others. For example, militant antiabortion groups, antigay groups, and others can become violent and destructive. Tragically, some groups' efforts to create a better world can mean rejecting others or trying to deny out-group members of their rights and beliefs. Consider the following:

> Jen is a college student who experiences depression. Her family includes a variety of people with affective disorders, including a brother with bipolar disorder. Jen gets involved in the university's campus ministry community action association to give her something to do in addition to her studies. She quickly becomes interested in homelessness and organizes campus ministry students to work in a local shelter. She further studies issues about homelessness as a sociology and religious studies double major. She reports that she feels energized by her work in this area and finds herself having fewer episodes of depression, saying,

It's weird that by being engaged in the homeless issue and trying to help others I have really helped myself not only in feeling less depressed but by giving me an education and career direction that I've never had. I feel that God has helped me find a better path by helping others.

Although Jen feels very satisfied with her work at the homeless shelter, her engagement has left little time for her studies. Her grades slip, and her parents worry that she is spending too much time in these extracurricular activities and not enough time on her schoolwork. They are concerned that she is not getting the most of her college education and that she may not be in a good position for graduate studies or employment once she graduates.

Jen found a way to engage in social justice activities through her religious community. In doing so, she felt needed and wanted and improved her psychological well-being. However, her grades slipped, which created tensions with her parents. Jen's therapist provided time management strategies and helped her develop a long-term plan to best manage her priorities and energy. Jen agreed to cut back on some of her extracurricular activities to have the time and energy to put into her schoolwork and could understand the need to maximize her school performance in order to graduate on time and successfully. Her therapist spoke with her about how she could perhaps do more for the homeless as a successful college graduate than in her current volunteer position, which helped motivate Jen to work harder in school. Jen also enlisted several other students to work on some of these projects, which helped to reduce her responsibilities and agreed to work more intensely on her volunteer activities during the summer months, when she is on school break.

Learning From Spiritual Models

All religious traditions use spiritual models to help followers live a more spiritual, religious, ethical, and perhaps exemplary life. Islam refers to Muhammad as a "beautiful exemplar" (*uswa husana*, Qur'an 33:21). Hindu texts state, "What the outstanding person does, others will try to do. The standards such people create will be followed by the whole world" (Bhagavad Gita 31). Many are familiar with the popular question "What would Jesus do?" often referred to simply as "WWJD?" Research on observational learning (e.g., see Bandura, 1986) has clearly shown the advantages of learning by watching models. Ancient examples such as Jesus, Mohammed, and Buddha, or more contemporary examples, such as Mother Teresa, Gandhi, Martin Luther King, and the Dalai Lama, as well as unknown yet very important personal models, such as family and friends, help others live more spiritually and ethically. Research has found that having effective spiritual models also increases life satisfaction and a variety of health behaviors (Bandura, 2003; Oman & Thoresen, 2003).

Spiritual models can be used in psychotherapy by asking clients to name the people whom they admire and wish to emulate. Research has found that spiritual models are often family members who seem to exemplify living a high-quality life (Oman & Thoresen, 2007). Religious–spiritual leaders, such as church pastors, priests, and rabbis, can also be good models for living spiritually and ethically.

Oman and Thoresen (2007) suggested that spiritual modeling includes four important psychological processes that parallel those offered by Bandura (1986) in his research and understanding of observational learning: attention, retention, reproduction, and motivation. *Attention* refers to the need to attend to the behavior of the model. For example, once a spiritual model has been identified, a client can work to attend to their behavior to experience the model in action. *Retention* refers to remembering the behavior of interest. Clients must find a way to remember the behaviors that they have seen in order to incorporate them into their lives. *Reproduction* refers to actually engaging in similar behaviors as the model. They must mimic the target behavior. Finally, *motivation* refers to the desire to behave like the model in question. One must believe it is worth the effort for them to follow the model's behavior.

For example, one might choose Jesus as a spiritual model. One might attend to his behavior by closely reading and reflecting on Gospel stories and read them over and over again, attend Bible study groups, listen to clergy and faith community members discuss his behaviors, and so forth to maximize retention. One may then try to behave as Jesus would, to reproduce these spiritual behaviors. For example, the popular question "What would Jesus do?" is a good example of trying to articulate what Jesus would do in any given contemporary situation and to replicate that model behavior. Because Jesus lived more than 2,000 years ago, one must speculate on how he would respond to contemporary issues and engage in modern behaviors, such as driving, voting, and recycling. Finally, motivation is enhanced in a variety of ways that might include church services, prayer, rituals, community fellowship, devotional, and educational activities.

Many people use family members as models. Perhaps a parent, grandparent, sibling, or other important relative, friend, or colleague in the life of a client exemplifies better living and can serve as an effective model. Having living family members, friends, and other contemporary persons act as models has the additional advantage of their being able to answer questions and discuss principles for living directly.

Therapists can ask clients whom they look to as spiritual models, including persons from both the past and present, ask what qualities these models have that are so appealing, and then help them nurture these qualities within themselves. Spiritual models need not be perfect and thus perhaps harder to relate to by clients. Spiritual models may have both outstanding and problematic qualities that clients can learn to appreciate. See the following example:

> Matthew considers Martin Luther King Jr. an important spiritual model. As an African American, he thinks Dr. King has done more to help the African American community than anyone and feels inspired by his teachings and life. Matthew is committed to nonviolence and credits Dr. King's legacy and model for this commitment. He hosts a MLK party on the MLK long weekend, has memorized Dr. King's famous "I have a dream" speech, and has read many of his writings and biographies. Matthew says "I think that I'm a better person in general by experiencing Dr. King as a model for me." Sometimes he says to himself, "What would Dr. King do?" in particular situations that he encounters.
>
> However, Matthew is troubled by Dr. King's reported plagiarism in his doctoral dissertation in education from Boston University and his reported marital infidelity. It upsets Matthew that this very important model for him was not perfect. Matthew states that these reports are "disappointing" and sometimes "just takes the wind out of my sails."

Matthew found an important model to emulate, someone who demonstrated patterns of thought and behavior that motivate him to live better. Matthew's therapist worked to help him accept the fact that even outstanding models such as Dr. King had weaknesses and that having faults in some ways makes accomplishments even more remarkable and inspiring. Matthew, although unhappy with Dr. King's reported shortcomings, acknowledged that no one is perfect or should be expected to be perfect, and that people such as Dr. King can be powerful and inspiring models nonetheless.

Other Tools

I now turn to several tools that often improve psychological and interpersonal functioning.

Acceptance of Self and Others (Even With Faults)

Perhaps Zen Buddhism is especially well known for acceptance of self and others even with faults, but this value also is found in most other religious–spiritual traditions (at their best). Religious–spiritual traditions generally offer hope for those in need of forgiveness, reconciliation, and acceptance, and many clients desperately need to work toward better acceptance of themselves and others. Of course, acceptance of self and others does not mean one cannot improve oneself or benefit from corrective feedback about one's behavior. Acceptance of self and others does not mean complacency. It perhaps means we could use the acceptance offered by religious–spiritual principles to be more at peace with ourselves and others even with the faults that we all have. Being more accepting of ourselves and others has implications for many of the mental health troubles that clients experience, such as depression, anxiety, low self-esteem, and interpersonal conflicts.

Perhaps the well-known Serenity Prayer, previously mentioned in chapter 2 of this volume, which states, "God, give us grace to accept with serenity the things that cannot be changed, courage to change the things that should be changed, and the wisdom to distinguish the one from the other" (Niebuhr, 1987, p. 251), illustrates the perspective of accepting self and others that many religious and spiritual traditions offer. Although this prayer is so well known and so often referred to that it might be a cliché, it is effectively used in AA and other self-help programs and can be effectively incorporated into psychotherapy with appropriate clients. Clients are likely to achieve better psychological functioning and well-being if they work hard to live by this prayer. Consider the following example:

> Zoe's sister, Monica, drives her crazy. Whereas Zoe has always been very responsible, Monica has always been very irresponsible. Zoe has always bailed Monica out of financial, housing, relationship, and job troubles. With therapy, Zoe finds herself better able to accept Monica for who she is and to set firmer limits on their interactions to prevent her from feeling victimized by Zoe's irresponsibility. Zoe tells Monica, "I love you and accept you, but I'm just not going to bail you out any longer." With time and experience, Zoe finds she can develop a more satisfying relationship with Monica by accepting her for who she is without expectations for different behavior or personality.

> However, Monica's behavior still irritates Zoe. She states,

>> Sometimes I just can't believe the kind of stupid decisions she makes. So often I find myself saying, "What is she thinking?" But at least now I say it to myself rather than to her. However, I did say to her the other day, "Boy, it must really suck being you," which she didn't take very well. I suppose I shouldn't have said that, and I know that it will continue to take time and energy to just let go of my upset with her and fully accept her however she behaves.

Zoe worked to accept herself and her sister more in order to have a better relationship with her and for her own psychological functioning and peace of mind. Zoe tried to incorporate other strategies discussed in this volume, such as mindfulness-based stress reduction, forgiveness, and bibliotherapy, to help her cope better with her sister's behavior, in addition to other cognitive–behavioral techniques.

Being Part of Something Larger Than Oneself

Religious traditions, organizations, and settings all help to underscore the point that there is something bigger, perhaps more important and timeless, than our current needs, desires, and place in time. For example, religious temples and churches through the centuries have been designed to suggest that the faith they represent connects to something very important and larger than life. The great European cathedrals, such as Notre Dame in Paris or the Durham cathedral in England, as well as other great religious–spiritual structures, such as the Vatican, Mecca, and the Temple Mount in Jerusalem—all inspire awe and wonder. Religious ceremonies that have been performed in a similar manner for hundreds and thousands of years with special vestments, incense, traditions, ritual, language, and so forth, which all contribute to the notion that the religious–spiritual community, buildings, faith, and activities are connected to something grander and maybe more lasting than either ourselves or our daily concerns. Being connected to something larger and more timeless than ourselves has many psychological benefits (Pargament, 2007). It can inspire awe and wonder as well as keep the daily stresses of life in better perspective. See the following example:

> Ann does not describe herself as religious per se but finds that when she attends her Jewish temple for High Holiday services she feels uplifted, inspired, and connected to her religious community. She says,
>
>> Somehow I feel connected to this ancient tradition and people and am aware that there is something special, important, and eternal about all of this. I don't attend services during the rest of the year, but there is something special about the High Holiday services, where it just all comes together for me.
>
>> However, other aspects of the services she finds hard to accept. For example, she says, "What's with all the Hebrew? . . . [I] can't understand it at all," and she thinks "it seems too ancient and impractical." Also, she complains that the "services go on for what sometimes feels like forever."

Ann found a connection with something eternal and bigger than herself in religious ceremonies and structures. Despite not having described herself as being religious–spiritual, she found something powerful in her religious tradition. She recognized that the services are not "perfect" and contain elements that are difficult or troubling for her. Her therapist pointed out that although perhaps they are not ideal , the services do, on balance, provide an overall positive experience for her. Ann agreed that it is foolish to think that the services should be perfect and that the big picture is that she still found them to be meaningful and satisfying.

Appreciating the Sacredness of Life

All of the religious traditions underscore the notion that life and people are sacred (Armstrong, 2006; H. Smith, 1991). In fact it is "the heart and soul of spirituality" (Pargament, 2007, p. 32). Most traditions believe that God or a divine spirit exists within all of us. For example, the Jesuit order within the Roman Catholic tradition is well known for its phrase "finding God in all things." The Jesuits are not alone in this regard. The perspective that all living things, including people, are sacred is part of nearly all religious–spiritual traditions and has important implications for how people engage with others (Armstrong, 2006; Pargament, 2007; Spohn, 2000). Well-known and often-quoted Jewish theologian and rabbi Abraham Heschel stated, "Every act of man is an encounter of the human and the holy" (Heschel, 1986, p. 273). If one believes God or something divine lives within all of us or that all people are sacred, then one is more likely to treat all people with a higher level of respect and compassion. Many clients go to mental health professionals for psychotherapy because of conflict in important relationships. Many struggle with getting along with their children, spouse, boss, and others. Maintaining a mind-set that all are sacred may help clients find a way to interact with others with greater and more thoughtful care, respect, compassion, and love. Consider this example:

> Lori hates her coworker, John. She describes him as being a narcissist and a bully at work. She says, "I know it is wrong to hate people, and certainly my faith encourages me to 'love your enemies,' but this guy drives me crazy." Sometimes Lori gets so frustrated that she says she might just find another job, but generally she acknowledges that running away from the problem is not likely to be productive and that the odds are reasonable that there will be "other Johns out there wherever I go." After exploring a variety of problem-solving ideas to cope with her work relationship with John, Lori's therapist suggests thinking of John as someone who is sacred, as all people are sacred, and Lori works to come to terms with the fact that she can dislike someone for a variety of compelling reasons but can still work toward seeing that person as sacred and a child of God. Lori says her pastor suggested praying for John because the New Testament says one should pray for one's enemies. After initially being repulsed by the idea, Lori prays for John and finds that her anger toward him diminishes over time. Lori says, "I don't have to like him, but I suppose I have to try and love him, as we are called to love all people since they are sacred in the eyes of God."

Lori used her spiritual tradition to find the divine or sacredness in everyone, which helped her to approach others with more compassion and respect and improved her relationships. Like Zoe in the earlier example, Lori struggled with her relationship with John but continued to try to love him as a person and see him as a sacred being. She was encouraged by her therapist to consult her pastor for spiritual direction. Lori's therapist also encouraged her to use a variety of other spiritual techniques, such as mindfulness, to help her accept John for who he is and not to attach too much to his behavior. The therapist helped her to acknowledge his problematic manner but to distance herself from it and accept it for what it is for her.

USING EXTERNAL AND OTHER TOOLS IN INTEGRATION

A clinical example that incorporates a variety of external and other religious–spiritual tools may provide a sense of how these tools can be used together. In the following case, Reggie has struggled with a number of difficult issues associated with his military experience in Vietnam but has benefited from several external and other religious–spiritual tools in his recovery.

Reggie is a 60-year-old African American man who has a history of homelessness, alcohol addiction, unemployment, and posttraumatic stress disorder associated with his tour of duty in Vietnam during his late teens and early 20s. Reggie is being seen at a local community mental health clinic affiliated with a homeless shelter for clients with mental illness. He works on and off as a shuttle bus driver at various airports and rental car companies but frequently finds himself fired after failing to show up to work, which is usually associated with a period of substance abuse. Reggie grew up in the Baptist tradition but has had long periods of his life when his religious faith offered no solace for him. He was married many years ago but divorced and never remarried. He has no children.

Reggie notices that when he attends church services, he is less likely to feel lonely and be tempted to abuse drugs. However, his attendance is off and on. With Reggie's permission, his therapist at the community mental health center speaks with his pastor about ways to increase the chances that Reggie would attend services and other church-related activities as part of his treatment plan. His pastor offers several roles to Reggie, such as greeting people as they enter the church, helping with the collections, and assisting with coffee and donuts after Sunday services. Giving Reggie a role at church makes him feel needed and important and increases the chances that he will stay connected with the church community.

Reggie's pastor suggests that he get involved with one of the ministries that offer support to veterans from the Iraq war. The pastor has a number of Vietnam and Persian Gulf veterans in his congregation and develops a ministry in which these vets can offer support to the younger vets in the congregation. Although initially reluctant, Reggie bonds with a younger and now disabled veteran whom he enjoys talking with and helping. Reggie says that after a while he felt like an "older brother" to the younger veteran, which he admits he enjoys.

Reggie has participated in AA for many years and generally feels connected to the people in the organization. He has a sponsor at AA who was also a veteran, whom he thinks is a good fellow. Reggie also feels connected to his pastor at church, who acts as a spiritual model for him. Reggie finds that Jesus is an excellent model and likes the popular question "What would Jesus do?" The question helps guide him in his daily decision making.

Reggie has a lot of anger about how he believes veterans are treated by "the system." He feels his experiences in Vietnam were awful and that it was unfair that generally "poor minority kids from the inner city" like him were fighting the war while "well-off rich White kids" got to go to college instead. His anger about what he perceived to be an unjust war fought by those who were poor and marginalized has contributed to his substance abuse and acting out over the years. However, he is involved with antiwar protests and other advocacy activities for veterans. These activities also give him an opportunity to feel he can make a difference in the lives of others. During one protest, he is briefly interviewed by a local television reporter, which he really enjoys. Seeing himself on television, even for just a few moments, makes him feel important, proud, and part of a cause.

Reggie's church involvement and his veteran advocacy and AA group meetings all contribute to his feeling part of something larger than himself. He reports he feels less alone and engaged in something that really matters.

Reggie's Vietnam experiences were very traumatic for him. Even many years later, he cries when he talks about the things he witnessed there and participated in. One of the outcomes of his experiences in Vietnam is the appreciation that life is sacred and can end at any time. His therapist works with Reggie to try to apply this view to himself and to better care for his body and mind by avoiding substances. With his therapist, Reggie adopts a mantra of "I'm sacred too."

Reggie has struggled with acceptance of himself and others over the years. His self-esteem is low, and he often refers to himself as a "screwup." He feels especially embarrassed that he has been homeless and has not stopped his substance abuse. Reggie works hard in therapy and in AA and other programs to be more accepting of himself and others. It is a struggle for him, but he makes progress slowly.

Reggie used a variety of external and other religious–spiritual tools in his efforts to cope better with his troubles. Although he continued to struggle, the tools helped him make very good progress. Furthermore, his church and AA involvement had the additional benefit of having others watch over him and both support and encourage his progress.

CONCLUSION

In this chapter, I focused on external and additional religious–spiritual tools that involve relationships with others or highlight a spiritually informed perspective toward them. Psychotherapeutic activities can be enhanced when religious–spiritual tools are used appropriately. As I mentioned in chapter 4, it is not necessary for the mental health professional to be an expert in each of these religious–spiritual tools or actually provide them to the client. It is enough to be aware of them and know when to discuss them with clients.

In the next chapter, I discuss ethical issues in religious–spiritual integrative psychotherapy, providing several principles to follow and examples of common pitfalls to avoid.

6

FIVE ETHICAL VALUES TO GUIDE PROFESSIONAL BEHAVIOR

The most recent edition of the American Psychological Association's (APA's) Ethics Code (2002) states that psychologists must consider religious issues as they do other types of cultural diversity, such as race, ethnicity, gender, and sexual orientation. Specifically, the Ethics Code states,

> Psychologists are aware of and respect cultural, individual, and role differences, including those based on age, gender, gender identity, race, ethnicity, culture, national origin, religion, sexual orientation, disability, language, and socioeconomic status and consider these factors when working with members of such groups. (APA, 2002, p. 1063, Principle E)

The Ethics Code therefore demands at least some degree of sensitivity toward religious diversity (see Koocher & Keith-Speigal, 2007). In addition, APA's multicultural guidelines further discuss the need to respect and be competent in diversity issues, including religious–spiritual diversity (APA, 2003). APA is not alone. The ethics codes of other mental health professions generally agree that religious issues should be considered in the same way as other diversity issues (e.g., see American Association for Marriage and Family Therapy, 2001; National Association of Social Workers, 1999).

RESPECT, RESPONSIBILITY, INTEGRITY, COMPETENCE, AND CONCERN

If psychology and related fields continue to integrate religious–spiritual matters into their professional work, many important ethical issues must be considered, and this chapter highlights the most compelling ones. Although there are many strategies and principles to consider, I use the APA Ethics Code here and, more specifically, the RRICC (i.e., respect, responsibility, integrity, competence, and concern) model of ethics, which readily applies to various mental health ethics codes (Plante, 2004), to consider the integration of religion–spirituality into psychotherapy by emphasizing the ethical values of respect, responsibility, integrity, competence, and concern. These values are represented in the ethics codes of not only psychologists but also social workers, marriage and family counselors, and mental health professionals in other countries. Therefore, these five ethical values are likely relevant for most mental health professionals in the United States and abroad. However, for efficiency I use the APA Ethics Code for quotes and as a reference. The other professional codes are more similar than different regarding these issues and do not all need to be repeated here (American Association for Marriage and Family Therapy, 2001; National Association of Social Workers, 1999; Plante, 2004). In most cases, I also provide several real-life case examples to illustrate both appropriate and inappropriate ethical decisions.

Respect

The quote noted earlier from the APA Ethics Code regarding respect for religious differences and diversity comes from the section that focuses on "respect for people's rights and dignity" (APA, 2002, p. 1063, Principle E). It is critical that therapists treat their clients (and people in general) with a high degree of respect regardless of religious perspectives or other differences. Psychology has a long history of sometimes being paternalistic toward others by smugly dictating what is and is not healthy psychological functioning. In previous decades, clients who were highly religious or spiritual were too often pathologized by the field of psychology and individual clinicians. These clients were often considered repressed, defended, insecure, and deluded; they were seen as living in a fantasy world and being in need of treatment for their attachment to religion (e.g., see Ellis, 1971; Freud, 1927/1961). Their beliefs were certainly not respected.

The APA Ethics Code and other ethics codes now articulate the need to respect religious–spiritual beliefs and values and to avoid pathologizing those who seek religious–spiritual identification, growth, and involvement. Although therapists certainly are not required to agree with all faith beliefs, behaviors, and rituals, and even may find some religious points of view highly distasteful and destructive to health and well-being, they are asked to be respectful of the religious–spiritual beliefs and traditions of others. Therapists also must be respectful of the role of clergy and spiritual models (both current and from the ancient past) in the lives of religious–spiritual clients. Clients might frequently refer to these models (e.g., Jesus; Buddha; Mohammad; their pastor, rabbi, priest) in glowing terms. The Ethics Code calls therapists to avoid bias in this regard, stating, "Psychologists try to eliminate the effect on their work of biases based on those factors, and they do not knowingly participate in or condone activities of others based upon such prejudices" (APA, 2002, p. 1063). Ethical Standard 3.01 in the Human Relations section of the Ethics Code further calls therapists to avoid any kind of discrimination based on, among other qualities, "religion" (APA, 2002, p. 1064).

Spiritual and Religious Bias

As mentioned earlier, most professionals interested in integrating religion–spirituality into psychotherapy have been involved in a religious–spiritual tradition. They may feel very knowledgeable about their own tradition yet uninformed about other faith traditions. For example, a Christian therapist may know a great deal about the Christian tradition from his or her denominational perspective (e.g., Catholic, Methodist, Seventh-Day Adventist) but very little about the non-Christian traditions or even other Christian denominations. Thus, it becomes important for professionals to keep their own potential biases in check, most especially when they know little about, or perhaps are even antagonistic toward, particular traditions and denominations.

Case Examples of Respect Issues in Treatment

Dr. A is a therapist who does not identify with any religious–spiritual tradition. He grew up in a secular home and never had much interest in religious–spiritual matters. Dr. A is proud to be a rational and empirically minded professional who specializes in behavioral medicine and health psychology and is associated with a large university medical center. He tends to believe that religion has done much more damage to the world than good and is a silly and delusional preoccupation for many. He is treating a client with cardiovascular disease who recently had a heart attack. Dr. A is asked to work on discharge planning that aims to improve the patient's lifestyle with diet and exercise. His patient is a devout Christian who peppers his speech with Bible quotes and references to "the Lord" and "the Lord's will." Dr. A has little tolerance for his patient's religious beliefs and language, rudely suggesting that he talk with a hospital chaplain and telling him to come back when he is ready to work on improving his lifestyle without all the "God mumbo jumbo."

Dr. A did not respect his client's religious beliefs and dismissed his spirituality as getting in the way of effective treatment. Although Dr. A is not required to agree with his client's views, he must respect them and work with them as effectively as possible without bias or discrimination. Dr. A may need ongoing consultation with a clergy member or appropriate mental health professional to ensure that the client is treated with respect.

> Dr. B is a therapist who does not identify with any particular religious–spiritual tradition and grew up in a mostly secular environment. Her clients, a highly devout and involved Mormon couple, have been having trouble managing the behavior of their teenage son. They report that he has been rejecting of their religious tradition and that he wants to be like many of his non-Mormon peers. They had hoped he would go to a Mormon college, such as Brigham Young University, where they had met, but he wants to go to a local state school and says he wants to live his own life. Although Dr. B acknowledges that she does not know a lot about the Mormon tradition, she wants to be respectful of it and perhaps involve either another therapist or a clergy member who is much more familiar with that faith. With permission, Dr. B consults a more knowledgeable peer and tries to help the family in a thoughtful and respectful manner. Although she is honest with the parents about her lack of knowledge, they want to continue working with her because of her excellent reputation.

Dr. B was respectful and honestly articulated her level of competence with her clients, getting consultation as needed.

Responsibility

High-quality research from multiple sources over many years clearly indicates that the vast majority of Americans (and most people around the globe) believe in God; are affiliated with a religious tradition and some type of church, mosque, or temple; wish to be more spiritually developed; and want their health care providers (including mental health professionals) to be aware and respectful of their religious–spiritual traditions, beliefs, and practices (Hartz, 2005; Koenig, 1997; Koenig et al., 2001; Myers, 2000a, 2000b). Because religion–spirituality plays such an important role in the lives of most people, therapists have a responsibility to address this critical aspect of peoples' lives as they work with them. Just as therapists have some responsibility to be aware of the importance of biological, psychological, and social influences on behavior and functioning, they must also be aware of and thoughtful about religious influences. If solid research tends to support the notion that health benefits can be expected for those engaged in religious–spiritual activities, then it would be irresponsible for therapists to ignore that finding.

Furthermore, when desired by clients, mental health professionals should work collaboratively with clergy and other religious leaders involved with clients' pastoral care (McMinn & Dominquez, 2005; Plante, 1999). The APA Ethics Code states that "psychologists consult with, refer to, or cooperate with other professionals and institutions to the extent needed to serve the best interest of those with whom they work" (APA, 2002, p. 1062, Principle B). Although therapists usually have no trouble working collaboratively with physicians, school teachers, guidance counselors, and attorneys, as needed by their clients, they now must add clergy and religious leaders to this list of collaborating professionals.

Case Examples of Responsibility Issues in Treatment

> Dr. C is treating a profoundly depressed adolescent patient who is pregnant from a sexual encounter with her high school boyfriend. The patient is deeply religious and comes from a very conservative Roman Catholic home. To her and her parents, abortion is just not an option. Dr. C thinks this point of view is crazy and that abortion is the best possible solution. Dr. C does not ask about her religious beliefs and does not feel a need to consult the girl's parish priest. After several weeks, the client makes a serious suicide attempt and is admitted at the local psychiatric hospital.

Dr. C chose not to engage the client's clergy or discuss the religious–spiritual issues of an unwanted pregnancy within the context of treating a devout, conservative Catholic client and family. A suicide attempt could have been averted with closer attention to the religious dimensions of the client's troubles.

> Dr. D is treating a depressed middle-aged Jewish woman who is upset that her daughter has decided to marry a non-Jewish man. She finds the young man very likeable but cannot help feeling that her daughter should marry someone who is Jewish. She and her daughter have had many arguments about this issue. Dr. D is not Jewish and knows little about Jewish traditions and culture. He communicates his lack of knowledge to the client and offers to consult a colleague and rabbi about the matter, with her permission.

Dr. D responsibly acknowledged his lack of understanding of the issues related to her religious tradition and offered to consult others to ensure the client received the best quality of treatment.

Integrity

Mental health professionals are required to act with integrity by being honest and fair toward all with whom they work, being open about their limitations as professionals, and avoiding any type of exploitive deception. Integrity requires them to carefully monitor professional and personal boundaries, which can be easily blurred when religion–spirituality is integrated into psychological services. Therapists must remember that they are mental health professionals and not clergy or theologians unless they have those credentials. Being an active member of a particular religious tradition does not make a therapist an expert in religious areas that were not part of his or her professional training. Even if a mental health professional is a member of the clergy, and thus maintains both roles, he or she must be very clear about professional boundaries to minimize role confusion.

Promoting Quality Science and Practice First

First and foremost, mental health professionals must be careful to always provide state-of-the-art mental health services based on sound clinical science and practice guidelines regardless of the religious–spiritual persuasion of the client. Although that point might seem obvious, sometimes mental health professionals, in an effort to respect religious diversity, fail to provide the same quality of service they would to nonreligious clients. For example, a client may engage in harmful behaviors toward self or others because of religious convictions, such as physical or sexual abuse, neglect, discrimination, or harassment. Yet because the client's behavior is conducted in the spirit of his or her religious beliefs, a therapist might feel compelled to support the client or perhaps not intervene in a way that state-of-the-art science and practice would suggest.

For example, a religious client who experiences anorexia nervosa may conduct a traditional Yom Kippur (if Jewish), Good Friday (if Christian), or Ramadan (if Muslim) fast in a manner that is destructive, given her psychiatric diagnosis. She might extend the traditional fast to include, for instance, all of the days during the High Holidays if Jewish or throughout Holy Week if Christian. Perhaps the fast continues long after these holidays are over. A therapist, in an effort to be sensitive to the client's religious tradition, may not intervene regarding the fast, which could have serious and even fatal consequences. Another client may wish to prevent his or her daughter from receiving medical attention or refuse to send her to school because of religious beliefs about the role of education and medical care for women. A parent may feel religiously justified in hitting his or her child with a belt or other object, attempting to deal with the child's sin or out of a belief that demonic spirits are motivating the child's misbehavior. Another client might feel justified in using and providing to others illegal mind-altering drugs for spiritual enhancement. It is important for mental health professionals to first and foremost provide quality care that is based on ethical and legal guidelines in addition to quality empirically supported treatment. They must be careful not to abandon these important principles when religious–spiritual reasons are invoked by their clients. Religious–spiritual motivations for behavior do not trump high legal and ethical standards for practice.

Blurred Boundaries and Dual Relationships

Many religious–spiritual people desire to work with professionals who share their faith community and interests, and it is very common for church members to refer to a therapist from their own group. This practice creates boundary conflicts when the professional now treats or evaluates many members of his or her own faith community. There are rarely hard and fast rules about these potential boundary conflicts other than to avoid exploiting others and confused roles. The nature of the work, the size of the religious congregation, the type of possible dual relationships that might emerge, and the need for clarity of roles and responsibilities all need to be carefully considered.

Case Examples of Integrity Issues in Treatment

> Dr. E is very active in the local Zen center. He conducts workshops on mindful meditation, takes yoga classes, and enjoys meditation retreats on a regular basis. He is also on the advisory board for the Zen center and has gotten to know most of the members of the community. Because Dr. E is an engaging person and has a thriving clinical practice, many members of the Zen center seek him out for professional psychological services for themselves and their family members. Boundaries are often blurred, and Dr. E talks about clinical matters with his current and former patients at various Zen center events with others within earshot of his conversations. A former patient gets very angry when she overhears Dr. E talking with someone about one of his patients with whom she is good friends.

Dr. E blurred professional and personal boundaries in a way that likely created dual relationships and the possibility of exploitation. Because Dr. E was so active and involved in the Zen center, it might have been wise for him not to see patients from there to avoid these conflicts.

> Dr. F is an active member of her church, serving on various committees and participating in a variety of church activities. Because fellow congregants know she is a psychologist, they wish to see her (and refer friends and family) for their psychotherapy needs. Dr. F appreciates the vote of confidence but feels that she cannot treat or evaluate people from her religious community because of possible conflicts of interest and dual relationships. She works out an arrangement with another therapist who has a similar situation in her own church across town so that they work with clients from each other's church community.

Dr. F thoughtfully made arrangements to avoid possible dual relationships yet still ensured that her fellow congregants obtained appropriate professional services from a colleague who was well versed in the religious tradition.

Competence

Because the vast majority of graduate and postgraduate training programs ignore religious–spiritual integration in professional training, how can mental health professionals competently provide the much-needed services of integration? Clearly most professionals are on their own to ensure that they get adequate training and supervision. Richards and Bergin (2005) offered several specific recommendations about training to better ensure competence in integrating religion–spirituality into psychotherapy: (a) reading the solid literature now available on this topic, (b) attending appropriate workshops and seminars, (c) seeking out supervision and consultation from appropriate colleagues, and (d) learning more about the religious–spiritual traditions most common among one's clients. As discussed earlier, Pargament (2007) offered a thoughtful list of problems that well-meaning mental health professionals may bring to religiously–spiritually integrated psychotherapy: bias, myopia, timidity, overenthusiasm, cockiness, and intolerance for ambiguity. In addition to the recommendations offered by Richards and Bergin, Pargament suggested that therapists take a course on comparative religion and that graduate programs offer appropriate courses in this area.

Luckily, many quality workshops, conferences, seminars, books, and articles exist, including a series of professional journals dedicated to the integration of religion–spirituality in psychology (see the Additional Resources section of this volume). Furthermore, establishing ongoing professional consultation with experts in religious–spiritual integration is now easier in many locations because of the popularity of psychology and religion topics. The professional organizations, such as APA and the Society of Behavioral Medicine, maintain special interest groups in this area and electronic mailing lists that allow for an electronic community of interested professionals to stay connected and consult each other.

Just because a mental health professional is a member of a particular religious–spiritual community does not mean he or she either is an expert in that tradition or can integrate religion–spirituality into his or her work. Members of faith traditions vary greatly in their knowledge and comfort level, and thus professionals must avoid using their religious–spiritual knowledge in a manner that gives the impression that they are experts in their faith tradition. Furthermore, they must be sure that they do not usurp the role of clergy and avoid falling into pastoral care, spiritual direction, or theological consultation unless they have expertise in those areas.

Supporting Tolerance and Fighting Inflexibility

Many of the problems and conflicts that therapists are likely to encounter in religiously–spiritually integrated psychotherapy involve client religious–spiritual inflexibility. In general, therapists can help clients in many ways when they support religious–spiritual tolerance and combat religious–spiritual rigidity (Pargament, 2007). Religious–spiritual inflexibility frequently leads to conflict in clients' social relationships as well as to anxiety, depression, and other problematic thoughts, feelings, and behaviors. For example, clients might feel that only their particular religious beliefs are correct and that everyone who disagrees with them is not only wrong but doomed to eternal damnation. Obviously, this perspective makes social relationships with friends, family, neighbors, and coworkers very challenging if not impossible. Clients might also expect from themselves and others what they believe is perfection in thoughts, feelings, and behavior because imperfection might be perceived as spiritual weakness or sin. This perspective can not only create a high degree of anxiety and depression among clients but also result in child abuse and suicidal and other self-destructive behavior.

Although therapists must stay within their area of competence and must not impose their value of tolerance on their clients, they can encourage clients to think more carefully about religious–spiritual inflexibility and perhaps consult clergy or religious experts within their faith tradition to develop a spirituality that is health promoting and adaptive rather than health damaging and maladaptive. Clients often behave much more intolerantly and rigidly than their religious–spiritual models and clergy members; this inflexibility is often based on fear and usually is not supported by the theology and doctrine of their faith tradition.

Attending to Overgeneralizations

Therapists as well as the general population too often overgeneralize when it comes to religious–spiritual traditions that they know little about. Sadly, most information about religious–spiritual traditions and perspectives is likely obtained from sensationalized media stories about the very worst religious traditions and communities have to offer. Furthermore, all faithful and involved members of a religious tradition and community do not necessarily believe all of the official teachings and guidelines of their faith tradition. For example, all Jews do not keep kosher, follow Shabbat guidelines, and support Israel's political decisions. All Catholics do not support the Church's positions on abortion, divorce, homosexuality, and female priests. All Christians do not necessarily believe that Jesus physically rose from the grave or that he was born of a virgin.

It is important for therapists to remind themselves of the great diversity in belief and practice even within faith traditions. This is true not only of individual members from a faith tradition but also of clergy themselves. It is especially easy to overgeneralize about those who come from traditions with which the therapist is unfamiliar, and thus therapists must be especially on guard when they work with clients from these traditions.

Attending to Transference and Countertransference

Although therapists always should attend to transference and countertransference issues with their clients, perhaps it is especially important to do so with clients who fall into one or more of the seven circumstances discussed in this chapter. Religious–spiritual beliefs and practices have a way of eliciting transference and counter transference issues in psychotherapy. For example, religious clients may behave toward their therapist as they would toward their clergy member. This is especially true if the therapist and client share the same faith tradition and if the clergy member referred the client to a particular therapist. Therapists are prone to countertransference issues with religious–spiritual clients, perhaps driven by their own religious beliefs, practices, and biases.

Getting Consultation

Although getting consultation as needed is an important principle for any therapist regardless of the nature of his or her clinical work and client profile, it is important to have strategies and appropriate professional contacts available when working in religiously–spiritually integrated psychotherapy. No therapist can be an expert on all religious–spiritual traditions and perspectives, and no therapist can be as fully informed about religious–spiritual matters as clergy or theologians. Furthermore, working closely with a representative of the client's religious–spiritual tradition can often be helpful to provide the best and most integrated psychotherapy (see chap. 8 for an in-depth discussion of consultation issues).

Case Examples of Competency Issues in Treatment

Dr. G is an active member of her Baptist church. Religion is important to her, and she finds herself talking about religious issues with many of her clients. Her views on theology, salvation, sin, and so forth are well integrated into her professional clinical services. When she treats fellow Baptists, she feels especially free to discuss religious issues and concerns.

Although Dr. G was an active and engaged Baptist, she was not a member of the clergy and had no theological training or professional experience in this regard. She inappropriately assumed that if she was a member of a particular faith community, she could integrate her views into her professional psychotherapy services.

Dr. H is a Catholic psychologist who is well known for his work with the Catholic Church. His patient experiences a great deal of guilt, which she attributes to her strict Irish Catholic background. She has panic disorder and worries that her thoughts, behaviors, and impulses might be sinful. She knows that Dr. H is a Catholic and asks whether some of her most embarrassing thoughts and feelings, which she is too uncomfortable to discuss with her priest, might be sins. She asks questions about life after death and about Church teaching on a variety of topics. Although Dr. H has thoughts on these matters as a Catholic, he informs her that these types of questions are best addressed in spiritual direction with a clergy member or church professional but psychotherapy could help her cope with the feelings associated with her beliefs.

Dr. H carefully articulated his area of competence and tried to provide his client with referrals to help address her religious questions.

Concern

At the heart of the mental health professions is concern for the well-being and welfare of others, and this concern must be nurtured and expressed among those who seek to integrate psychology and religion. Although therapists are asked to be respectful to those from various religious traditions, this respectfulness has limitations when religious beliefs and behaviors turn destructive. Concern for the welfare of others always trumps other ethical values.

Unfortunately, many people have suffered a great deal because of religious conflicts and beliefs over the centuries, and many still do today. There are too many examples of people being abused, neglected, and even killed for religious beliefs and behaviors. Others have been burdened with feelings of guilt and rejection because they did not live up to the standards expressed by their religious leaders or expectations set forth by their religious tradition. Many have been shunned because of choices they made regarding spouses, children, careers, or other decisions that were viewed as wrong by their religious leaders and traditions.

Tragically, religious beliefs can lead people to engage in highly destructive and even lethal behaviors. Although terrorism and suicide bombing in the name of religion are extreme examples, less fatal yet still destructive behaviors occur in the name of religion. For example, parents of particular religious traditions refuse medical treatment for sick children or believe that physical punishment of children and spouses is acceptable. Some believe that circumcision should be conducted on adolescent girls. Others believe denying females medical, educational, and other services is the right thing to do.

Although ethics codes require professionals to be respectful of religious traditions and beliefs, they certainly do not require therapists to be complacent or condone destructive thoughts, feelings, and behaviors, most especially when they result in significant physical or mental harm by both legal and ethical definitions. Their concern for the welfare of people must be paramount in their work, especially when religious beliefs create harm to self or others. Thus, when someone seeks to "kill infidels," commit terrorism, or oppress and abuse others in the name of their religious tradition, therapists' concern for others must force them to act to prevent harm. This concern might propel them to report child abuse, involuntarily commit someone to a psychiatric facility, or engage other legal means to avoid any serious harm to self and others.

Case Examples of Concern Issues in Treatment

Dr. I is a school psychologist who is evaluating an elementary school child with symptoms of attention-deficit/hyperactivity disorder. The child's teacher made the referral because of classroom misbehavior and inattentiveness. During the evaluation, it becomes clear that the child comes from a highly conservative, evangelical Christian home and that he is hit with a belt for even minor transgressions that his parents call sinful.

Concerned about the child's welfare, Dr. I contacted child protective services to report possible child abuse. Although Dr. I needed to be respectful of parenting styles and religious views, she also needed to follow the state laws regarding child abuse reporting because there was a reasonable suspicion of abuse.

Dr. J treats a family that comes from a very conservative Islamic background. Now that the daughter is of age, the father plans to conduct a female circumcision. The mother is terribly upset by the forthcoming circumcision and experiences a variety of anxiety and depressive symptoms. Dr. J feels that she must respect their religious tradition and does not seek consultation or discuss the case with child protective services.

Although it was important that Dr. J respect religious diversity, she still needed to ensure that child abuse did not occur and should have consulted appropriate authorities to protect the child.

CONCLUSION

I hope the ethical principle held by APA and other national mental health organizations to be respectful and knowledgeable about religious diversity (e.g., see APA, 2002, 2003) will result in more educational opportunities for both mental health professionals and students in training to better prepare them for working with clients from a wide variety of religious traditions. Closely monitoring ethical issues that emerge or are likely to emerge during the course of therapists' work is critical. Honoring ethical values such as respect, responsibility, integrity, competence, and concern for others and getting appropriate training and ongoing consultation can greatly help the professional navigating these often challenging waters.

In the next chapter, I focus on seven situations that mental health professionals often encounter when integrating religious–spiritual tools in psychotherapy. I also highlight a variety of guiding principles to follow during integrated psychotherapy.

7

SPECIAL CIRCUMSTANCES: SEVEN TYPES OF CLIENTS

Ria refers to herself as a "born-again Christian" and peppers her language with Bible quotes, comments such as "Praise be to God," and many references to Jesus. She is very active in her evangelical church. Ria seeks psychological services to find strategies to manage her son, who has autism, and her therapist wonders how she can use Ria's beliefs and religious community to help her with a challenging parenting situation.

Miguel is addicted to alcohol and other substances, divorced, and estranged from his teenage daughters. He had a job at a factory but lost it. Lately he has been suicidal. He began court-ordered therapy after his second arrest within 6 months for driving while intoxicated. Miguel discloses to his therapist that he was sexually abused when he was young by his parish priest and that he has a lot of resentment toward the Catholic Church in particular but all religions in general, saying, "It's all a bunch of bullshit."

Lai has Stage 2 breast cancer but refuses medical treatment. She states that she and her faith community will pray about her illness and that she expects God will cure her. She believes medical intervention is unnecessary for those who believe in God's healing power. Lai and her husband seek the services of a "Christian counselor" to discuss marital and parenting issues. Her husband is concerned about his wife's illness and thinks medical intervention is a reasonable idea. Lai dismisses his concerns as lack of faith.

Ria, Miguel, and Lai presented clinical situations that are typical in working with clients who are especially religious, damaged by their religious tradition or leaders, or make decisions about their health and well-being on the basis of religious beliefs that may ultimately hurt them or their loved ones. Mental health professionals are likely to find themselves working with clients with similar concerns and issues.

Each client offers a unique story and set of circumstances that challenges the therapist to provide professional services tailored to the individual. The integration of spirituality and psychotherapy also must be tailored to the individual because religious–spiritual experiences and interests vary even within the same religious community. Although each person and clinical situation is unique, therapists may find themselves in any of seven common situations when using religious–spiritual tools in psychotherapy:

- working with clients who are very religious,
- working with clients who are not religious,
- working with clients outside one's religious tradition,
- working with clients within one's religious tradition,
- working with clients victimized by their religious leaders or community,
- working with clients who feel damaged by their religious tradition, and
- working with clients with destructive religious views and behaviors.

WORKING WITH CLIENTS WHO ARE VERY RELIGIOUS

Because religion–spirituality is such a large part of the worldview and lifestyle of very religious clients, it makes sense to integrate it into psychotherapy in a way that is productive. Of course, clients must be willing participants for integration to occur, and these clients usually welcome the invitation to bring their religious–spiritual perspectives into treatment.

Because clergy often have an important role in the lives of those who are very religious, and because they can help the mental health professional better understand the interaction between religious perspectives and daily living and problem solving, ongoing consultation with clergy members may be especially helpful with these clients. This is especially true with clergy who are supportive of mental health services in general. Of course, clients' permission to consult with their clergy on treatment is always necessary.

Many highly religious clients have what Pargament (2007) referred to as "spiritual inflexibility" (p. 302). At the extreme, they can be rigid, obsessive–compulsive, dogmatic, perfectionistic, and authoritarian. These clients may believe their religious–spiritual perspectives are the only correct ones and that those who disagree with them are theologically misguided. Because of this attitude, these individuals can be hard to live and work with, and thus interpersonal conflicts are often what bring them to a mental health professional. Significant conflicts with a spouse or children are often the presenting symptoms in these cases.

Pargament (2007) maintained that "fear lies at the root of spiritual inflexibility" (p. 299). By rigidly holding onto particular religious beliefs and practices, the client binds the anxiety that can emerge with uncertainty and a host of unanswered life questions. The inflexibility can give the client a structure, stability, and security to cling to. Although living in a more "black and white" world has its appeal, it comes at great cost to interpersonal relationships and quality of life. Obsessive–compulsive tendencies are usually part of spiritual inflexibility, which may generalize to other areas of the person's life.

Spiritual resources can be used to help these clients become more flexible. For example, most of the highly regarded religious models that the devout emulate, such as Jesus, Mother Teresa, Mahatma Gandhi, Buddha, Pope John Paul II, and Moses, have all had well-documented periods of doubt and challenging spiritual journeys. These exemplars were not rigidly confident in their beliefs and practices throughout their lives. Even in the Hebrew Bible, God actually changes his mind a few times because of the behavior and reasoning of his followers. If God can change his mind, perhaps humans can too. In addition, the highly devout may quote scripture passages to support particular beliefs and practices but take these passages out of context. It is tragic that sacred scripture has been used to justify many unethical, immoral, and harmful behaviors, including murder. Therefore, therapists should encourage these clients to work with clergy and knowledgeable others in their religious tradition to help them better understand the entire context of the scripture writings.

Not all very religious clients are spiritually inflexible. Many of the devout are tolerant of others and open to other ways of being religious–spiritual. In working with these clients, it is important to try to understand and respect their religious–spiritual points of view while helping them attend to the psychological, behavioral, and relational issues that brought them to psychotherapy. Religion–spirituality is more likely to be part of the solution than part of the problem for the spiritually flexible client. Consider the following case examples:

> Robert is a devout Orthodox Jew, and his parents were both Holocaust
> survivors. He belongs to a highly conservative temple, keeps a kosher

home, and takes the Sabbath very seriously. He and his wife are working with a mental health professional on parenting issues with one of their children who has attention-deficit/hyperactivity disorder. The therapist is also Jewish but from a more secular, liberal, and reconstructionist tradition and is able to use the language, references, and traditions of the Jewish faith and culture to develop rapport with Robert. Although devout, Robert does not have spiritual–religious inflexibility. He acknowledges that his religious beliefs and practices work for him and his family, but he does not feel a need to impose his view on others or reject other traditions or approaches. He feels comfortable with his therapist even though he is more conservative than the therapist.

Aamaal is a devout Muslim. He prays five times each day and takes his faith tradition very seriously. He feels conflicted about living in the West because he believes the secular traditions of America are sinful and insulting to God. He thinks how American women dress and act are especially disgraceful. This causes troubles for him at work because he supervises both men and women and must follow American employment laws and company policies. After some conflicts at work, his human resource manager suggests that he use the employee assistance program to obtain consultation about his conflicts with female employees in particular. The mental health professional assigned to Aamaal is not a Muslim and knows little about Aamaal's religious and cultural traditions. However, with Aamaal's permission, the therapist consults a clergy person well known to Aamaal to assist with treatment. Aamaal appreciates his therapist's desire to better understand his religious–spiritual perspective. Aamaal is not concerned that his therapist is not a Muslim, and he likes the fact that his therapist is willing to discuss his religious perspectives and traditions.

Robert and Aamaal, devoutly involved in their respective religious traditions, benefited from working with professionals who respect their beliefs and practices.

WORKING WITH CLIENTS WHO ARE NOT RELIGIOUS

The tools from religious thought are helpful to not only religious–spiritual clients but also nonreligious clients. Even those who consider themselves to be agnostic or atheist can benefit from spiritually based tools. This may come as a surprise. Many believe that anyone who is scientific and rational must conclude that religious–spiritual views are outdated delusions. Recent highly popular books have promoted the view that religious–spiritual perspectives and traditions are actually unproductive and dangerous (e.g., see Dawkins, 2006; S. Harris, 2005; Hitchens, 2007). So, how can religious–spiritual tools be of any help to those who are nonspiritual or even highly antagonistic to anything that seems religious–spiritual?

Many tools discussed in this volume can indeed be helpful to nonreligious clients. Mindfulness-based stress reduction is an excellent example. Although the techniques from this meditative tradition come from religious–spiritual sources, most of the religious–spiritual underpinnings have been removed, and therefore these techniques can be useful to nonreligious clients. Nonreligious clients can also benefit from ritual and community support, which can be secular experiences. For example, a weekend long-distance bike ride with family or friends might offer some of the benefits of ritual and support without religious–spiritual associations. Behaving in an ethical manner will likely reap its own rewards even if the ethical behavior is not motivated by one's religious tradition or faith community.

It should also be mentioned that nonreligious persons can also be spiritually inflexible. However, in these cases, the spiritual inflexibility is often an inflexible hostility toward anything religious–spiritual. For example, some people who highly value science and reason find that their perspective is incompatible with religion and spirituality. Some focus on the terrible behavior that some people engage in that is motivated by their religious beliefs, such as terrorism. In fact, many of the popular books that highlight atheism or are highly critical of religion–spirituality maintain a remarkably angry and virulent tone (e.g., see Dawkins, 2006; S. Harris, 2005; Hitchens, 2007). Often these individuals feel victimized by either their religious background or someone else's tradition. Inflexible nonreligious clients may initially reject any suggestions from mental health professionals that sound religious–spiritual. These clients' views should be respected; however, their therapists may wish to determine the source of their rejection of all things religious–spiritual, especially if the clients have been victimized by religious persons or institutions. Here are a few case examples:

> Jake describes himself as an atheist. He is a scientist and strongly believes that unless science can prove otherwise, there is no God or supernatural higher power. However, he belongs to his Jewish temple, attends services and study groups, and is very active within the Jewish community in general. Jake is retired and acknowledges that he enjoys the social connections he has nurtured within his religious community and believes that active engagement with his temple and Jewish community keeps him stimulated and socially involved. He says,
>
> > I am an atheist, and I think you have to be crazy to believe in anything supernatural. However, I am proud to be a Jew, and I fully support Israel and the Jewish community. Maybe I identify to some degree with Einstein. He was, of course, an amazing scientist yet also a Jew.
>
> Carlos says he has no interest in religion–spirituality. He grew up in a secular home and never found religion to be of interest. However, after attending stress management training at work, he begins to use mindfulness-based stress reduction and meditates daily. He states,

> Somehow I find that I really need to do my meditation practice to keep myself centered, calm, and focused. It seems to help me in both my personal and professional life. I don't really care if the techniques originated in the Eastern religions. All I know is that it works and helps me have a better quality of life.

Jamal is not religious and has no particular spiritual practice. He has had troubles with substance abuse. He tries to remind himself daily that he should interact with others with loving kindness. He states,

> I used to be pretty bitter, and I suppose it rubbed off on others around me. When I'm more loving and kind to people, I'm happier and so are they. It took a while to finally figure this out. I notice that when I try to focus on being loving and kind, good things tend to happen. Besides, I think I'm less likely to drink or use drugs as well.

Jake, Carlos, and Jamal all benefited from tools from spiritual–religious thought without any engagement with religious–spiritual communities, traditions. They found ways to secularize these tools in a way that improves the quality of their lives.

WORKING WITH CLIENTS OUTSIDE ONE'S RELIGIOUS TRADITION

As discussed in chapter 6, therapists who are unfamiliar with various religious communities may assume much about how their clients think, feel, and behave on the basis of stereotypes. This form of bias is not uncommon and can be insulting and highly destructive to clients.

Therefore, therapists working with clients from religious traditions different from their own may wish to discuss these differences with their clients and be sure they understand the unique religiously based issues and perspectives of their client. A respectful openness is needed. Therapists might also consider finding out what (if any) concerns clients might have about working with a professional from a different faith tradition or perhaps no faith tradition. The possibility of a religious mismatch between client and therapist should be considered as well. For example, someone who comes from a highly conservative, fundamentalist, and evangelical religious tradition may find it challenging to work with a therapist who comes from either no religious tradition or one that the client believes will result in eternal damnation. Consider these examples:

> Claire is a devout Catholic who works as a secretary at a Catholic university and attends daily Mass on campus. She is pregnant with her fourth child and has recently found out that the baby has Down's syndrome. She consults a therapist for help with depression and stress related to this

situation. Her therapist, who is not Catholic and has had very little experience with Catholics, assumes that abortion is "off the table" and fails to discuss any options other than delivering the baby to term, out of respect for what she assumes is the client's religious belief.

Aala is being treated for anorexia nervosa and depression. She is a Muslim who wears a head scarf and is always fully covered, even in warm weather. Her therapist feels uncomfortable treating someone fully covered because she feels that it is challenging to examine treatment progress without looking at her body shape and form. The therapist wishes to weigh her without so many clothes on but is unsure of how to discuss this with her.

Claire and Aala were involved with a religious tradition different from their therapist's, creating challenging issues for the therapist. Therapists must be attentive to their own potential religious and cultural biases and may wish to consult colleagues or clergy members and consider discussing these issues with their clients directly.

WORKING WITH CLIENTS WITHIN ONE'S RELIGIOUS TRADITION

There can be many advantages to working with clients from a similar religious tradition. Plenty of research has suggested that therapist–client matching on a wide variety of variables, such as gender, ethnicity, native language, and religious identification, tends to be associated with better treatment outcomes and client satisfaction (e.g., see Norcross, 2002). Under these circumstances, the therapist is more likely to understand the client's religious–spiritual and cultural issues and resources and therefore it may be easier to establish rapport and a positive working alliance. Also, the therapy itself might be easier. The therapist can draw from his or her knowledge of psychotherapy science and practice as well as his or her religious tradition more thoughtfully and, one hopes, more effectively.

As a psychologist who is Roman Catholic and does a great deal of consultative work for various Catholic diocese and religious communities, I have found myself receiving many referrals from sources who are looking for a mental health professional who well understands and relates to Catholicism. Furthermore, I have found that many Catholic clergy, such as priests, nuns, brothers, and deacons, want to refer to a mental health professional who shares their faith tradition because they feel assured that the faith tradition will be respected and appreciated in psychotherapy. Perhaps they feel they can better trust someone who is from the same religious faith community. Therefore, religiously–spiritually integrated psychotherapy and work with religious–spiritual clients and referral sources in general often benefit from the therapist and client being from the same faith tradition.

However, there may be some disadvantages to client–therapist religious matching. Clients may assume that because the therapist shares their religious tradition they will share similar beliefs and practices and may become uncomfortable if they find that the therapist holds more liberal or more conservative beliefs than their own. Furthermore, clients may attempt to blur professional and personal boundaries while working with someone from their same religious tradition. For example, they may expect the therapist to pray with them or participate in other shared religious practices. As stated in previous chapters, therapists must practice in a manner consistent with their professional training, experience, and license and thus must be careful not to engage in professional behavior with their clients that they ethically and legally should avoid. Finally, clients may experience particular transference issues with therapists from their own religious tradition. For example, they may behave toward their therapist as they might behave toward their clergy person. They may relate to the therapist as they would to a clergy person and perhaps expect an approach more like pastoral counseling or spiritual direction. Therapists may also be tempted to act on their countertransference impulses and issues or blur professional boundaries in these situations. For example, they might offer spiritual or theological advice, impose their religious–spiritual beliefs and practices on their clients, or make assumptions about clients' religious practices and beliefs on the basis of their own personal religious–spiritual perspectives and experiences.

Therapist–client matching regarding religious–spiritual matters can thus offer both advantages and disadvantages in professional treatment. Therefore, therapists must be attentive to these issues while working with clients from similar religious–spiritual backgrounds. They must be especially concerned about client expectations, transference and countertransference, and blurred professional boundaries. Three case examples are as follows:

> Father Jim is a Catholic priest struggling with his homosexual orientation. He seeks psychotherapy from a Jewish female therapist, stating,
>
>> I really want a fresh and different perspective that is outside of and not influenced by the Catholic Church. I could see a Catholic therapist, but I think they might have too much baggage working with a priest who is homosexual. I guess I just don't want to deal with that potential.
>
> Mei is a devout Christian from an evangelical tradition. She has been anxious and depressed regarding managing three young children, including one who has learning disabilities, and she was sexually abused by her former husband. She seeks the professional services of a "Christian counselor" who is a psychologist, stating,
>
>> It is really important to me for someone to understand my faith and respect the role of Jesus in my life. I really feel more comfortable talking about my troubles with someone who shares my faith. They'll understand me better, I bet.

A local convent would like help managing psychological and behavioral problems among some of their sisters. They seek the services of a psychologist who can conduct psychological testing and provide consultation on a variety of matters. The mother superior thinks it very important to obtain the services of an active and practicing Catholic professional in order to secure the trust of the sisters involved. Furthermore, she is concerned that non-Catholics might find it challenging to understand and respect some of the religious traditions of the cloistered religious community.

In these examples, clients thoughtfully considered the possible advantages and disadvantages of working with a mental health professional with a similar religious background. Father Jim decided to work with someone outside of his Catholic tradition to get a "fresh perspective," whereas Mei and the mother superior of a convent both concluded that it is important to work with someone from the same religious tradition.

WORKING WITH CLIENTS VICTIMIZED BY THEIR RELIGIOUS LEADERS OR COMMUNITY

Many people have felt damaged by their religious tradition because of the behavior or statements of religious representatives. Perhaps an unkind word, a guilt-inducing comment, or even abusive behavior occurred that was terribly upsetting and destructive to a congregant. I have heard many stories of clergy engaging in illegal, unethical, or immoral behavior. The crisis in the Roman Catholic Church concerning sexual abuse by priests is an excellent example (Plante, 1999, 2004). Victims of sexual abuse by priests often find it very difficult if not impossible to set foot in a Catholic Church again, attend Mass, or interact with Catholic clergy in any capacity.

Of course, many non-Catholics also feel victimized by their religious institutions. Fundamentalist Christian groups have their share of former members who feel damaged for being judged, rejected, or ostracized for not believing or behaving in ways acceptable to their religious leaders or faith communities. Jews sometimes feel victimized as well when they choose to live in a way that is perceived to be wrong by temple leaders and particular family members (e.g., marrying a non-Jew, refusing to raise their children Jewish, not attending High Holiday services or celebrating Passover). In general, the more exclusive, fundamentalist, conservative, and spiritually inflexible the religious institution tends to be, the more likely there will be a number of former members who feel victimized.

Although it is important for therapists to understand the dynamics of this religiously based sense of victimization and how powerful these influences can be on clients, it may be important for therapists to help their clients avoid "throwing out the baby with the bathwater." A remarkably common response to religiously based damage and victimization is to overgeneralize it and be completely rejecting of the religious institution or religious influences in general. For example, someone who was sexually abused by a priest, pastor, rabbi, or other clergy member may come to believe that all (or at least most) clergy from that tradition are corrupt, immoral, abusive, and so forth. Tragically, this tendency to overgeneralize the victimization creates a block to reconciliation for many clients. These clients cut themselves off from the more positive aspects of the religious tradition and from clergy members who may be able to help and heal them.

Therapists can help their clients cope with and process their sense of victimization and damage while also helping them differentiate their particular experience from more positive general aspects of their religious tradition. Often clients need help to appreciate that the behaviors of a particular clergy member or of a particular church community do not necessarily generalize to the entire religious–spiritual tradition.

I am fond of pointing out to clients that religious leaders are as human as anyone else and that although we may wish they were perfect and expect much from them, they, like all of us, are flawed, and some can be destructive. Furthermore, many religious communities are very old and do not change easily. They struggle to maintain traditions and beliefs that have foundations perhaps thousands of years old. They often do not respond quickly to contemporary times and ways of thinking. Finally, when reflecting on an organization's behaviors and decisions of the past, it usually is easy to find fault. All institutions that are old enough, whether religious or not, have parts of their history they might not be proud of when viewed through a contemporary lens. For example, the history of the U.S. government includes having tolerated slavery. Although therapists must understand and appreciate their client's anger at their religious clergy or organizations, they can help clients keep their feelings of victimization in perspective and avoid throwing out the baby with the bathwater. Consider these examples:

> Lai is sexually violated by a priest during the course of pastoral counseling related to her divorce. Lai is seduced by the priest during a period of time when she feels highly vulnerable. After several months of sexual encounters, she breaks off the relationship and contacts the local bishop. The bishop handles the accusations in a responsible manner, and ultimately, the priest is defrocked by the Vatican. Lai finds herself unable to return to the church and has a highly negative reaction whenever she sees a priest or passes by a Catholic church. Over time, she becomes more isolated and lonely because she had previously used church activities as a primary social support system. In therapy, Lai works on her feelings toward the priest who violated her trust and on better appreciating that all priests are not the same as the one who harmed her. Eventually, she is able to return to church in another city with assistance from a compassionate and helpful priest who is aware of her history and experiences.

Gerry and Anne are engaged to be married and are looking for a rabbi to perform the ceremony. Gerry is Christian and Anne is Jewish. The rabbi from Anne's home temple, whom she has known and liked her entire life, is angry at Anne for wanting to marry a non-Jew. The rabbi also expresses his displeasure with Anne's parents and refuses to allow Anne to be married at the temple. Anne feels devastated. The temple and rabbi were very important to her when she was growing up, and now she feels rejected for reasons that seem unreasonable. Gerry and Anne agree to raise their potential children Jewish, but that does not convince the rabbi to support the marriage. They decide to marry in a civil ceremony at a hotel, and Anne stops going to Jewish events and services. However, after their first child is born several years later, Anne longs to reconnect with her Jewish tradition. With therapy, Anne begins to look at other temples in her area and finds a young female rabbi who makes her feel accepted. Over time, Anne reconnects to her tradition with the help of therapy and a more accepting rabbi.

Feng grew up attending an evangelical Christian church. He was active in youth activities, and his parents had spent some time overseas as missionaries. During college, Feng begins to question much of the dogma and beliefs associated with his faith tradition. Over time, he takes courses in comparative religion and other religious subjects, ultimately graduating with a degree in religious studies. Eventually, he no longer believes in the teachings of his church. His parents and pastor are appalled by his new views and say that he is lost to Satan. They refuse to have anything to do with him until he corrects his beliefs and returns to the ways and teachings of his church. In fact, his pastor encourages his parents to ignore him and cut him off from family affairs and speaks poorly about him to community members. Feng ultimately becomes very depressed and seeks psychotherapy. After several months, he develops an interest in Zen Buddhism and mindfulness meditation, which he finds very useful. He also reconnects with some extended family members who are sympathetic to his conflict with his parents and pastor and nurtures these and other supportive relationships.

In these examples, Lai, Anne, and Feng all felt victimized by their religious leader and tradition, and their feelings of rejection and loss led to depression and isolation. Psychotherapy in collaboration with more accepting religious leaders and communities helped each of them heal and return to a spiritual community that ultimately was more satisfying for them.

WORKING WITH CLIENTS WHO FEEL DAMAGED BY THEIR RELIGIOUS TRADITION

Many people feel damaged by their religious tradition even without identifying any particular event or victimizing person representing their faith community and tradition. Psychotherapy clients may also feel victimized by church dogma and policy without any direct experience of victimization from a particular church leader or representative. For example, many church groups may seem rejecting to those who are homosexual, have had an abortion, been divorced, or dress and act in ways that appear "unholy" to some people. As a Roman Catholic who works with many Catholic clients, I have heard numerous stories of client anger toward the Roman Catholic Church as an institution concerning its policies prohibiting divorce, homosexual unions, female or married priests, and so forth. For example, many Catholics from particular cultural and geopolitical backgrounds (e.g., Ireland) feel they were damaged by an overemphasis on sin and guilt that they believe was just part of their cultural as well as religious community. Furthermore, many clients feel victimized by the Catholic Church about matters from the distant past that did not personally impact them or anyone they know. For example, many refer to the Crusades from the Middle Ages as a reason for being angry with the Catholic Church. Some from particular Jewish backgrounds feel that their cultural influences also encouraged guilt and a certain level of distrust of non-Jews. Some Jews feel that their cultural tradition focused on their history of victimization, which ultimately led to highlighting the negative rather than positive aspects of being a part of the Jewish community. Some from conservative Christian backgrounds also feel damaged by an emphasis on guilt, sin, and very strict dogma and expectations for both thought and behavior. Another example may be gays and lesbians who feel they are perceived as damaged or disordered in the eyes of their religious community. Many of these clients feel angry with religion and with faith communities, and their anger may manifest by rejecting not only the religious communities and faith traditions but also those who represent those communities.

As in the previous section on clients who feel directly victimized by their religious leaders or communities, these clients may feel damaged by just being part of a faith tradition that was harmful to them in some way. They may come to fully reject religious traditions in general, even ones that are different from their own. It is important to help these clients cope with their feelings but also help them avoid overgeneralizing their experience and rejecting potentially beneficial religious–spiritual, and perhaps secular yet humanistic, activities and perspectives. A few case examples are as follows:

> Kathy grew up in an Irish Catholic home with 15 brothers and sisters all from the same parents (no blended family members or twins). She jokes that she had so many siblings that she did not even meet all of them until she was an adult. She feels that the Irish Catholic tradition was damaging in that her parents felt they could not use birth control or divorce from their unhappy marriage. Kathy says,
>
>> When I was a teenager, I remember getting slapped by my mother when I told her that if the Church makes all these rules about birth

control and divorce maybe the priests should babysit all these kids and pay to feed them. I don't think I ever saw my mother so angry with me as when I said that.

As an adult, Kathy fully rejects any religious or spiritual perspectives, beliefs, or activities, saying that "it's all a bunch of crap used to control uneducated people." However, after struggling with breast cancer in her 40s, Kathy longs for some religious–spiritual connection. During the course of medical and psychological therapy, she decides to talk with an Anglican priest in the community whom she knew and liked. She begins attending Anglican services and activities, including a church-sponsored cancer survivors group.

Asa grew up in the Jewish tradition but says he never felt connected to it. Overall, he feels his religious experience emphasized guilt and that all non-Jews hate Jews. He states,

> I [feel] it glorified victimhood. We spent so much time learning about how we almost got wiped off the face of the planet so many times and how everyone hates us. We also learned more about Israel than I care to know. It's halfway across the world, and I've never been there.

Asa no longer identifies with his Jewish tradition, but he embraces Zen Buddhism, stating, "I really like the emphasis on meditation and the nonjudging nature of Zen. No guilt and no being a victim to boot."

Ryan grew up in the Mormon tradition. During his missionary year, he struggles with depression, anxiety, and homesickness. Furthermore, he is robbed on several occasions and feels traumatized by the experience overall. After he returns to his home, he finds that his faith has faltered, and he feels used. He states, "I can't believe they forced us young and impressionable kids to basically do free labor for them . . . seems like slavery to me."

Kathy, Asa, and Ryan all felt damaged by their religious tradition and ultimately rejected it. Kathy and Asa found other religious–spiritual traditions and communities that were satisfying to them, but Ryan did not.

WORKING WITH CLIENTS WITH DESTRUCTIVE RELIGIOUS VIEWS AND BEHAVIORS

Although mental health professionals strive to be respectful of religious diversity, some religious community members engage in beliefs that can lead to destructive behavior toward themselves or others, such as abuse or neglect of children or dependent adults, suicidal behavior, religiously inspired terrorism, rejection of much-needed medical attention, and denial of basic human rights. Many of these issues have important legal implications requiring the mental health professional to break confidentiality and report their concerns to civil authorities such as the police or child protective services (e.g., serious and immediate danger to self or others, child abuse or neglect). For example, some may justify physically abusing their children by referring to the "spare the rod, spoil the child" perspective or suggest that God commands them to beat the devil out of them for their own good. Others might justify racism and bigotry because of references to a religious view or scripture quote. For example, over the years some Christians have justified violence against Jews on the basis of quotes from scriptures taken out of context. The daily newspapers provide much evidence of violence motivated by religious differences.

More subtle or less severe religious beliefs and behaviors may not pose any significant safety risks or legally require breaking confidentiality but still lead to psychological, behavioral, and relationship problems among clients. These behaviors or perspectives may never come to the attention of newspaper reporters, the police, or child protective services but may still be highly destructive to the well-being of clients and others. For example, for many, religiously inspired guilt, prejudice, inter- and intragroup conflict, and bias can destroy relationships and psychological well-being. Parents refuse to attend or support their child's wedding because of religious or ceremonial disagreements. Couples divorce over differences in religious beliefs. Children are told they are doomed to hell for not behaving or believing in a particular way. Important medical advice is ignored because of a particular religious view. In these situations, mental health professionals must balance respect for clients' religious beliefs with the need to avoid or minimize health damaging behaviors. This balancing act can be very challenging. While respecting religious diversity, therapists must still provide mental health services based on the highest standards of science and practice. Consider the following:

> Mark has severe back pain associated with his work as a laborer. After visiting a doctor who recommends surgery, he decides that his pain can be treated only through prayer. He refuses medication as well and feels that if his faith is strong enough and it is God's will, his pain will be relieved. He consults a psychologist about issues associated with workmen's compensation. His psychologist notices his discomfort during a session and asks him about his pain. Mark insists that modern medical intervention would only insult God's divine healing process.

> Marcia is a mother of three small children. She tells them that God watches and judges their every move and thought, stating that sinful children will be doomed to hell. Although her children are very well behaved as a result of these fear- and guilt-inducing techniques, they show evidence of anxiety disorders and were referred to a school psychologist for highly anxious classroom and playground behavior.

Angelica feels depressed and guilty because she cannot measure up to her expectations for charitable works. She says the Bible states that you should give away all of your possessions and follow Jesus, and she has tried to do so. She has very few possessions and gives of herself as much as she can. Others often take advantage of her willingness to be so giving by asking her to do constant favors. Although her efforts are often appreciated, she still feels selfish and disheartened because she thinks it is not enough. Her husband and children feel neglected by her because she seems to always be doing something for others, including many strangers.

The religiously based destructive behaviors that Mark, Marcia, and Angelica engaged in were damaging to themselves and their loved ones. The mental health professional must be respectful of such religious beliefs without condoning their health damaging actions. Consultation with the client's clergy may help treatment and should be considered.

CONCLUSION

Each client offers the mental health professional a unique story, clinical situation, and perspective on their religious upbringing, tradition, beliefs, and practices. Therefore, mental health professionals must tailor their interventions with the uniqueness of each client in mind. However, seven client–therapist situations are frequently found when religious–spiritual issues are integrated into psychotherapy. Being aware of these seven common situations and their challenges and having some principles to manage them may help mental health professionals better prepare them.

Frequently, ongoing professional consultation with clergy or other representatives of religious–spiritual traditions is needed to provide high-quality integrated services. In the next chapter, I discuss the issues relevant to consultation in order to work collaboratively with these professionals in the best interests of the client.

8

CONSULTATION WITH RELIGIOUS PROFESSIONALS: AN OFTEN-OVERLOOKED TOOL

Dimas is very active in his Episcopal church. He sings in the choir, volunteers to visit hospice patients, and visits prisoners in the local correctional facility. Now that his three sons are grown and out of the home, he would like to become even more involved with his church and has decided to apply to the diaconate program. He is referred to Dr. A, a psychologist, for a psychological evaluation to determine whether he is suitable for the diaconate. The religious superior who is in charge of the vocations office asks Dr. A, "Will Dimas make a good deacon? Is he fit for duty?"

Rabbi Irene is worried about several of her congregants who lost their jobs during recent layoffs in the computer industry and, because of slow economic times, are having significant trouble finding suitable employment. Rabbi Irene asks Dr. B, a psychologist, whether she could consult her to better counsel these now-unemployed congregants and wonders whether Dr. B would offer some group sessions at the temple for them. Rabbi Irene says, "I'm not trained to deal with their job-related stress, with so many appearing despondent, but maybe you could help them and counsel me on knowing how I might better help them in my role as a rabbi."

Fr. Damian is stressed by his responsibilities as a pastor for a Catholic university. He thinks many of those who come to him for spiritual direction and pastoral counseling have significant problems with depression, sexual identity, relationship conflicts, and both academic and career pressures. One of the students recently made a suicide attempt and was sent to the psychiatric ward at the university medical center. Fr. Damian worries that he does not have enough training to work with people with serious mental health issues and wonders whether he could consult Dr. C, a psychologist, on a regular basis to help him better understand some of the people who come to him for spiritual help. Fr. Damian states,

> I find that so much of what I do involves counseling students who have major life stressors or problems. Often I feel like I'm flying by the seat of my pants. I really need a mental health professional to help me best manage these issues. They never trained me on these issues in seminary.

These case examples are typical referrals that result in collaborative relationships between mental health professionals and clergy. Clergy are often faced with congregants who have significant mental health issues and severe stressors. In fact, a clergy member is often the first person outside of family and friends whom people with emotional, behavioral, and psychiatric troubles confide in, and when that happens many clergy feel they are in over their head. At such times clergy can greatly benefit from working closely with a mental health professional. Likewise, mental health professionals can often make additional gains with their clients when they consult clergy and work in concert with them. Consultation between mental health professionals and clergy is often needed to provide high-quality clinical and pastoral care.

It is surprising that very little has been published on clergy–therapist collaboration and consultation (McMinn & Dominquez, 2005; Milstein, Manierre, Susman, & Bruce, 2008; Plante, 1999). Although several books and professional journal articles are available, it is remarkable that so few empirical studies have been published that examined the principles of effective consultation between the mental health and religious communities. In this chapter I discuss consultation between these professionals, including outline principles to enhance consultation and common problems to avoid.

WHY CLERGY AND THERAPISTS SHOULD CONSULT EACH OTHER

To provide high-quality mental health services, it often is important for therapists to consult professionals in other fields. For example, therapists often consult medical professionals when their clients are taking psychotropic or other medications. Therapists working with the court system often regularly consult attorneys, judges, law enforcement professionals, and case workers, and those working with children and adolescents frequently consult school personnel such as teachers, guidance counselors, and school-based mental health professionals. Likewise, with client permission, it can be very helpful for therapists to work collaboratively with clergy when clients are receiving pastoral care or spiritual direction or are actively engaged in their religious community. Sometimes it is reasonable to consult clergy even when the client is not involved with a religious–spiritual congregation. For example, clergy may be well aware of grief support networks, meditation and retreat centers and practices, and other services that might benefit psychotherapy clients regardless of religious–spiritual affiliation. Therefore, whatever the religious–spiritual orientation of the client, consultation with clergy can be productive and valuable.

A couple of typical examples illustrate these points.

> Jack and Jessica are about to marry. They have been meeting with their pastor for marriage preparation classes, and the wedding is scheduled to take place in just a few weeks. As the wedding date gets closer, Jessica seems more and more stressed during their preparation sessions. Jack and the pastor both seem to think that Jessica's anxiety is typical wedding jitters. Ten days before the wedding, Jessica privately confides to the pastor that she cannot go through with it. She says that although she loves Jack, she believes he is not the right partner for her. After a heart-to-heart conversation with Jessica, the pastor contacts Dr. D, a local psychologist who is also a member of the religious congregation and well known to the pastor, to see whether he can work with the couple immediately to figure out how best to proceed. Dr. D schedules daily sessions with the couple to work through the crisis, and it becomes clear that the wedding must be canceled. Dr. D helps them manage the enormous stress of the breakup and resolve practical issues such as informing family and friends that the wedding has been called off. The pastor is grateful that Dr. D, whom he knows and trusts, can help with the crisis.

Clergy often face this scenario of a last-minute wedding crisis. Sometimes performing several marriages a week and hundreds each year, they often have remarkable stories to tell about marriages cancelled at the last minute, families who become violent at wedding ceremonies and receptions, crises regarding gender identity and sexual orientation that emerge a few days before a wedding, and so forth. Although clergy may be well trained to deal with these situations from a pastoral–spiritual perspective, they often need consultation when a significant conflict, psychopathology, or relational crisis emerges. An ongoing collaborative relationship with a mental health professional who can quickly and effectively help the clergy member best manage these wedding crises can be very helpful for all parties.

Similar family and relational crises frequently emerge with other life transitional events, such as births, deaths, baptisms, and confirmations. For example, an interfaith couple might find themselves in a family crisis when one member of the couple cannot go through with a baptismal event for their child. A calamity may unfold at a funeral when a previously unknown child quietly born out of wedlock through an extramarital affair attends the service. Clergy very often appreciate the ability to consult with an appropriate mental health professional when life transition emergencies occur.

> Fr. Paul is concerned about a woman at his church who tends to get overly involved with church activities and seems to volunteer for just about every committee and function. Although initially Fr. Paul was happy to have such an enthusiastic and dedicated church volunteer, he has found that she alienates other congregants with her controlling and emotionally unstable behavior. Fr. Paul says in exasperation, "It is hard to fire volunteers, but this woman is driving me crazy, and I've noticed that some of our other church volunteers are refusing to work with her." After a consultation session with Fr. Paul, the consulting psychologist feels that the woman may have a psychiatric disorder, perhaps borderline personality disorder. Fr. Paul asks about how to interact with this church member–volunteer. He says, "I can't ask her to leave our church, and somehow I have to manage her behavior and volunteer efforts without losing the rest of my congregation in the process."

Clergy must deal with congregants with all sorts of psychological and psychiatric issues, conflicts, and disorders. Furthermore, most church communities must rely on volunteers to manage their many social, educational, and liturgical activities. Volunteers tend to receive less screening, training, and corrective feedback than do employees, and thus it is common to have church members who become a problem for the religious community. Many clergy in this situation feel frustrated and value consultation with mental health professionals to better manage these challenging relationships.

The previous examples demonstrated how clergy can benefit from consultation with mental health professionals. However, the benefits are not one way: Mental health professionals can greatly benefit from consulting clergy. Here is an example:

> Originally from India, Aruna is a devout Hindu. She is very accommodating with her extended family and sometimes feels they take advantage of her goodwill. She discusses her concerns with Dr. E, whom she initially consulted about educational and psychological testing for her young son. Dr. E wonders how her religious beliefs and customs might create a situation in which her relatives could take advantage of Aruna's graciousness. Because Dr. E is not very familiar with the Hindu faith, she asks Aruna whether she would allow her to regularly consult a Hindu clergy person to help her better understand how Aruna's faith and culture are related to her family stressors.

In this example, a mental health professional was able to provide better services when she consulted clergy.

In addition to learning how religious beliefs and practices affect clients who seek mental health services, therapists who consult clergy get an opportunity to coordinate care. In addition to psychotherapy, many clients are receiving pastoral counseling services, spiritual direction, marriage counseling. Both therapists and clergy can help clients manage the various conflicts, stressors, and challenges they face, but success is more likely when these efforts are coordinated and informed by each other. Without consultation, these professionals may actually work toward opposing goals. For example, perhaps a therapist is working with a client with the goal of ending an abusive marital relationship while a clergy member is working on trying to "save" it. A therapist might be working to maximize a young single woman's use of contraception while a clergy person is discouraging it. Although clergy and mental health professionals may not always agree on treatment goals even with ongoing consultation, they are more likely to understand and appreciate each other's point of view if ongoing collaboration occurs.

There is another compelling practical reason to regularly consult clergy members: They are a great referral source. Because a substantial number of people are engaged with a religious community of some sort and because the most likely professional they will turn to in a crisis is a clergy member, who usually is not fully prepared to deal with the psychological problems of congregants, a close working relationship with clergy likely will result in ongoing referrals.

HOW CLERGY AND THERAPISTS SHOULD COLLABORATE

There are a number of important principles that mental health professionals should keep in mind to maximize effectiveness when collaborating with clergy. Although certainly not an exhaustive list, these principles include (a) maintaining mutual respect and reciprocity, (b) understanding the faith tradition, (c) using a shared language, (d) avoiding jargon, (e) appreciating clergy stressors, and (f) respecting boundary issues. Each of these six principles is discussed briefly and illustrated with examples.

Maintaining Mutual Respect and Reciprocity

Perhaps one of the fundamental errors that mental health professionals can make in collaboration with clergy is to behave in a manner that suggests the mental health professional has all of the answers and the clergy person has little, if anything, to offer the consultation relationship. In fact, survey research has supported the view that mental health professionals sometimes behave in a somewhat arrogant manner with clergy by not seeing them as professionals who bring much to the consultation relationship (McMinn et al., 2003). As in any professional collaboration, mutual respect and reciprocity are needed for it to be effective. The spirit of the arrangement must that it is a partnership of equals who both offer something important and unique to providing the client with the best treatment. Also, a spirit of learning from each other and working as a team must permeate all communications and consultations (McMinn & Dominquez, 2005). Consider this example:

> Dr. F and Rabbi Ariel work together on weddings and circumcision crises. Dr. F specializes in family and couples therapy, and Rabbi Ariel runs a large temple that has many interfaith couples and families in the congregation. Rabbi Ariel finds that the non-Jewish members of the family often experience some degree of conflict prior to a wedding or bris. Sometimes these conflicts become a crisis when a couple wonders whether circumcision is right for their child or whether the wedding should occur after all. Extended family members can contribute to these problems when they refuse to attend the special event or protest something about the ceremony. Rabbi Ariel appreciates Dr. F's expertise, and they work together to solve many of these crises. Because Dr. F is Jewish and very familiar with Jewish culture and traditions, she is especially helpful during these times of need.

In this case example, a mental health professional worked closely and collaboratively with a clergy member in a respectful, reciprocal manner. She provided consultation to the clergy member that greatly helped him manage the needs of his congregants, while the clergy member provided helpful services to clients in need during important and stressful transitions in their lives.

Understanding the Faith Tradition

It is critical that mental health professionals have a solid understanding of the faith traditions with which they work, including enough knowledge of the beliefs, customs, and diversity of perspectives associated with these communities. They cannot be expected to be an expert on all the various religious groups and subcultures within each one, but they should know enough to be effective in their services and minimize insensitive, disrespectful, and otherwise problematic assumptions and suggestions. If the mental health professional has personal experiences with a particular religious group by being a member of that congregation, it may be a natural fit to consult clergy from that religious community. Therapists who know very little about the faith tradition they have been consulted about should make that known to the clergy from that group to determine whether they are the best person to help with the consultations needed.

Religious communities tend to be very complex, and trying to be aware of the dynamics, theology, customs, traditions, worldview, and such within and between each faith tradition can be overwhelming. Thus, it is important for mental health professionals to monitor their areas of competence and get consultation themselves to best serve their clients who are engaged in various religious communities. An example is as follows:

> Dr. G is a psychologist and Mormon bishop. He provides family and couples therapy to a number of Mormons in the community. He is well aware of Mormon beliefs and traditions and finds that this familiarity greatly helps him in his clinical work. He serves as a consultant to other Mormon bishops and church elders in a large multistate area and to marriage preparation and family education programs offered by the church.

Dr. G can rely on his understanding of his religious tradition to better assist clients who share the same tradition. He better understands the culture, language, rituals, and dynamics as a result of his own experience with the faith community.

Using a Shared Language

It is critical that mental health professionals understand and speak the language of the religious groups with whom they work. Again, they do not have to be experts, but they must be comfortable with and knowledgeable of the types of language used in various religious traditions. For example, many Americans from the Jewish tradition interject Yiddish words and phrases into their speech. Many evangelical Christians use frequent Bible quotes and references in conversation. Understanding and engaging in the language of the religious tradition or culture is often necessary to more effectively communicate with clients and build trust and rapport. Consider the following example:

> Dr. H is well versed in the Bible and other sacred writings. He works with Christians who seek out his services specifically because he is a "Christian counselor." Dr. H's familiarity with the Bible is very helpful in his work when his clients use Bible quotes and sayings in their conversations. He provides consultation to various clergy in the area, and they feel comfortable with him because he is so familiar with the shared language of the congregations and churches.

Dr. H can use his understanding of and comfort with religious–spiritual language to better communicate with clients. This ability likely results in enhanced rapport, client comfort, and improved professional services.

Avoiding Jargon

It is important that mental health professionals minimize or avoid the use of jargon, which can be off putting to clergy and others who are not mental health professionals. Mental health professionals, like other professionals, can become immune to the use of technical, diagnostic, and other terms that usually are unknown by those not in the field. It is important to know one's audience and avoid language that might make good communication and consultation difficult. Consider this example:

> Dr. I works very hard to avoid professional language when working with non-mental-health professionals, including clergy. She jokes that she always tries to speak in a manner that her grandmother would understand. Occasionally, a more technical phrase or word such as "borderline personality" or "corrective emotional experience" slips out, but she has trained herself to define these words and phrases when they are used.

Attention to minimizing jargon helps Dr. I maintain an equal, comfortable, and productive collaborative relationship with clergy.

Appreciating Clergy Stressors

Unlike mental health professionals, who can often limit their client interactions to neatly packaged 50-minute segments in a professional office, clergy are called on 24/7 and work in many challenging environments outside of a comfortable office. They can be asked to rush to a hospital, crime scene, or congregant's home on a moment's notice. Also, congregants' expectations for their behavior can be so high that no human could come close to meeting them. Mental health professionals must understand these and other unique stressors experienced by clergy, and in doing so they can tailor their interventions and consultations to better meet clergy needs. An example illustrates these points:

> Dr. J provides consultation to a local pastor who has a fairly large low-income congregation that focuses on social justice issues. The church hosts a homeless shelter and soup kitchen and is active in civil disobedience activities. The pastor and a number of church members have been arrested on many occasions for sit-ins and other demonstration activities. Dr. J periodically gets crisis phone calls from the pastor to obtain referrals or advice about issues related to his church members, sometimes at odd hours. Dr. J tries his best to offer assistance within his area of expertise, understanding the unique stressors of this pastor.

Dr. J is thoughtful and attentive to the pastor, mindful of the unusual stress on clergy members, and he does not try to impose his views on him about how to behave as a professional.

Respecting Boundary Issues

Clergy are often asked to fill multiple and complex roles with congregants that tend to be much more challenging than those of mental health professionals. They may go to the home of congregants for meals and attend important life-cycle ceremonies such as births, weddings, and funerals, as well as the receptions that accompany them. They may coach a church sports team, teach various classes to both parents and children, manage church finances, and be present to oversee liturgical celebrations. Boundary conflicts are sure to unfold. It is important for mental health professionals to appreciate these boundary issues to provide both effective and realistic consultation and support. Here is an example:

> Dr. J is well aware of the challenging boundary issues of the pastor and his congregation. In fact, the pastor has shared a jail cell on more than one occasion with members of his congregation. The pastor finds himself offering marital and other pastoral counseling care to church members with whom he also goes on social justice trips and works closely in the church-sponsored soup kitchen. The pastor also frequently requests that congregants use their skills to help each other, which is well intended but can blur boundaries. For example, a congregant who is a police officer is asked by another congregant to check on a congregant who is accused of having an extramarital affair, and the pastor asks a wealthy congregant to help support another congregant who is an unwed teen mother. Because boundaries can become very blurred in the pastor's church community, Dr. J discusses ways to avoid any exploitation of congregants and manage the stress of multiple roles.

Dr. J was attentive to professional boundaries and was well aware of how his views about boundaries as a mental health professional may be different from the perspectives held by clergy. However, being mindful of boundary issues and how they may apply to church settings can be helpful in collaborative relationships with clergy, especially given their often highly complex roles and expectations of them.

TYPICAL PROBLEMS IN CLERGY–MENTAL HEALTH CONSULTATION

Typical problems in consultation between mental health professionals and clergy include (a) conflicting values and goals, (b) confidentiality, and (c) boundary issues. Several comments are offered on each potential problem along with an illustrative case example.

Conflicting Values and Goals

Often mental health professionals have treatment goals that conflict with goals supported by the religious tradition. This is also true with certain values. For example, a mental health professional might be working toward helping a client become pregnant using artificial means such as in vitro fertilization, whereas a clergy member might insist that only natural methods are acceptable. A mental health professional might believe marital partners are equal, whereas a clergy member might insist that the man may dominate a woman in a relationship. A mental health professional might help a pregnant teenager learn about possible options, including abortion, whereas a clergy member may not see abortion as an option at all. There are many ways that the treatment goals and values of clergy and mental health professionals can conflict, and being encouraged to proceed in two opposing directions at the same time can be devastating for clients. Therefore, it is important for clergy and mental health professionals to discuss these potential conflicts in advance. Of course, sometimes agreeing to disagree in a respectful manner is the best one can hope for when these conflicts are unavoidable. Consider the following:

> Dr. K is working with a 16-year-old high school student, Janet, about possible options for managing her pregnancy. She and her parents consider themselves to be conservative and active Roman Catholics, and they are terribly distraught about this unwanted pregnancy. When they consult their parish priest, Fr. Allen, he encourages them to give up the child for adoption, stating that abortion is just not an option. Janet and her parents think abortion should be considered and feel conflicted about Church teachings because of the practical needs of their family. Because they all like their church and Fr. Allen, they feel they could never face him again if they went through with the abortion. Dr. K tries to discuss the pros and cons with them in a neutral manner but tends to believe that abortion is a reasonable possibility. With the family's permission, Dr. K and Fr. Allen consult about the situation and, although respectful of each other's position, cannot come to an agreement.

Although Dr. K and Fr. Allen had different points of view regarding how to proceed with and best help the family, the best solution would be for them to respectfully disagree and continue to consult with each other and the family and allow the family members to make their own informed decision.

Confidentiality

Confidentiality can be challenging during any consultation, but the way mental health professionals value and manage confidentiality may be more restrictive than the way many other professionals manage it. Mental health professionals experience these differences in confidentiality management when working with school and medical personnel, for example. Thus, it is critical that expectations about confidentiality be articulated both verbally and in writing with not only the client but also the clergy or other professionals who are part of the church consultation experience. An example is as follows:

> Dr. L is working with a couple contemplating divorce. The man is a well-known sports star for a local professional basketball team and thus at-

tracts a good deal of media and public interest. The family is also actively engaged in a local Baptist church. Having met with their pastor several times about their marital troubles, they are referred to Dr. L for marital counseling. Dr. L maintains strict confidentiality. However, after consulting with Dr. L about the situation (with client permission), the pastor mentions the marital troubles to a few people working at the church. Within a few days, the local newspapers report that the couple have marital problems and are in professional counseling. Dr. L is mentioned in the article by name.

Office gossip can easily jeopardize confidentiality, especially in environments that do not maintain the kind of vigilance needed to best manage confidential material. Mental health professionals must be hypervigilant about confidentiality yet also respectful of the fact that clergy and others may have different perspectives on how best to manage confidentiality matters within the church community. Mental health professionals may choose to offer clergy and other professionals a statement from their written consent form about how they manage confidentiality.

Boundary Issues

As in most social environments, clergy often use the services of those they know. For example, clergy get to know their congregations and may naturally feel more comfortable referring to professionals from within the ranks of their own church community. Thus, mental health professionals who happen to be congregants of a particular faith community may expect to get referrals as well as consultation requests from clergy within the faith tradition and religious community, and that provides some challenging boundary issues that must be closely considered. For example, clergy may wish to refer congregants who are in need of mental health services to a therapist who is a member of congregation. Clergy may want to consult the mental health professional about congregants who are experiencing significant personal troubles. The possibility of complicated dual relationships can easily emerge when the mental health professional is also part of the religious community, and thus the vulnerability to dual relationships may result in therapists avoiding professional relationships with any members of their religious congregations. Consider this example:

Dr. M is a member of the local Jewish temple. The rabbi knows Dr. M from various committee meetings, liturgical events, and social activities that the congregation sponsors. Having been a member of the temple for a number of years, Dr. M is now on the board of the directors and knows just about everyone affiliated with the local Jewish community. Because Dr. M is also a talented mental health professional and a likeable person, people in the community are drawn to her and see her as their "shrink." In addition, the rabbi depends on her for consultations on various issues she has with members of the community. At first Dr. M is flattered to be considered such an important resource for the temple. However, the situation becomes complicated when the rabbi wants to discuss her conflict with congregation members who are Dr. M's friends. Dr. M also finds some of her current and past clients on the same committees on which she serves.

Any time clergy consult, refer to, and depend on mental health professionals who are also members of their religious communities, boundary issues and conflicts are sure to arise. Mental health professionals must also be hypervigilant about managing these potential dual relationships in a thoughtful, professional, and ethical manner and generally avoid treating those within their congregations unless there is a compelling ethical reason to do otherwise (e.g., rural environments where no other appropriate professional is available).

CULTIVATING A SUCCESSFUL CONSULTATIVE RELATIONSHIP WITH CLERGY

McMinn and colleagues (Chaddock & McMinn, 1999; McMinn et al., 1998, 2003) conducted a national interview survey with psychologists and clergy to investigate the nature of their consultation experiences with each other. On the basis of their findings, McMinn and Dominquez (2005) offered several principles to maximize the consultation relationship between these professionals: (a) nurturing the relationship, (b) communication, (c) respect, (d) common values and goals, (e) complementary expertise, (f) psychological and spiritual mindfulness, and (g) trust. These authors further discussed basic and advanced consultation relationships, with basic services defined as focusing on communication, respect, and shared goals, and more advanced consultation emphasizing psychological and spiritual mindfulness and mutual trust (McMinn et al., 2003).

In addition to these values, I offer several practical principles to nurture successful consultations: (a) Remember there is nothing like face-to-face time, (b) do a good job, (c) be an educator, and (d) ask for and adjust to feedback. Each is explained in further detail in the sections that follow.

Remember There Is Nothing Like Face-to-Face Time

Ongoing consultation relationships benefit from face-to-face time. Regular interactions in person with clergy members provide opportunities for both spontaneous and planned consultations as well as build the trust and rapport that are so vital to consultation relationships. Without regular meetings in person, it is easy to experience an "out of sight, out of mind" relationship that will atrophy over time. Face-to-face time is easier to arrange when the mental health professional is a member of the same religious community as the clergy member or if they have other activities together (e.g., serving on the same board of directors for a community organization, belonging to the same health club, shopping at the same grocery store). Much consultation activity occurs in the few moments before and after church services or unrelated meetings. Here is an example:

> Dr. N is on an advisory board for a local homeless shelter. A local Seventh-Day Adventist pastor is also on the board. The board has monthly meetings, and the pastor and Dr. N enjoy getting to know one another on the committee. As time passes, the pastor asks Dr. N for consultation about congregants and invites Dr. N to give presentations at the church on several topics related to parenting. The pastor begins to refer congregants who need professional counseling services to Dr. N. Because they see each other regularly at board meetings, they can more easily maintain and grow their professional relationship.

Dr. N developed professional consultative relationships with clergy that emerged as by-products of getting to know them through unrelated activities that met regularly.

Do a Good Job

Nothing promotes success more than success. Doing a good job tends to mean more referrals are on the way. Of course, all mental health professionals expect to do a good job, but offering friendly and attentive consultation that is respectful, efficient, and effective certainly helps to better nurture the collaborative relationships needed in consultation. Too often clergy and others are appropriately disappointed with the attention and service either they or their congregants receive from health care professionals. Thinking in terms of superb customer service and professional services that exceed expectations is sure to create good consultative relationships and more business for the mental health professional. Consider this:

> Dr. O works with couples in crisis. Local clergy find that he works especially well with couples who are either considering divorce or thinking about canceling wedding plans. Dr. O finds ways to work quickly and effectively with relational crises, and the clergy are especially grateful that he can usually see couples on short notice. Dr. O says,
>
> > I know that when I get a call from a clergy member, there is a relational crisis on the way, and crises need attention immediately. I always try to reserve at least some time in my daily schedule to help manage a potential crisis, and I know how much it is appreciated by both my clients and the clergy referral sources.

By offering a high-quality service that was efficient and flexible, Dr. O became the therapist of choice for a variety of religious groups.

Be an Educator

Mental health professionals sometimes seem to forget that they can be very helpful in providing education to clergy and those with whom they work in consultative relationships. They can help clergy better understand psychopathology and what can be expected from people with particular diagnoses or conditions, as well as help them better anticipate the conflicts and stressors people may experience during weddings, funerals, marital discord, and so forth. An example is as follows:

> Pastor Scott notices that several of the children in the educational program have attention-deficit/hyperactivity disorder (ADHD). He is not quite sure how to manage these children at the meeting house and consults Dr. P about it. Dr. P specializes in school-based mental health programs for children and assists the pastor in developing a program that considers the special needs of the children. Dr. P helps to educate Pastor Scott about ADHD and what can be expected from children who have it.

Dr. P educated clergy about the psychological and behavioral issues that congregants experience and what contributes to challenging behaviors, thereby helping clergy avoid inappropriate assumptions and provide better services to their community.

Ask for and Adjust to Feedback

Getting ongoing corrective feedback can better ensure that the consultation relationship is working and that the clergy members are getting what they hoped for from an ongoing relationship with a mental health professional. Often, unless the professional asks for it, he or she will not get vital feedback needed to ensure effective consultation. Negative feedback usually is provided silently, by having referrals withheld and consultation requests no longer emerge. It is important that mental health professionals obtain corrective feedback, but it is perhaps even more important that they be willing to adjust their practices in response to the feedback. It is critical that mental health professionals not engage in defensive behavior and reject corrective feedback from their customers. Consider the following:

> Dr. Q regularly tells his clients who are clergy members that he very much wants and appreciates feedback in order to ensure that the clergy members and congregants get the best possible service from him. He routinely uses a client satisfaction questionnaire and often asks his client clergy members whether their needs are being met by his efforts.

Dr. Q was careful to obtain regular feedback from clergy members about his service to ensure their needs were being met and so that he could make efforts to correct any problems that might result in client dissatisfaction.

Furthermore, the clergy likely appreciated his efforts to ensure they too were satisfied.

CONCLUSION

Ongoing consultation between clergy and mental health professionals offers a variety of advantages for both parties. Clergy have much to offer mental health professionals, and mental health professionals have much to offer clergy. Both have much to offer clients. Furthermore, the odds are high that clients will receive superior coordinated care if clergy and mental health professionals talk with each other about common goals in serving their clients and congregants. Consultation between clergy and mental health professionals is a neglected area of research (McMinn & Dominquez, 2005; Milstein et al., 2008; Plante, 1999), and there is much to learn about best practices to make it most effective for all involved.

In the next chapter, I introduce several examples of best practices and programs that illustrate religiously–spiritually integrated psychotherapy. In addition, I present several more detailed case studies to better demonstrate how religious–spiritual tools can be used successfully with actual clinical cases.

9

BEST PRACTICES IN ACTION

Eduardo has a heart attack at age 40. Part of his treatment program for cardiovascular disease includes mindfulness-based stress reduction. He says,

> At first I thought, "You've got to be kidding! I had a heart attack, and now I've got to sit on the floor saying 'om' with a bunch of wackos?" But my doctor insisted on it as part of a whole lifestyle management program working with a psychologist, and I have to admit that I found it helpful.

Ana enters a 12-step program to help her with overeating. She says,

> I've tried everything and probably have gained and lost 50 pounds a bunch of times. My therapist suggested that I try the 12-step program, and I figured I had nothing to lose—plus it was free. The whole higher power thing really makes sense for me even though I am not especially religious. I see that it makes sense for the folks in my group, too. I've lost a good deal of weight and thus far have kept it off longer than after any of my other weight loss attempts.

Bo has troubles with anger and is fired from several jobs because of losing his cool. He reports,

I've always been a bit of a hothead, and it has been a problem for me on and off in both my personal and professional life. I went to a therapist as part of my employee assistance program, and one of the things she said to me that really stuck was to look at everyone as being sacred. When I try to see everyone, even people who drive me crazy, as sacred, and try to see the divine living within them, I just cannot get so angry with them. It's made a big difference for me.

Eduardo, Ana, and Bo all benefited from the integration of spirituality into psychotherapy and related services. In this chapter I provide in-depth clinical examples to better illustrate the use of religiously–spiritually integrated psychotherapy. The examples are not intended to imply a gold standard of religiously–spiritually integrated psychotherapy.

Mental health professionals working with clients in psychotherapy have been using religious–spiritual resources and concepts for years. Richards and Bergin (1997, 2005) reviewed the literature on religious–spiritual interventions used by more than 1,400 mental health professionals, including psychiatrists, psychologists, and various types of licensed counselors, and concluded that the most frequent religious–spiritual interventions used by these professionals with their clients include (a) offering private prayers for their clients' well-being, (b) teaching religious–spiritual principles and concepts, (c) encouraging forgiveness of self and others, and (d) referring to sacred scriptures for guidance.

Research suggests that some therapists already integrate religious–spiritual principles into psychotherapy in their overall eclectic, secular, and mainstream practices. For example, a survey of clinical psychologists who are members of the American Psychological Association's (APA's) Division 12 (Society of Clinical Psychology), and who do not identify themselves as particularly spiritually or religiously minded, found that 91% routinely assessed their client's religious background, 57% used religious language and concepts with clients in treatment, and about one third recommended religious participation, including church attendance and religious readings (Shafranske & Malony, 1990). More recent surveys have found similar results and that 82% of psychologists think there is a positive relationship between religion and mental health functioning (e.g., see Delaney et al., 2007). Among a large group of Christian psychologists associated with the Christian Association for Psychological Studies (CAPS), prayer, discussion of religious concepts, and references to scripture were the most common spiritually oriented interventions used in psychotherapy (Ball & Goodyear, 1991). Thus, it appears that a large percentage of practicing mental health professionals are already integrating religious–spiritual principles and concepts into psychotherapy. This is true even for practitioners who are not specifically identified as religious counselors or members of religiously oriented professional groups, such as CAPS or Division 36 of APA (Psychology of Religion).

What can be learned from these professionals in terms of best practices in spirituality and psychotherapy integration? Unfortunately, although some helpful information exists about what they are doing to integrate spirituality into psychotherapy, little is known about how they do it. Several surveys have focused on religious–spiritual interventions in psychotherapy, but they tend to provide a rather broad picture of psychotherapy services using various categories of religious–spiritual interventions rather than specific principles and examples that other mental health professionals could learn from. We know that a sizable number of therapists pray for the well-being of their psychotherapy clients, encourage them to forgive themselves and others, attend religious community events, read sacred scripture, and discuss religious–spiritual concepts, but we do not clearly know how they do it. In addition to survey results, therapists need examples to learn about spirituality and psychotherapy integration.

In this chapter, I present several illustrative examples of religiously–spiritually integrated psychotherapy and offer suggestions about best clinical practices. I hope this chapter will help therapists learn something about how to do religiously–spiritually integrated psychotherapy that goes beyond the findings of survey research.

It is important to mention several precautions before discussing best and illustrative practices in religious–spiritual integration in psychotherapy. It is very important to be sure that mental health professionals are respectful of their client's interest or lack of interest in religiously–spiritually based interventions. The professional must secure some assessment of the client's religious–spiritual affiliations, interests, and commitment (if any) before offering religious–spiritually minded intervention strategies. It is also important for mental health professionals to be sure that they practice this type of integrated psychotherapy in a competent manner within their areas of expertise. Thus, mental health professionals may encourage their clients (when appropriate) to pursue religious–spiritual benefits, but the professional must avoid offering services that he or she is not competent or licensed to provide as well as avoid proselytizing in any way. These issues were discussed more fully in chapter 6 of this volume, but it is critical to mention these points at least briefly here.

There are several excellent examples of best practices in spirituality and psychotherapy integration. Although some of these programs are not exclusively about psychotherapy, their importance and usefulness for mental health professionals indicate that they should be mentioned and discussed here.

12-STEP PROGRAMS

Although 12-step programs such as Alcoholics Anonymous (AA) are peer rather than professionally organized and led (Alcoholics Anonymous

EXHIBIT 9.1
The 12 Steps of Alcoholics Anonymous

1. We admitted we were powerless over alcohol—that our lives had become un-manageable.
2. Came to believe that a Power greater than ourselves could restore us to sanity.
3. Made a decision to turn our will and our lives over to the care of God as we understood Him.
4. Made a searching and fearless moral inventory of ourselves.
5. Admitted to God, to ourselves and to another human being the exact nature of our wrongs.
6. Were entirely ready to have God remove all these defects of character.
7. Humbly asked Him to remove our shortcomings.
8. Made a list of all persons we had harmed, and became willing to make amends to them all.
9. Made direct amends to such people wherever possible, except when to do so would injure them or others.
10. Continued to take personal inventory and when we were wrong promptly admit-ted it.
11. Sought through prayer and meditation to improve our conscious contact with God, as we understood Him, praying only for knowledge of His will for us and the power to carry that out.
12. Having had a spiritual awakening as the result of these steps, we tried to carry this message to alcoholics, and to practice these principles in all our affairs.

Note. From *Alcoholics Anonymous: The Story of How Many Thousands of Men and Women Have Recovered From Alcoholism* (2nd ed., pp. 59–60), by Alcoholics Anonymous, 1955, New York. Copyright 1955 by Alcoholics Anonymous. The Twelve Steps are reprinted with permission of Alcoholics Anonymous World Services, Inc. ("AAWS"). Permission to reprint the Twelve Steps does not mean that AAWS has reviewed or approved the contents of this publication, or that AAWS necessarily agrees with the views expressed herein. AA is a program of recovery from alcoholism only—use of the Twelve Steps in connection with programs and activities which are patterned after AA, but which address other problems, or in any other non-AA context, does not imply otherwise. Additionally, while AA is a spiritual program, *AA is not a religious program.* Thus, AA is not affiliated or allied with any sect, denomination, or specific religious belief.

World Services, 1955, 1977, 1990), their remarkable popularity and frequent use among mental health professionals to supplement treatment (Hopson, 1996) call for my mentioning them in this chapter about best practices in psychotherapy. In addition to AA, numerous other 12-step programs have been developed using the same core principles of intervention and recovery: Sexoholics Anonymous, Narcotics Anonymous, Gamblers Anonymous, and Overeaters Anonymous, among others. On reading the 12 steps listed in Exhibit 9.1, it is clear that the program's philosophy and orientation are strongly based in religion–spirituality. In fact, about one half of the 12 steps specifically refer to God.

The 12-step program encourages participants to confess their problem-atic and addicted behavior, seek forgiveness from God as well as from those harmed by their behavior, place their trust in God or a higher power, pray for personal improvement, become closer to a divine power, encourage others who struggle with addictions to follow a similar path of recovery, and prac-tice these principles in all aspects of their lives, even beyond problems asso-ciated with alcohol or other addictions. Twelve-step meetings often begin with a reciting of the Serenity Prayer (i.e., "God, give us grace . . .") and often end with a reciting of the Lord's Prayer (i.e., the Our Father). Clearly the 12-step program well integrates religious–spiritual principles into its self-help and fellowship-based addiction treatment. Mental health professionals tend to work closely with 12-step programs by encouraging their clients to participate in them.

BIOPSYCHOSOCIAL APPROACHES

Dean Ornish, a physician affiliated with the University of California, San Francisco Medical Center, is well known for his Opening Your Heart program (Friend, 1995; Ornish, 1990), which involves a comprehensive treatment for coronary heart disease and prevention. It provides a biopsychosocial approach to heart disease treatment and prevention that, among other things, integrates spiritual principles, including yoga, visualization, prayer, religious devotion, and meditation, and encourages forgiveness, altruism, and compassion (Ornish, 1990). He stated,

> Your mind, body, and spirit are all intimately interconnected . . . coronary heart disease occurs on emotional and spiritual levels as well as physical ones. . . . If we also address the emotional and spiritual dimensions, then the physical heart often begins to heal as well. (p. 250)

Other physicians and health care professionals who specialize in heart disease and behavioral medicine in general have included religious–spiritual beliefs and practices such as meditation and prayer in their treatment protocols as well to treat patients holistically (Benson, 1996; Borysenko & Borysenko, 1994). Because many patients with cardiovascular disease, and others who suffer from serious physical problems associated with lifestyle factors, benefit from work with mental health professionals to alter lifestyle patterns, improve interpersonal relationships, and better cope with the stress of having a chronic and often life threatening disease, psychotherapy and psychoeducational services are often incorporated into these medical treatment approaches.

MANUALIZED RELIGIOUSLY–SPIRITUALLY INTEGRATED PSYCHOTHERAPY PROGRAMS

In an era of empirically supported treatment programs and manualized protocols, a number of high-quality structured programs have emerged that well integrate religious–spiritual and psychotherapy principles for a variety of important clinical problems: the Christian Marriage Counseling Approach for Christian Couples (Worthington, 1989, 1990), Becoming a More Forgiving Christian (Worthington, 2004), Coping With Divorce (Rye & Pargament, 2003; Rye, Pargament, Pan, Yingling, Shogren, & Ito, 2005), Solace for the Soul (Murray-Swank, 2003; Murray-Swank & Pargament, 2005), Lighting the Way (Pargament et al., 2004), Spiritual Renewal (Richards, Hardman, & Berrett, 2000), Re-Creating Your Life (Cole & Pargament, 1998), and From Vice to Virtue (Ano, 2005), among others.

Most of these spiritually integrated psychotherapy intervention programs that have research support and have been published in quality, peer-reviewed, professional outlets involve brief (i.e., 4–10) treatment sessions that offer treatment manuals and typically focus on particular clinical problems, such as social anxiety, HIV/AIDS, other serious medical problems, sexual abuse victimization, eating disorders, and high-conflict divorce. Most of these treatment programs have emerged from a Christian perspective. However, some programs are nondenominational and can be used with clients from any or no religious faith tradition. For example, the Eight-Point Program (EPP) discussed in the next section in some detail is a good example of an empirically supported treatment approach that can be integrated into psychotherapy with clients from just about any faith tradition or no faith tradition (Easwaran, 1991; Oman et al., 2007). Many of the mindfulness-based stress reduction programs also are excellent examples of integrative treatment programs that can be used with any religious background (or for those without any spiritual or religious affiliations or interest) for a variety of clinical problems and issues (Kabat-Zinn, 2003).

A number of these treatment programs have been developed by Everett Worthington at Virginia Commonwealth University and Kenneth Pargament at Bowling Green State University, along with their colleagues and doctoral students. Although it is beyond the scope of this chapter to provide details about all of the available treatment programs, several are briefly mentioned and highlighted to provide the reader with a sense of what is available with these best practices in religiously–spiritually integrated psychotherapy.

Christian Marriage Counseling

Marriage counseling provided within the context of a religious tradition is common among most faith communities. Thus, church-based marriage enhancement and therapy services are common among a large number of diverse religious communities. This is not surprising because many people turn to a clergy member or other religious leader in their church environment when confronted with marital troubles. Perhaps this has led to the development of treatment approaches targeted to particular faith communities and offered as part of church services. Worthington's (1989, 1990) Christian Marriage Counseling Approach for Christian Couples is an excellent example of a high-quality marriage therapy program that well integrates religious–spiritual principles from a Christian perspective. It is especially appealing to those of a

Protestant faith. The goal of the therapist is to "help people grow spiritually and psychologically by . . . helping them solve their marital problems" (Worthington, 1990, p. 5). The treatment approach includes praying with clients, reading self-help books on marriage from a Christian perspective, and focusing on forgiveness, among other integrative techniques.

Lighting the Way

The Lighting the Way program is an eight-session group treatment approach for women who struggle with HIV/AIDS (Pargament et al., 2004). Each of the eight sessions has a theme or focus, such as anger (Session 4), shame and guilt (Session 5), and hopes and dreams (Session 7). Religious–spiritual integration occurs in each session. For example, during the session on letting go of anger, participants are encouraged to discuss their resentment toward God for their contracting and suffering from a serious illness, whereas during the hopes and dreams session participants are encouraged to reflect on what God's purpose for their lives might be, given their illness.

Spiritual Renewal

The Spiritual Renewal program is a 10-session approach for women with eating disorders (Richards et al., 2000). As in the Lighting the Way program, each session has a particular theme, such as the healing power of faith and spirituality (Session 1), affirming your divine worth (Session 3), and belonging and gratitude (Session 9). Also, as in other programs, religious–spiritual concepts and themes are integrated into each treatment session. For example, during the belonging and gratitude session, participants are encouraged to discuss their feelings of belonging with others and with God as well as developing a sense of gratitude for God's gifts and blessings.

Re-Creating Your Life

The Re-Creating Your Life program is a six-session nondenominational group treatment for those experiencing a serious medical illness, such as cancer (Cole & Pargament, 1998). The program focuses on spiritual coping strategies, such as securing community support, meditation, spiritual visualization, and so forth. The program's goal is to use religious–spiritual principles of coping to improve overall adjustment to medical troubles. These principles can be used for chronic as well as terminal illnesses.

Research on these and other religiously–spiritually integrated psychotherapy treatment programs and packages has generally found that they are effective relative to either no treatment or secular treatment approaches (D'Souza, Rich, Diamond, Godfrey, & Gleeson, 2002; Lampton, Oliver, Worthington, & Berry, 2005; Wachholtz, 2005; Wachholtz & Pargament,

2005). These findings are also encouraging when examining non-Christian interventions, such as Muslim approaches (Azhar, Varma, & Dharap, 1994). Although these research findings are encouraging, it is important to mention that additional quality randomized clinical trial research is still very much needed in this fairly new area of research because there is much still to do in evaluating these and other religiously–spiritually integrated approaches. In addition, non-Christian or nondenominational treatment programs are especially needed. Even if religiously–spiritually based treatment does not provide more benefits than secular interventions, many spiritual clients prefer it (Pargament, 2007). Therefore, religiously–spiritually integrated interventions do not have to be superior to secular psychotherapy, just at least as good.

THE EIGHT-POINT PROGRAM: AN INTEGRATIVE APPROACH TO SPIRITUALITY AND PSYCHOTHERAPY

Like mindfulness-based meditation, EPP (Easwaran, 1978/1991; Flinders, Oman, & Flinders, 2007) is another excellent example of how to use the tools offered by religion–spirituality high on the metaphorical mountain (i.e., spiritual tools and practices common to all of the major religious traditions) to help clients in psychotherapy practice. Initially developed in the 1960s at the University of California, Berkeley, and used in a variety of secular settings (Flinders et al., 2007; Oman et al., 2007, 2008), the program teaches eight spiritual principles manage stress, improve interpersonal relationships, and enhance well-being:

1. Passage meditation
2. Mantra repetition
3. Slowing down
4. One-point attention
5. Training the senses
6. Putting others first
7. Spiritual association
8. Inspirational reading

Each of these principles or points can be applied to clients from any religious tradition or no tradition. Definitions of each of the eight points and case examples follow.

Passage meditation involves concentration on a spiritual or sacred text or perhaps a quote from an important spiritual model. Those who are not affiliated with any religious tradition may choose a text that does not refer to any religious–spiritual tradition but focuses on values or qualities they strive toward, such as compassion or equality. The person is asked to close his or her eyes, sit comfortably, and repeat the passage for 30 minutes as slowly and deliberately as possible. Of course, many newcomers to meditation practices have trouble sitting quietly for 30 minutes and thus might start with shorter time intervals and gradually increase their meditation session over time.

> Marcia experiences generalized anxiety disorder. As part of her treatment, she agrees to a passage meditation exercise. She is a Christian and active in her Methodist church. One of her favorite Bible quotes that helps her relax is Romans 8:28 from the New Testament, which states, "And we know that all things work together for good to them that love God, to them who are called according to his purpose." Marcia meditates on this passage as part of her passage meditation exercise, which helps her feel more at peace.

Mantra repetition involves the use of a short word or phrase that is repeated either silently or aloud. One could choose a mantra that suits one's religious–spiritual tradition (e.g., *Jesus* for Christians and perhaps *Rama* for Hindus) or a word that is not associated with any particular religious tradition, such as *one* or *peace*. They are encouraged to use the mantra as they conduct their daily activities, and perhaps most especially during times of stress, or to relax and calm the mind when needed, such as before sleep. This technique is essentially the same as used in transcendental meditation or Herbert Benson's popular *relaxation response* (Benson, 1976).

> Marcia uses the mantra "Bless me, Jesus" throughout the day. She finds herself repeating her mantra regularly as she engages in her daily activities and finds that it helps her to relax and be more at peace.

Slowing down refers to behaving with care and deliberation rather than living at a frantic pace. It focuses on maintaining priorities and limiting activities to avoid multitasking, time urgency, and stress.

> Jim considers himself fairly Type A, and his family does as well. He believes a car accident he had while multitasking was a wake-up call that his Type A behaviors were going to kill him, so he seeks the services of a psychologist to help him become "more Type B." One of the treatment interventions the psychologist uses with Jim is "slowing down." Jim and his therapist discuss letting go of many of his activities and commitments and work on a number of slowing down exercises. Jim has much trouble making these adjustments, but over time he improves a great deal.

One-point attention requests that people give full attention to one thing at a time and avoid multitasking. It attempts to keep a person centered and focused on the present and to avoid the constant interruptions that stress so many.

> Jim is also taught about one-point attention. He finds it challenging because he prides himself as a multitasker. He practices the technique and makes gains over many weeks and months.

Training the senses attempts to help discriminate lifestyle choices to avoid common destructive behaviors such as smoking, drinking excessive alcohol, overeating, and other compulsions.

> Jim eats too much and occasionally drinks too much alcohol. He finds that stress contributes to his poor eating and drinking habits. Jim's therapist works with him on training the senses to be more mindful about his drinking and eating. Over time, he improves his habits and loses 20 pounds.

Putting others first refers to finding ways to avoid self-centeredness and selfish behavior. It focuses on developing empathy and compassion for others and teaches that following one's own needs and desires at the exclusion of others' often leads to disappointment.

> Asha is embarrassed by her often self-centered behavior. She admits that she can find herself turning people off by being so self-focused. After being rejected by a new boyfriend, she feels she could use help being less selfish. Her therapist speaks with her about putting others first and gives her exercises to hone this skill both at work and in her personal life. Asha finds it challenging but cannot help noticing the positive response she receives from her coworkers and associates.

Spiritual association involves encouraging people to find a community of support with others who share similar values and perspectives. This may involve traditional church communities within a particular faith tradition or some other community in which social support and group cohesion can occur.

> Irene feels isolated and lonely after moving to a new community to start a new job. She begins to feel that her move may have been a mistake. Although the job is going well, she feels that she is too isolated in her new surroundings. Irene has a history of being involved with her Jewish temple and decides to join a temple in her community to nurture relationships with people of similar backgrounds and points of view.

Inspirational reading helps people support their religious–spiritual practices through reading inspirational or devotional material. Reading the Bible, the Hebrew scriptures such as the Torah, the Koran, or even nonreligious but yet inspirational reading can be used, depending on the interests of the client.

> Irene joins a women's book club associated with her new temple that focuses on religious–spiritual readings. She finds both the books and the community of women inspiring.

These eight points are not orthogonal but interactive. Clients learn how to integrate these principles into their lives and daily routines to achieve better psychological, physical, and interpersonal functioning. Research using the EPP on health care workers, HIV/AIDS patients, college students, schoolteachers, and others have found it to be very productive in improving overall psychological and physical functioning (Flinders et al., 2007; Oman et al., 2007). The EPP illustrates using the collective wisdom of religious–spiritual traditions and adapting these principles to contemporary life for those who come from a wide variety of religious traditions or even no religious tradition.

In the next section, I provide five clinical examples of using religious–spiritual tools with actual clients in psychotherapy. Although it is impossible to provide a structured cookbook of exactly how to use the religious–spiritual tools introduced in this book with all clients, I hope providing several clinical case examples in more detail than in other sections of the book will give the reader a better understanding and appreciation of religiously–spiritually integrated psychotherapy. Of course, these religious–spiritual tools must be used and adapted according to the unique clinical situations and persons (both clients and therapists) involved. To focus on the integrative use of religious–spiritual tools, the cases do not discuss the details of the traditional psychotherapy interventions and orientations being used. The interested reader may also wish to review a few other APA books that provide highly detailed case studies and examples of spiritually integrated psychotherapy (e.g., see Richards & Bergin, 2004; Sperry & Shafranske, 2005).

USING RELIGIOUS–SPIRITUAL TOOLS TO ENHANCE PSYCHOTHERAPY: EXTENDED CASE EXAMPLES

Martha: How Spiritual Direction Helped With Anxiety

Martha is a 62-year-old married woman with two adult children. She has a long history of struggles with anxiety disorders, including panic attacks and agoraphobia. Many members of her family also have experienced anxiety and depressive disorders, including panic disorder. Martha's troubles with anxiety and panic began when she was a teenager and have resulted in her developing a lifestyle that is very restrictive. For example, she never continued her education beyond the high school level. Furthermore, she has never been employed as an adult, learned to drive a car, or traveled beyond her home state. Over the years, Martha has been overly dependent on antianxiety medications such as Xanax and Valium, prescribed by several internal medicine physicians. She first sought psychological treatment in her mid-40s to better manage her anxiety symptoms and has been in and out of treatment for almost 20 years.

Martha identifies herself as Roman Catholic on her initial intake forms. When asked during an initial assessment interview about her religious involvement, she proudly mentions that several family members have been priests and that her husband had been in seminary to become a Catholic priest before they decided to marry. She reports that she closely identifies with her faith tradition but that it has been a source of both comfort and discomfort for her, saying she often feels guilty about her thoughts and frequently wonders about her perceived sins. She maintains that she attends Sunday Mass each week and that periodically she attends daily Mass as well but reports that she occasionally has panic attacks in church when she is feeling especially guilty and sometimes avoids taking communion when she feels most vulnerable to panic.

Martha states that she has been anxious as far back as she can remember and that her family is full of relatives who have struggled with anxiety and related disorders. She reports that both of her now-adult children have a history of anxiety, depression, and panic yet are doing well enough to maintain satisfying jobs and marriages. She claims that they also have been treated for panic and anxiety by mental health professionals.

Martha is very interested in integrating her religious perspectives into psychotherapy when the opportunity is offered to her.

Religious Self-Disclosure

The therapist informs Martha that he is also Roman Catholic and thus is familiar with Catholic traditions and beliefs. Martha is grateful to be working with a fellow Catholic, who she feels can understand her and her worldview better than someone who is not Catholic. Martha feels she is working with someone who respects her religious tradition and can perhaps help her better integrate her faith with her treatment. She is also pleased that she will not have to do a lot of explaining about her faith to someone who is from the same religious tradition. She says that a previous therapist frequently asked her to help him understand her religious tradition and that she does not want to have to educate another mental health professional about Roman Catholicism.

Consultation With Clergy

Martha is reluctant to agree to any kind of collaboration between her priest and her therapist. She says her parish priest is very nice but elderly, being in his early 80s, and that she does not feel comfortable talking with him about her psychological problems and does not think it would be helpful. She says,

> Fr. B is a dear old-fashioned parish priest who does a fine job saying Mass and all, but I wouldn't feel comfortable talking with him in much detail about my personal life, never mind having him talk with my psychologist. In fact, I do not think he looks too favorably on psychologists. In general, he thinks prayer and confession are the way to handle personal problems, and certainly not talking to some shrink.

However, Martha appreciates the suggestion by her therapist that she might wish to consult a priest who is not connected to her parish to receive confidential spiritual direction to better help her integrate her faith with her treatment. The therapist refers her to several priests and lay spiritual directors for possible consultation. After careful consideration and discussion with her therapist, she chooses to work with a priest affiliated with a local Catholic university who is also a licensed psychologist. She seeks his consultation as well as confession several times each year and agrees to have her psychologist and spiritual director talk together as needed to provide coordinated care. She signs a release-of-information form to allow her therapist to engage in ongoing consultation with the priest.

Forgiveness, Gratitude, and Kindness

Martha has a great deal of trouble forgiving herself for what she perceives are sins and various transgressions. For example, although she reports that she loves her husband and that they have been best pals since high school, she does not feel particularly attracted to him sexually and they have infrequent sexual encounters. She says she feels guilty that she is not very attracted to her husband and denies him the kind of sexual life he wants. Although she reports she had never has marital affairs, she finds herself being sexually attracted to other men, including friends and acquaintances as well as movies stars and celebrities. She asks her therapist whether these feelings are sins. The therapist tells Martha that he cannot appropriately comment on what is or is not a sin because he is not clergy and these topics are out of his area of competence. However, he refers her to her spiritual director and priest consultant for questions about sins and is willing to discuss her guilt about her feelings and her beliefs about them. He offers a variety of cognitive–behavioral strategies to cope with her feelings as well as a focus on forgiveness of herself for being less than perfect in her mind. He discusses the role and benefits of forgiveness in both religious and psychological terms and again suggests that she also discuss these issues with her spiritual director.

In addition, Martha has trouble forgiving several extended family members for various transgressions over the years. She feels that some relatives were greedy, rude, and not gracious during special holiday celebrations. She also feels disappointed with her daughter in-law for behaviors and comments that she thinks were rude or disconcerting. Her anger with her relatives leads to ongoing stress and an increase in panic symptoms, periodic sleeping difficulties, and dissatisfaction with a number of her family relationships. The therapist talks with her about maintaining reasonable expectations about the behavior of others and better ways to maintain satisfying family relationships even with relatives with whom she does not see eye-to-eye. He also focuses on ways to forgive her relatives for various transgressions in order to improve her relationships with them and secure better quality of life and more peace of mind for herself.

Prayer

Periodically, Martha reports a serious illness or death in her family. For example, her brother dies unexpectedly from a heart attack and her sister is diagnosed with Stage 4 cancer that has spread to several internal organs. Martha asks her therapist to pray for her relatives and for her to better cope with these stressors. Although the therapist does not pray with Martha during the therapy sessions, he does agree to add her and her family members to his regular prayer list. Martha is grateful for his willingness to support her by praying for her and her relatives, stating that it means a great deal to her.[1]

Bibliotherapy

Martha occasionally talks about theological concerns and wonders about the validity of some of her church teachings, such as Jesus being born of a virgin and performing various miracles. Her doubts lead to further guilt and panic, and she feels she cannot talk with her parish priest about these doubts because they are too embarrassing. Her therapist suggests she talk about these concerns with her spiritual director and also suggests several books she might find useful that focus on the types of theological issues she is most concerned about. Their conversations about the benefits of forgiveness lead Martha's therapist to suggest several popular self-help books on this topic as well.

Acceptance of Self and Others (Even With Faults)

Martha is often anxious about aspects of her behavior and thoughts and those of people close to her, such as her husband. Her frustration often leads to feelings of anxiety, depression, and panic as well as stressful conflicts in her interpersonal relationships. Her therapist reviews the Serenity Prayer with her and discusses the benefits of living this popular but wise prayer, which focuses on changing what one can and accepting what one cannot change. Martha reports that she knows the Serenity Prayer very well and likes it. After her discussions on this topic with her therapist, she decides to put a framed copy of the prayer in her home to remind herself of the wisdom of the prayer.

Conclusion

Martha struggled with anxiety, panic, depression, and several conflictual family relationships. As a devout and engaged Roman Catholic, her faith tradition was important to her and could be effectively integrated into her clinical care by the use of several religious–spiritual tools, such as forgiveness, prayer, bibliotherapy, and acceptance of self and others, as well as ongoing consultation with her spiritual director, who was a priest. Although Martha likely would have benefited from secular high-quality psychotherapy without regard to her religious–spiritual concerns, thoughtful attention to these issues enhance treatment and likely result in a better clinical outcome.

---

[1]Therapists who do not feel comfortable praying for their clients might offer to keep them and their well-being in their thoughts.

Thuy: Navigating Her Call Toward Integrity and Community

Thuy is a woman in her mid 50s who seeks psychotherapy because of frustrations with her husband, her youngest son, and her career as a human resources professional. Thuy feels that she married her husband primarily for financial security because he was a successful business executive but has found that over time their relationship has turned more frustrating and uncomfortable. She reports that they no longer have a sexual relationship, and they basically just tolerate each other. She has had several marital affairs with coworkers and business associates over the years. She claims that because of her children's well-being, her religious views, and financial considerations, divorce is not an option for her. Thuy is also concerned about her youngest son because he has a learning disability that makes school challenging for him. He enters high school and begins to behave in oppositional ways consistent with being a teenager, desiring more independence from his parents. Finally, Thuy is feeling burnt out in her career. She fell into human resources work and has failed to pursue her perceived ideal career as an attorney. Now that all of her children are older and more independent, her career frustrations cause her more stress.

Thuy discloses on her intake forms that she is a member of the Presbyterian Church and has had periods in her life when she was very active in her religious community. During a follow-up initial interview, she says her feelings about her husband and periodic affairs make her feel guilty, and during these times she becomes less involved with her church and faith tradition.

Meaning, Purpose, and Calling in Life

Thuy says she wanted to be an attorney when she was growing up and while in college. She reports that one of her uncles was an attorney and that she respected, admired, and loved him. Furthermore, he worked with social service agencies, and she was impressed with his passion for social justice.

After college, Thuy wanted to take some time off before going to law school. She decided to take a position in a human resources department at a large company, thinking she would spend a year or 2 earning money to help her pay for her law school plans. While in her position, she met her husband, who was a successful and older business executive. She maintains that one thing led to another and that she found herself intimately involved with him. Although she claims that she never felt in love with him, he was financially secure and could offer her the lifestyle she longed for. They married, and she got pregnant soon after. After having several children and taking time off from work to raise them, she returned to human resources work because it suited her needs for part-time employment and was "family friendly." Over time she abandoned her dream to become an attorney.

Thuy's therapist uses the calling protocol to help her discuss and reflect on her vocation in order to develop more meaning and purpose in her life. Over time, Thuy decides to apply to law school after all and hopes to focus her efforts on heath care law as it relates to services for older people. She says,

> Now that my kids are pretty much grown and independent, I can pursue my career dreams that have taken a back seat during the past few decades. Working in human resources all these years, I have had a pretty close look at some of the problems with health care benefits and access, especially for the elderly, who really need quality health care, and so I think I would like to pursue these issues as an attorney.

Attending Community Services and Rituals

Thuy discusses her on again, off again relationship with her church and discovers that she misses some of the community support and the ritual of Sunday services. She realizes that her avoidance is usually related to feeling guilty about her marital infidelity and that she feels like a hypocrite going to services while violating her marital vows. Her therapist discusses the notion that church services are not for only those who are perfect or without problems. With encouragement from her therapist, Thuy decides to talk over her concerns with one of the clergy in her church who runs the marital and divorce support outreach programs. After an open discussion with the clergy member, she decides to return to church services and reports she feels that even if she is not perfect she is entitled to be involved with her church community.

Ethical Values and Behavior

Thuy's guilt about her marital affairs lead to a series of conversations with her therapist about marital and general ethics. Thuy says she feels foolish that she is known for being an honest and ethical person at work but is engaged in the deceit of marital infidelity at home. Thuy feels that she needs to reconcile her view of herself as an ethical person while having marital affairs. Over a number of conversations, Thuy decides that she has to deal more directly with her marital troubles and that having affairs is not a productive way to distract herself from them. She decides to end her affair and work with another therapist on couples issues. Although reluctant, her husband agrees to attend marital therapy sessions with another therapist. Thuy says,

> I pride myself on being an ethical person. I pride myself on being honest, responsible, and being a person of integrity. This obviously does not jive with my affairs. Somehow I need to face this fact and, I suppose, prove to myself that I can be more ethical in my personal as well as professional life.

Social Justice

Thuy is disgusted by some of the remarkable hassles her parents went through with their health insurance and the lack of care they experienced during their last years of life. As a human resources professional, she also has been involved with a number of cases of employees being victimized, in her mind, by the health care industry. She finds it especially disturbing that this occurs among those who have low-paying jobs and few financial resources. Her therapist and she discuss ways to channel her anger into social justice activities, which leads her to consider pursuing health care law as a career change. Furthermore, she decides to become involved with several social justice activities through her church and finds meaning and fellowship in them. One of the activities she is especially excited about is church-sponsored visitations to nursing homes and hospitals, working alongside chaplains and deacons. She finds this ministry very rewarding and engaging. She also feels that she can use some of her skills as a human resources professional to help some of the patients she interacts with.

Acceptance of Self and Others (Even With Faults)

Thuy's frustrations with herself, her husband, and her son are addressed in psychotherapy regularly. One aspect that is highlighted is the notion that it would be helpful to work on her acceptance of herself and her family members (even with faults) and to better live the Serenity Prayer of changing what one can and accepting what one cannot change. She is familiar with and likes the Serenity Prayer and knows it offers wisdom that can help her.

Conclusion

Thuy struggled with marital troubles, career dissatisfaction, feeling disconnected from her religious community, and several other important interpersonal conflicts. An emphasis on developing a sense of vocation along with reengaging with her spiritual community, focusing on living her ethical values, better accepting herself and others, and nurturing her interests in social justice added value to her psychotherapy. Although Thuy would no doubt have benefited from traditional psychotherapy services without any regard to religious–spiritual tools, thoughtful use of these tools likely enhanced her psychotherapy treatment and improved clinical outcomes.

Zach: Recharting a Productive Life With Chronic Illness

Zach begins psychotherapy right after his 30th birthday. He feels very depressed and upset about turning 30 because he thinks his life "stalled out" after being diagnosed with ulcerative colitis immediately after graduating from college 7 years earlier. He had planned on going to graduate school to study theater arts but ended up moving back into his parents' home and working on and off in part-time low-level jobs that were unsatisfying. Furthermore, he reports that his parents are feeling that he should move out of their home and live on his own now that he is 30, but he feels he cannot afford to do so. He says they have been very supportive but thinks he should be more independent and "move on with [his] life."

Zach grew up in the Jewish tradition. He reports that although it is important to him to maintain his cultural and faith tradition, he stopped being very active in it when he began struggling with his illness. He claims that he no longer attends services or participates much in the Jewish holidays and traditions, saying, "Since I got sick, I find myself just avoiding the whole thing and being more isolated."

Meditation

Zach is open to meditative practices to help him better manage his stress and illness. He was introduced to mindfulness-based stress reduction while participating in a support group for coping with chronic illness at the local hospital after he was initially diagnosed with colitis. He maintains that he found the meditative exercises useful at the time but failed to continue the practice after he stopped going to the group sessions. After a discussion about the possible benefits of meditation, Zach agrees to again practice mindfulness-based meditation and begins attending a meditation program in his community. He enjoys the group as well as the practice, and he experiences satisfying stress-reducing effects over time.

Meaning, Purpose, and Calling in Life

Zach experiences a crisis in meaning, purpose, and calling, feeling derailed from his interest in theater. He had hoped to attend graduate school in fine arts or drama and pursue a career in the entertainment industry as an actor but was open to other roles in the theater industry. But now he says that managing the symptoms and treatments of his illness make pursuing his career interests too demanding and unrealistic. In psychotherapy, Zach agrees to participate in the calling protocol and discusses how he might be able to find a sense of calling and meaning given his illness and the concerns that he has about trying to manage his illness and a demanding career effectively. He decides to take some courses in creative writing at a local college and thinks he might be able to pursue writing more easily than acting, given the limitations he feels are imposed on him by his illness. He finds that he enjoys writing and receives helpful feedback from his instructors. He writes a screenplay that his instructor encourages him to further develop and submit to entertainment industry members. This energizes him and helps him see a possible new direction for his talents.

Attending Community Services and Rituals

Zach reports that he feels lonely and wants to connect to others in the community. He also expresses a desire to feel more connected to his religious tradition but wants to be separate from his parents' faith community. He says,

> I do not want to be going to services in the temple I grew up in with my parents at age 30. I feel infantilized, and I hate all those

questions from my parents' friends about why I'm not married and not working in some impressive career. It just depresses me.

Zach decides to attend a temple in another part of town that seems to have more young people as members. He attends several services and likes the rabbis there. After several months of attending temple events, he decides to join the temple and volunteers on several committees that interest him. During Purim celebrations, his new temple puts on a humorous play acted by the temple staff. The rabbi knows about Zach's talents and asks him to help them with the project, which Zach eagerly agrees to. Zach says that participating in the production makes him feel connected to people with a shared goal and distracts from his illness.

Volunteerism and Charity

Zach discusses his feelings of "being useless" because he feels that he is not "offering anything important to anyone." He feels that without a spouse, child, or meaningful career, no one depends on him and he feels unimportant. After a number of discussions about his feelings, Zach decides to volunteer at a local boy's club to teach low-income children how to swim. Zach states that he loves swimming and enjoys teaching young people. After a number of weeks he finds himself feeling more important, connected, valued, and useful, and he feels gratified by positive feedback about his teaching and easy manner with children.

Learning From Spiritual Models

Zach begins to read stories of people coping with chronic illness, including those he considers to be religious–spiritual giants. He finds a book in a local bookstore that discusses how some people use their illnesses as a way to grow spiritually. Zach is intrigued by the notion that he could improve his spirituality and quality of life by viewing his illness differently. He enjoys learning about how others manage their chronic illness. He finds out that one of the rabbis at his new temple has a chronic illness as well (i.e., lupus), and he has several productive conversations with her about how she manages her illness and how she has grown spiritually as a result. Over time, she becomes a spiritual model for him, and Zach is impressed by how well she copes with her illness and manages to live productively and spiritually.

Acceptance of Self and Others (Even With Faults)

Zach works hard in psychotherapy to learn to better accept himself with his chronic illness. He focuses on the notion that although his personal and career plans were derailed after college, he has no choice but to learn to better accept himself with his physical and other limitations. Zach is intrigued by the Buddhist notion that suffering is expected in life and often due to attachments and desire. He works on trying to be less attached to the particular life plan and vision that he had for himself prior to his medical troubles and on better accepting his current reality and life situation. He finds that his meditation group and practice as well as psychotherapy and conversations with his rabbi help him make progress on accepting himself and others.

Conclusion

Zach did not expect to develop a serious chronic illness at such a young age and found his life plans derailed. He became depressed and at a loss for how to proceed with his life, most especially after his 30th birthday. A variety of religious–spiritual tools—meditation, developing a sense of calling, volunteerism, and participating in a religious community, among others— were integrated into his psychotherapy with positive results.

Rico: A Nonreligious Client's Journey Toward Valuing Self and Others

Rico is a 50-year-old man who grew up in a secular home without any formal religious training. He seeks psychotherapy because he is depressed and experiences significant stress associated with his job as well as challenges coping with several serious chronic illnesses. Rico has Type I diabetes as well as hepatitis C. He married late in life, at age 48, and has no children. Rico hopes to find better ways to cope with stress in his life, manage his illnesses better, and improve his relationship with his wife Cindy. He reports that Cindy is understanding about his work stress and medical issues and is generally very accepting of him. However, he says the stress often makes him angry and grumpy, which he admits he occasionally takes out on her.

Meditation

Rico is very interested in learning about mindfulness-based stress reduction. He heard about it from a variety of sources and wonders whether it might help him cope better. He also likes that mindfulness-based stress reduction is not associated with any particular religious organization that mandates membership or believing in any particular dogma. He takes a series of classes at the local hospital and finds the training helpful. He reports, "Somehow it centers me and cools my jets. It's like taking a chill pill."

Ethical Values and Behavior

Rico prides himself on being an ethical person and a "man of integrity." Although he says he had no religious training growing up, his family was very interested in ethical behavior, which "rubbed off" on him. His interests led him to become a community advocate and attorney, which he finds rewarding and meaningful. He says, "I like working for the little guy, the people who have no voice. I like to take on the big organizations, or those with power and influence, on behalf of those that have so little." Rico is attracted to social justice issues and says he is always upset when people with power and influence exploit others for their gain.

Although Rico sees himself as being ethical, he admits that he sometimes is not very respectful or compassionate with others. In discussing the RRICC (respect, responsibility, integrity, competence, and concern) model of ethics (Plante, 2004), he admits that he could work to be "less of an ass" with others, saying, "I can get angry and frustrated and, in hindsight, have used my verbal skills and emotion to tear people up. I'm not proud of that." Rico feels that he can work on the respect and concern for others part of the RRICC model better.

Forgiveness, Gratitude, and Kindness

Rico admits that he sometimes feels angry about the behavior of political leaders, lobbyists, special interest groups, and those with power, money, and access. He admits he sometimes treats his enemies or opponents with anger and distain. He laughs when he tells several stories about how he behaves to opposing attorneys during some of his lawsuits and proudly states, "Most lawyers don't like going up against me." However, he also admits, "I guess I sometimes go over the top in advocating for my clients, and sometimes I treat people pretty badly in doing so." With further discussion, he admits that he also gets frustrated with drivers or store clerks whom he feels are incompetent or "screwing up." For example, he admits that he recently was a bit too harsh with a clerk at a bakery when the worker made errors with his order when he was feeling rushed. He says, "I really shouldn't have treated the clerk that way. I could be more gracious. We all make mistakes."

Rico admits that his illnesses and stress level often worsen when he acts in ways that are hostile and disrespectful. His therapist discusses with him the benefits of treating others (even his opponents) in a more loving, forgiving, and gentle way. They discuss that he can still do a good job for his clients even "without being an ass." After many weeks of therapy, he acknowledges benefits to altering his interpersonal style. After trying to be more gracious toward others, he enjoys some of the shock effect his new behavior has on those who know him well. Over time, he notices less stress and fewer problematic physical symptoms when he behaves in a more caring manner with others. He states, "I guess I can actually still defend my clients and work for the underdog without being a total ass to others." He learns to let go of his angry impulses better and is better able to see the benefits to both himself and others when he is more loving and caring.

Social Justice

Rico feels strongly about social justice and thinks his career gives him the opportunity to help create a more just world. Over time, he sees that his social justice activities need to be motivated solely for the benefit of his clients rather than the pleasure he experiences "bringing down the powerful." He states,

> I suppose I got such thrills out of watching the powerful brought down to earth and suffer rather than being just concerned with

having my clients get the justice they deserved. I noticed that when I tried to work on focusing my efforts on my clients and tried not to get invested in bringing the powers-that-be down, I felt more peaceful and less stressed out.

Acceptance of Self and Others (Even With Faults)

Rico says he thought he always had a "good guy, bad guy" view of the world that fit well with his community advocacy and legal work. However, in psychotherapy he realizes that this point of view was simplistic and contributed to his stress level and physical symptoms. He works on the notion of acceptance of others (even his enemies and opponents) and finds himself more peaceful over time. He says, "I really see the benefits in acceptance. I know the Serenity Prayer is overused, but I saw it somewhere while shopping, and somehow it hit me that it makes total sense."

Appreciating the Sacredness of Life

Rico works on finding the sacred or specialness in all people, including his opponents. Although he does not report any interest in religious views of the sacred, he sees the benefits of seeing everyone as important and special, even those whom he does not like or agree with. He reports,

> I suppose you really do treat people better when you try and remind yourself that everyone is special and important, even people you don't like or you are opposed to in court. Everyone has or had a mother who loved them or, perhaps, is one of a kind.

Conclusion

Rico struggled with serious chronic illnesses and had a personality style that was highly aggressive and often hostile toward others. Although not religious–spiritual, he found that religious–spiritual tools could be useful to him in psychotherapy and was willing to use them in a secular manner. They included meditation, nurturing ethical values, approaching others in a more gracious and kind manner, and other religiously–spiritually based tools. The use of these approaches improved his treatment and functioning in ways that likely would not have occurred without them.

Lea: Using Religious–Spiritual Tools to Overcome Clergy Abuse

Lea is a 40-year-old woman who enters psychotherapy highly depressed and with suicidal ideation. She reports that she has a tumultuous relationship with her husband, whom she feels is sexually obsessed and is losing a lot of money on gambling, including day-trading activities. Furthermore, Lea mentions that she was sexually exploited by a Catholic pries at a nearby parish church when she sought pastoral counseling about her marital troubles.

Although Lea grew up in a working-class Catholic home and sees herself as a "good girl," she claims that she has always been drawn to "naughty guys." She reports that she has always enjoyed men who are sexually assertive, enjoy parties and socializing, and are "a bit on the edge." She claims, "I hate to say it, but nice guys bore me, I suppose. The naughty ones were fun and exciting." Lea ultimately married a Hindu man from India. Lea, having been born and raised in the American Midwest, finds him to be "exciting and exotic." Once married, she maintains that his charm quickly faded and that he engaged in a good deal of drinking, gambling, and online pornography and also went to strip clubs. Over time, their relationship deteriorated. Lea, who has always felt that getting a divorce is not an option because of her religious beliefs, sought consultation from a priest across town for spiritual direction and pastoral care. After several sessions he encouraged her to have a sexual encounter after their session. In a troubled and confused state, Lea participated in sexual liaisons with the priest for several months before breaking it off because she thought the priest's behavior was becoming more and more bizarre. With worsening depression and suicidal ideation, Lea now seeks treatment from a professional psychologist referred to her by a friend. Lea wants a therapist who shares and understands her religious tradition and can integrate religious perspectives into psychotherapy.

Prayer

Lea feels that prayer is an important part of her life and asks her therapist to pray for her and her well-being. Her therapist agrees to keep her in his prayers, which she is very grateful for. She states, "It gives me a sense of peace and solace knowing that my therapist will pray for me. It means a lot to me." Lea discusses her prayer life in therapy, including the times she feels her prayers are connecting to God and the times she feels they are not. She discusses how prayer helps her cope with stressors and helps her talk through her troubles with God. Her therapist encourages her to continue to use prayer in her efforts to cope better and suggests that she consider consulting with a spiritual director who may help her find ways to enhance her prayer life.

Meditation

Lea finds some of the Eastern meditative traditions fascinating and helpful. She learns about mindfulness meditation and tries using it in her daily life. She also enjoys yoga and finds it to be helpful for her as well. Although her relationship with her husband has soured, she appreciates what she has learned from him and his circle of family and friends about meditation from the Hindu tradition.

Bibliotherapy

Over time, Lea feels shocked and angry at both the priest who violated her trust and the Catholic Church in general for having a priest who would behave in exploitative ways during pastoral counseling. Lea is interested in learning more about clergy sexual abuse and their victims but does not trust the sensationalized stories in the media. She wonders about how many priests have behaved in this manner with adults or children and feels that she cannot trust what she learns from the victim advocacy groups or from the news, which she thinks always has some agenda other than the truth. Her therapist recommends several thoughtful books on the topic, which she reads with great interest. She says that the books "helped me put this all in better perspective and helped me to think more logically about the problem."

Attending Community Services and Rituals

Lea's anger at the priest and Catholic Church results in her refusing to attend Catholic services or talk with any other Catholic clergy. However, she misses the weekly services and the support that she has felt from fellow parishioners. She had been active in several church groups but dropped out after she broke off her relationship with the priest. She says that she is just too angry and embarrassed to continue her church involvement.

Her therapist refers her to an Episcopal priest, who is also a licensed therapist, for consultation and spiritual direction. Given her experiences with the priest who abused her, she feels more comfortable talking with a clergy member not affiliated with the Catholic Church. Over time, she decides to attend Episcopal services and activities while she continues her work in psychotherapy. She expresses the need to continue weekly worship activities and support groups but is not ready to return to the Catholic Church. She finds the Episcopal Church to be similar enough to the Catholic Church to be comfortable and familiar yet different enough to help her feel more at ease while she works in psychotherapy.

Lea feels that starting anew with an Episcopal church helps her to continue her need to be part of a religious community but without the baggage that she experienced with the Catholic Church.

Volunteerism and Charity

During the course of psychotherapy, Lea mentions that two of the things that give her joy are music and children. Although Lea does not have children of her own, she reports that she very much enjoys being with young children and teaching music classes. She offers her music-teaching services to low-income children. She says she finds her volunteer work very rewarding and meaningful and that it helps to get her out of herself and focused away from her troubles. Her therapist encourages her to continue and to expand her volunteer activities as part of her overall treatment plan. She also decides to work toward a music-teaching credential so that she can consider pursuing her interests as a career in the school system.

Forgiveness, Gratitude, and Kindness

Lea is very angry with her husband, the priest who violated her, the Catholic Church in general, and herself for failing to live up to her own (and others') high standards and expectations of behavior. Her anger contributes to sleepless nights, depression, and a great deal of upset. Although she acknowledges that she has a right to be angry, she also understands, over time, that her anger needs to be channeled in a way that is more productive for her and consistent with who she feels she is as a loving person. Her therapist works with her on nurturing a more forgiving, loving, and kind style that includes working toward forgiving the priest, her husband, the Catholic Church, and others who have treated her unjustly. After many months of psychotherapy, she is able to talk in a more matter-of-fact manner about those who violated her and comes to forgive them more fully. She also leaves her husband but is able to forgive him and herself for the "failed marriage." She states,

> I can choose to be angry with them, which ultimately . . . harms [only] me, or I can choose to forgive them so that I can be at peace. It isn't easy to forgive, but I can see how it helps me be more at peace and less bitter about things.

Acceptance of Self and Others (Even With Faults)

Lea experiences a number of stressful relationships with several family members and has a great deal of trouble accepting herself and her perceived faults. Her depression and suicidal impulses are often directly related to her inability to accept herself and those around her. Lea's therapist focuses on her need to accept herself and others (even with faults). Lea works hard to change what she can about herself and her behavior while learning to accept those elements of herself and her life situation that are unchangeable.

Being Part of Something Larger Than Oneself

Lea reports that she loves the majesty of liturgical celebrations because they make her feel that she is part of something eternal and larger than herself. When she stopped attending Catholic services following her experiences with the priest, she missed the rituals and said she felt more ordinary and less connected to what came before her and what will come after her. In discussing the Episcopal services and tradition, Lea can see that this non-Catholic group maintains much of the liturgical majesty that the Catholics provided, with "less baggage." Lea's involvement with the Episcopal Church helps her to continue to feel part of something larger than herself. She says her teaching music to children also contributes to these feelings.

Conclusion

Lea experienced a dysfunctional, conflicted marriage, and her efforts to secure pastoral counseling and spiritual direction led her to be sexually violated by a priest. As a result, Lea experienced depression and suicidal ideation. A number of religious–spiritual tools were helpful to her in psychotherapy treatment: prayer, meditation, bibliotherapy, volunteerism, and attending community services and rituals, among others. These tools were productively integrated into her psychotherapy treatment with positive outcomes that would have been challenging to secure without them.

WHEN INTERVENTIONS DO NOT WORK

In reviewing the cases previously mentioned, it may appear that religious–spiritual tools in psychotherapy always work. Of course, this is far from true. It is important to acknowledge that religious–spiritual tools are perhaps no different from any other psychotherapeutic tool in that sometimes they work well and sometimes they do not. Furthermore, many of the interventions may not be successful at one point in time yet may be put to good use at a later date. Therefore, it is important for clinicians as well as clients to maintain realistic expectations regarding the use of these religious–spiritual tools and to understand that their use can be a process that may have both ups and downs. Relapse prevention strategies as well as flexibility are needed to prepare for and adapt to successes and failures while using religious–spiritual tools in psychological treatment.

For example, the clients discussed in detail in this chapter did not always respond successfully to the interventions offered, and some interventions worked better than others. Martha, for instance, continued to struggle with forgiveness and acceptance of herself and others. At times she found it just impossible to accept the behavior of her son, her daughter-in-law, and others in her life. Sometimes she just could not forgive. Sometimes her progress in treatment seemed to be lost during stressful and upsetting situations. During those challenges she focused on forgiveness as a process and something to strive for and tried to stay mindful of the fact that forgiveness does not always seem possible. Additionally, Martha at times got very angry when her prayers were not answered in ways she expected. Sometimes she reported that her prayers seemed empty and hollow and she questioned her faith and belief in God. At other times her anger was such that she lashed out at those who upset her (including God). Thus, it is important to adapt and be flexible with such challenges and maintain an accepting attitude that religious–spiritual tools may not work out as planned in all circumstances. At times progress is made, whereas at other times progress seems lost.

Furthermore, Thuy continued to struggle with anger and resentment toward her husband. Zach continued to feel underemployed and struggle with the challenges of a serious chronic illness. Rico's anger ultimately found it way into the courtroom, and Lea found herself enraged about her sexual victimization.

In these and perhaps most cases, religious–spiritual tools may not always work as well as hoped. By having a variety of tools to work with and being able to adapt to what works and what does not, therapists have a better chance of finding the treatment package that will ultimately be most productive for their clients and themselves.

CONCLUSION

There are many examples of high-quality programs that model spiritually integrated psychotherapy or similar services. Perhaps the 12-step programs are high-quality program that well integrate spiritual principles, concepts, and tools that can be applied to problems in living with alcohol and other addictions. There are a number of other programs as well that professionally and responsibly integrate religious–spiritual tools into self-help as well as professional mental health and health care services. In this chapter I presented several clinical examples of integrating religious–spiritual tools into psychotherapy services. They all are based on actual cases I have treated. The cases are not meant to be model cases but merely more in-depth examples of integration than presented earlier. I hope they provide a sampling of ways to use religious–spiritual tools in psychotherapy that are easy to understand and learn. Because every client, therapist, and clinical situation is unique, it is impossible and inappropriate to suggest that religious–spiritual tools should be used in a particular way for all parties. Each clinician must thoughtfully consider how and when to use them in psychotherapy in ways that make sense for their particular client and their particular clinical situation.

In the next and final chapter, I briefly discuss where research and training should go in the future and several principles that might make research and training in this area more productive so that the scholars and clinicians of tomorrow are better able to use religious–spiritual tools in psychological treatment.

10

NEXT STEPS:
FOCUSED RESEARCH AND TRAINING

Throughout this book I offered a variety of tools readers may find of use in clinical practice that are based on the best available clinical science as well as clinical practice. Although there is a long way to go in terms of understanding how best to offer psychotherapy, and psychological services in general, appreciating religious–spiritual tools is good place to begin. Religion–spirituality in psychology is a field that is in its infancy in terms of research support. Although individual clinicians may have tried to integrate religion–spirituality and psychotherapy for many decades, only in more recent years have these efforts been subjected to research using high-quality, state-of-the-art methodological and statistical techniques. Almost all empirical research studies, literature reviews, and books that try to incorporate research findings end by calling for more research. This book is no different. The good news is that more and more excellent research is being conducted by a number of skilled researchers; the bad news is that they have a very long way to go to answer the important research questions that might greatly improve clinical services (e.g., What types of interventions work best with clients and in certain circumstances?).

So much of the practice of state-of-the-art spiritually–religiously integrated psychotherapy is art rather than science. Mental health professionals need to move this field forward by letting more science better inform the art of clinical practice. The critical request is not so much a call for more research but for particular types of research projects that are most needed to better understand how to treat particular types of clients with particular types of clinical problems in particular types of circumstances. For example, how can religious community support best help those in need, and how can particular meditative approaches help those who are greatly stressed, anxious, or depressed? Thus, strategic efforts are required to conduct the kind of research that is needed now and that will most likely better inform clinicians so that they can best serve their clients.

In this brief final chapter, I discuss the importance of clinical research by specifying areas that need research and commenting on how this research might help to improve both clinical practice and professional training in the near future. I also discuss what can be done to ensure successful research efforts, and I highlight what has been learned from past successes and failures.

This book is certainly not the first to offer ideas about future research in this area. For example, Worthington, Kurusu, McCullough, and Sandage (1996) and Richards and Bergin (2005) together offered a thoughtful list of 10 proposed research agendas in the area of religion, mental health, and psychotherapy. These authors suggested that future research should, for example, use actual clinical clients rather than those who volunteer for a research study but do not have any particular diagnosis seeking professional services. They also called for studies that examine why religion–spirituality can sometimes result in positive effects and other times result in negative effects to determine what elements of religion–spirituality interventions promote health and relationships and what elements are damaging. They suggested that research should also focus on which clients can most benefit from spiritually and religiously oriented interventions as well as studies that examine the benefits and liabilities of different treatment modalities, such as individual, couple, group, inpatient, outpatient, brief, and family treatment services. They recommended that more emphasis be placed on treatment outcome studies, including those offered by clergy and lay religious counselors. Finally, they called for research that more closely examines religious and cultural diversity. These suggestions for future research still ring true today. Certainly, there is no lack of important research topics that need further and careful examination in this area. However, researchers must be thoughtful and strategic in order to triage their research agenda to get the most benefits from their efforts.

MAXIMIZING THE SUCCESS OF RESEARCH

Because this area of research is in its infancy, there are many important research questions that should be investigated (e.g., Does spiritually informed intervention result in better outcomes than secular approaches? Do religious rituals and practices improve psychological functioning for anxious and depressed clients?). However, it can be overwhelming and perhaps impossible to articulate them all. So much needs to be done. What appears most critical now is conducting high-quality research using the best available methodological and statistical techniques (e.g., randomized clinical trials) to determine how the religious–spiritual tools discussed in this book might be beneficial (or not) for various populations of clients. Randomized clinical trials, where possible, should be used with diverse clinical populations with assessment techniques that are multimodal and not based solely on self-report measures. As a rule, longitudinal studies that include appropriate follow-up are needed for these treatment outcome approaches, and control groups should be used wherever possible.

So, how can mental health professionals get the most for their efforts? Three principles immediately come to mind: (a) learn from successes, (b) benefit from the synergy of collaboration, and (c) secure useful resources and networks.

Learn From Successes

There are a number of important successes in this area of research from which to learn. Perhaps one of the best examples is the research on mindfulness-based stress reduction. As I discussed in several places throughout this book, mindfulness-based stress reduction is an empirically supported treatment intervention based on religious–spiritual tradition that can be successfully used in a variety of clinical arenas. State-of-the-art research using randomized clinical trials among different patient populations has been conducted and published in peer-reviewed professional outlets (e.g., see Shapiro, Schwartz, & Bonner, 1998). Conferences and conventions that highlight mindfulness have been well attended. The approach has found acceptance among not only those who have a special interest in religious–spiritual issues and interventions but also among those professionals who do not maintain these interests. Mindfulness has become an acceptable and mainstream intervention approach for a wide variety of clinical issues that is now empirically supported (e.g., see Hayes et al., 2004; Linehan, 1993; Shapiro & Walsh, 2007).

Having learned from the success of mindfulness-based stress reduction, researchers are conducting similar efforts with other religiously–spiritually based interventions. These include the Eight-Point Program (EPP) discussed in chapter 9 of this volume (see also Easwaran, 1991; Oman et al., 2008) and forgiveness training (e.g., see Rye et al., 2005; Worthington, 2004; Worthington et al., 1996). Solid research studies using randomized clinical trial methodology are being conducted to determine whether these interventions can be empirically supported among various clinical populations.

Perhaps the success of mindfulness-based stress reduction is due in part to the efforts to study the benefits of this approach using (a) the best available research methodology in prestigious university and medical center settings with well-established and highly respected researchers and (b) a more secular version of the technique that is palatable for those who come from a wide variety of faith traditions, including no faith tradition at all (e.g., see Kabat-Zinn, 2003). It is difficult to ignore results from high-quality, state-of-the-art studies published in top research outlets by leading researchers, especially when those studies used a technique that is generally agreeable to multiple diverse populations, including those who have little interest in religious–spiritual tools in psychological treatment.

Benefit From the Synergy of Collaboration

Although there may be many people interested in religiously–spiritually informed psychological treatment, a fairly limited number of researchers are conducting empirical research in this area. Although this group appears to be growing, most of the research studies published in this area are being conducted by the same group of a few dozen professionals (many of these researchers are mentioned by name in the Acknowledgements section of this volume). The fairly small number of researchers in this area is not surprising given the historical conflicts between psychology and religion. As this research continues to gain acceptance among mainstream psychologists and other health care and research professionals, more graduate students and young professionals may feel comfortable pursuing this area of research. The professional organizations have already recognized this issue and have begun to provide mentorship and networking opportunities.

Professional organizations listed in the Additional Resources section of this volume, such as the Spirituality and Health Special Interest Group (SIG) of the Society of Behavioral Medicine (SBM) and the American Psychological Association's (APA's) Division 36 (Psychology of Religion), are excellent examples of those that allow professionals and students alike to network and learn from one another. In fact, the Spirituality and Health SIG of SBM is the largest and fastest growing SIG in the organization. Furthermore, collaborative research efforts have many advantages, bringing different resources and expertise together to potentially allow for higher quality and more thoughtful research studies. For example, the Spirituality and Health Institute at Santa Clara University includes junior and senior colleagues from a variety of academic disciplines and from several San Francisco Bay Area universities (i.e., Santa Clara University, Stanford University, the University of California at Berkeley, and the Graduate Theological Union) who bring different skills and interests to collaborative research projects, allowing for more thoughtful and well-conducted studies. Other universities and research institutions can certainly do the same, even with limited financial resources.

In collaborative research, often the whole can be greater than the sum of the parts.

Secure Useful Resources and Networks

Securing critical financial resources and developing collaborative networks are vitally important in conducting quality research in this area. For example, rarely do good research ideas get turned into actual research studies without significant financial support. This is especially true when investigating treatment outcome studies with actual clinical populations. Sometimes research that involves religious–spiritual practice has difficulty securing funding sources, such as federal grants for psychologists and other health care professionals. However, foundation grants from a variety of sources may help. For example, several private foundations, such as the John Templeton Foundation and the Fetzer Institute, have generously offered to fund research and training in this area over a number of years.

In addition to resources, researchers should develop networks that include collaborative research teams, clergy, and various religious–spiritual communities, which may be cultivated to obtain access to appropriate clinical, spiritual, religious, and other populations. As I discussed in chapter 8, clergy may be an underused resource in the research endeavor. They have access to large populations of congregants and facilities, such as temples, churches, and social halls, where research might be conducted. They also have access to lay ministers and others who may provide appropriate interventions to various populations. Ongoing collaboration with clergy should be encouraged not only for the clinical care of clients but also for research possibilities and opportunities.

TRAINING THE NEXT GENERATION OF SCHOLARS AND CLINICIANS

We cannot advance research in the relationship between psychology and religion–spirituality without attending to the educational needs of graduate and postgraduate students. As I discussed in chapter 1 of this volume, although APA's various policy documents have clearly indicated that religion and spirituality are important multicultural aspects that should be considered in psychology training and practice (e.g., see APA, 2002, 2003), very few graduate and postgraduate educational training programs offer any training in religious–spiritual diversity. How can mental health professionals expect to make progress in research if students are inadequately trained? Shafranske and Malony (1996) proposed a thoughtful agenda for a graduate curriculum in psychology and religion that is still relevant today. It has four key areas: (a) values in psychological treatment, (b) the psychology of religion, (c) comparative religion, and (d) working with religious issues.

Values in Psychological Treatment

It is important that graduate and postgraduate training in psychology include training on values in general and religious–spiritual values in particular. Certainly, training in ethics should include some emphasis on the role of values in decision making and especially in psychotherapy approaches. It also should include "an investigation of the role of personal values of the clinician as they are expressed in clinical thinking and practice" (Shafranske & Malony, 1996, p. 578).

The Psychology of Religion

A great deal of literature is now available on the psychology of religion, with numerous solid empirical studies available for review. Sadly, some professionals assume that the work of William James, Sigmund Freud, and Carl Jung are the only sources available in this area and have neglected the wide and fairly comprehensive contemporary empirical research in the psychology of religion. This research includes how humans use religious–spiritual beliefs and practices to cope with stressful life events, the relationship between religious–spiritual approaches and both physical and mental health benefits, and a wide variety of topics on which psychology's forefathers had no empirical research support to comment. Thus, the psychology of religion literature should be reviewed and evaluated in graduate and postgraduate studies with a focus on application to clinical concerns. Although certainly writers such as Freud and Jung offer much in this area, it is critical to also be aware of the numerous contemporary empirical research studies that have been conducted and published that can inform our understanding and clinical practice.

Comparative Religion

It is clear that as our community and country become more and more ethnically diverse that religious diversity will only increase as well. Religious diversity is found not only between religious traditions but within them. Clinicians must develop some understanding of various religious–spiritual traditions and the great diversity that can be found among and between them. Graduate programs might enlist the resources available in university departments of religious studies to secure education in comparative religion, which would enhance their psychology graduate training program offerings.

Working With Religious Issues

Clinical training is necessary concerning (a) assessing and treating clients from various religious–spiritual traditions and (b) integrating religious–spiritual interventions into psychological services. As I mentioned throughout this book, the traditions may offer tools that are currently underused by most mental health professionals. As more research that demonstrates empirically supported religious–spiritual integration approaches to treatment (e.g., mindfulness) becomes available, clinicians will need to consider using them or referring clients to others who may provide such services. Of course, if research conclusively fails to support their use, these tools should no longer be used with clients.

In addition to the recommendations of Shafranske and Malony (1996), others have also offered specific guidance for training (e.g., see Brawer, Handal, Fabricatore, Roberts, & Wajda-Johnston, 2002; Richards & Bergin, 2005; Young, Cashwell, Wiggins-Frame, & Belaire, 2002). The possibilities mentioned include mentoring programs that use faculty and other educators who have specialties in the interface of psychology and religion and the integration of these topics into courses already offered, such as ethics and multicultural psychology, and who know what resources, such as conferences, books, and articles, are most beneficial for interested students.

Educating graduate and postgraduate students in psychology and religion as well as helping them better understand and be sensitive to how religious–spiritual issues impact their clients would go a long way to improve not only clinical training but also professional services to clients and future research projects. A cohort of well-trained and thoughtful professionals are required to conduct the state-of-the-art clinical work and the research of the future necessary to move religion–spirituality as it relates to psychology forward and to provide clinical services that are informed by and based on the highest quality research findings. Overall, much must be done to provide adequate training to graduate and postgraduate students to prepare them not only for clinical work but also for training the next generation of scholars to conduct the research that is sorely needed.

FUTURE DIRECTIONS

So where should one go from here? I recommend reading some of the books listed in the Additional Resources section. The suggested books cover a wide range of topics for consideration.

In addition to reading, I recommend attending professional conferences, seminars, workshops, and other professional events that highlight spiritually integrated psychotherapy. One may wish to consider contacting some of the organizations listed in the Additional Resources section for information about events and activities. Many of the organizations offer free or low-cost memberships, newsletters, electronic mailing lists, and other ways to keep informed of events that might be useful both now and in the future. Many of the organizations also host yearly conventions and conferences that provide a wonderful opportunity to learn more about religiously–spiritually integrated psychotherapy and related topics with others who are interested in the topic.

I also recommend finding local professionals who have similar interests in religiously–spiritually integrated and informed psychological services. One may wish to consider obtaining supervision or becoming part of a local ongoing case consultation group with other mental health professionals who share similar interests. One may also wish to contact organizations listed in the Additional Resources section to inquire about additional networking opportunities.

Finally, I recommend using the tools I discussed in this book in an ethical, respectful, responsible, and professional manner so they may benefit both clients and mental health professionals alike.

ADDITIONAL RESOURCES

A number of resources might be helpful to mental health professionals interested in learning more about spirituality and psychotherapy integration. Many professional organizations, Web sites, books, journal articles, and so forth are available and easy to access. Because much of this information changes quickly and new resources appear on a regular basis, one might keep in contact with colleagues and professional organizations to get the latest information about professional resources in this area. As of this writing, the following resources are especially helpful.

MAJOR AND LARGE PROFESSIONAL ORGANIZATIONS

American Psychological Association's Division 36 (Psychology of Religion)

American Psychological Association
750 First Street, NE
Washington, DC 20002-4242
Phone: 800-374-2721, 202-336-5500; TDD/TTY: 202-336-6123
http://www.apa.org/divisions/div36

Several high-quality professional organizations are likely to be of interest to those who would like additional information or perhaps might be interested in joining others who share an interest in the integration of spirituality, religion, and psychotherapy. Psychologists in particular may be interested in the American Psychological Association's (APA's) Division 36 (Psychology of Religion). In addition to regular newsletters and access to the membership electronic mailing list, the division hosts and sponsors various meetings, symposium, paper presentations, workshops, and conferences at the annual APA convention and elsewhere and can act as a resource for those with a special interest in this area. The division mission statement states that it

> promotes the application of psychological research methods and interpretive frameworks to diverse forms of religion and spirituality; encourages the incorporation of the results of such work into clinical and other applied settings; and fosters constructive dialogue and interchange between psychological study and practice, on the one hand, and religious perspectives and institutions on the other. (Division 36 of the American Psychological Association, 2008, ¶ 1)

For psychologists, Division 36 is probably the best starting place to get useful information and consultation.

Spirituality and Health Special Interest Group, Society of Behavioral Medicine

Society of Behavioral Medicine
555 East Wells Street, Suite 1100
Milwaukee, WI 53202-3823
Phone: 414-918-3156
Fax: 414-276-3349
http://www.sbm.org/sig/spirituality

The Society of Behavioral Medicine offers a special interest group that focuses on spirituality and health broadly defined. Although the group focuses mostly on the interaction between spirituality and physical health, mental health–related issues are also of interest. Those who are especially concerned with spirituality and health from a behavioral medicine or health psychology perspective and are interested in multidisciplinary approaches might find this group especially appealing.

SMALLER AND SPECIALTY PROFESSIONAL ORGANIZATIONS WITH A RESEARCH FOCUS

International Association for the Psychology of Religion

http://www.iapr.de

For additional information, contact:
Dr. Sebastian Murken
Psychology of Religion Research Group
University of Trier
Franziska-Puricelli-Str. 3
D-55543 Bad Kreuznach
GERMANY
Fax: ++49 / (0)6 71 / 7 96 71 20

The International Association for the Psychology of Religion is based in Europe and provides a forum for the exchange of scholarly information for those interested in the psychology of religion across the globe. Those professionals who are interested in multicultural and diverse points of view might find this organization appealing.

Society for the Scientific Study of Religion

Division of Social Sciences
Alfred University
1 Saxon Drive
Alfred, NY 14802
http://www.sssrweb.org

For additional information, contact:
Dr. Arthur E. Farnsley, II
Indiana University–Purdue University Indianapolis
Center for the Study of Religion and American Culture
Cavanaugh Hall 341
425 University Boulevard
Indianapolis, IN 46202-5140
afarnsle@iupui.edu

The Society for the Scientific Study of Religion publishes the *Journal for the Scientific Study of Religion* and works to stimulate and communicate important scientific research on religious institutions and experiences. Multidisciplinary professionals from a wide variety of fields who are interested in the scientific exploration of religion are involved in this organization.

Santa Clara University Spirituality and Health Institute

http://www.scu.edu/ignatiancenter/spirithealth/index.cfm

For additional information, contact:
Thomas G. Plante, PhD, ABPP
Department of Psychology
Alumni Science Hall, Room 203
Santa Clara University
500 El Camino Real
Santa Clara, CA 95053-0333
Phone: 408-554-4471
Fax: 408-554-5241

A variety of universities and other educational organizations have groups that conduct research or offer presentations on the integration of psychology and religion that are likely to be of interest to mental health professionals. For example, the Spirituality and Health Institute (SHI) at Santa Clara University is devoted to exploring the complex relationship between spirituality and health from an interdisciplinary, multicultural perspective. Faculties from several universities participate in a variety of collaborative research, teaching, and outreach projects. The intention behind SHI is to bring creative, thoughtful, and rigorous scholarly pursuit to better elucidate the relationship between spirituality and health as broadly defined.

Association for Transpersonal Psychology

P.O. Box 3049
Palo Alto, California 94303
Phone: 650-327-2066
Fax: 650-618-1851
http://www.atpweb.org

The Association for Transpersonal Psychology is a membership-based international organization for scientific, social, and clinical transpersonal work that serves the world community, stating, "Recognizing the reciprocity inherent between our actions and our world, the Association is dedicated to encouraging practices and perspectives that will lead to a conscious, sustainable, co-evolution of culture, nature, and society" (Association for Transpersonal Psychology, n.d., ¶ 1).

SMALLER AND SPECIALTY PROFESSIONAL ORGANIZATIONS WITH A CLINICAL FOCUS

Association for Spiritual, Ethical, and Religious Values in Counseling, American Counseling Association

American Counseling Association
5999 Stevenson Avenue
Alexandria, VA 22304-3300
Phone: 800-347-6647
Fax: 800-473-2329
http://aservic.org

For additional information, contact:
University of Central Florida
College of Education
Department of Child, Family and Community Sciences
P.O. Box 161250
Orlando, FL 32816
Phone: 407-823-2835
Fax: 407-823-5135
erobinso@mail.ucf.edu

The Association for Spiritual, Ethical, and Religious Values in Counseling is a special interest division of the American Counseling Association. It includes counselors and human development professionals who are interested in spiritual, ethical, and religious values that impact the development of the person and are committed to integrating these values into the counseling process. Counseling psychologists and marriage and family therapists may be especially interested in this organization.

American Association for Pastoral Counselors

9504A Lee Highway
Fairfax, VA 22031-2303
Phone: 703-385-6967
Fax: 703-352-7725
info@aapc.org
http://www.aapc.org

The American Association for Pastoral Counselors represents a broad group of theological and spiritual traditions and work among a wide variety of health care providers and settings. Although the majority of pastoral counselors come from a Christian perspective, they provide services within increasingly multicultural, interfaith, multidisciplinary, and racially diverse communities and within a more interconnected, conflicted, and technically sophisticated environment.

International Association of Pastoral Counselors

P.O. Box 140182
Dallas, TX 75214
http://www.angelfire.com/tx6/anglican

The International Association of Pastoral Counselors is an association of clergy members interested in the support and development of pastoral counseling. Its mission statement reads as follows:

> To encourage and promote excellence in the use of pastoral counseling by qualified clergy; to advance scientific research, education and standards of practice in pastoral counseling, and to advise others about the value, application and ethical use of pastoral counseling. (International Association of Pastoral Counselors, n.d., ¶ 1)

Christian Association for Psychological Studies

P.O. Box 310400

New Braunfels, TX 78131-0400
Phone: 210-629-2277
Fax: 210-629-2342
http://www.caps.net/index.html

The Christian Association for Psychological Studies (CAPS) is an organization of Christian mental health professionals that began in 1956 and that now includes more than 2,000 members in about 30 countries. CAPS supports the consideration of therapeutic, research, theoretical and theological issues.

American Association of Christian Counselors

AACC Member Services
P.O. Box 739
Forest, VA 24551
Phone: 800-526-8673
Fax: 434-525-9480
http://aacc.net

American Association of Christian Counselors is a professional association of Christian counselors and other licensed professionals, pastors, and church members interested in integrating religious–spiritual concepts from a Christian perspective with pastoral counseling by both professionals and laypersons.

ORGANIZATIONS THAT FOCUS ON SPIRITUALITY AND AGING

The Center for Aging and Spirituality

Luther Seminary
2481 Como Avenue
St. Paul, MN 55108
Phone: 612-641-3581
Fax: 612-641-3425
http://www.spirituality4aging.org/about.htm

The Center for Aging and Spirituality was begun in 1987 by a group of Lutheran clergy. It currently includes a multifaith community interested in the relationship between aging and spirituality.

Forum on Religion, Spirituality and Aging, American Society on Aging

American Society on Aging

833 Market Street, Suite 511
San Francisco, CA 94103-1824
Phone: 415-974-9600
Fax: 415-974-0300
http://www.asaging.org/networks/index.cfm?cg=FORSA

The Forum on Religion, Spirituality and Aging (FORSA) is a national, multidisciplinary, and nondenominational community of professionals interested in

> examining and fostering the spiritual dimension of human existence as a central element in the aging process and to fostering an appreciation for the importance of incorporating an awareness of this dimension into all the disciplines that make up the fascinating world of gerontology. (American Society on Aging, 2008, ¶ 3)

FORSA is a subgroup of the American Society on Aging, reported to be the largest professional membership association in the field of aging. The FORSA mission statement further reports that, "Some members come at the topic from traditional faith perspectives and are active in various churches, synagogues and mosques, while others approach the issues from the perspective of 'mindful' or 'conscious' aging" (American Society on Aging, 2008, ¶ 4).

WEB SITES

Each of the professional organizations previously listed have Web sites that not only present detailed information about the organizations but also provide additional links to information, services, and activities that professionals may find useful. In addition to the Web sites provided earlier, the following Web site is worth exploring.

Psychology of Religion

http://www.psywww.com/psyrelig

Professor Michael Nielsen from the Georgia Southern University maintains this very helpful Web site offering a great deal of information and links that explore a wide variety of issues pertaining to the psychology of religion.

VIDEOS AND DVDS

With the help of leading clinicians and researchers, APA offers a series of helpful videos and DVDs on spirituality. Topics include Christian counseling, addressing spiritual and religious issues in psychotherapy, mindful therapy, mindful therapy with addictions, and spiritual awareness psychotherapy. See http://www.apa.org/videos/series6.html for details.

BOOKS

Those who are interested in the integration of psychology and spirituality might find a number of books useful to themselves or their clients. I provide a list of them here and offer brief comments for each one. They are divided into several general categories, including general reading, physical health, meditation, and specific religious–spiritual practices.

General Reading

Batson, C. D., Schoenrade, P., & Ventis, W. (1993). *Religion and the individual: A social-psychological perspective*. New York: Oxford University.
An excellent overview of the field using Gordon Allport's theory as a foundation.

Beit-Hallahmi, B. (1996). *Psychoanalytic studies of religion: Critical assessment and annotated bibliography*. Westport, CT: Greenwood.
Likely to be of interest to those especially interested in religion and psychology from a psychodynamic and scholarly point of view.

Beit-Hallahmi, B., & Argyle, M. (1997). *The psychology of religious behavior, belief and experience*. London: Routledge.
Focuses on why people maintain religious beliefs and how these beliefs impact various aspects of their lives.

Browning, D. S. (1987). *Religious thought and the modern psychologies*. New York: Fortress Press.
Discusses the ethical, religious, and metaphysical assumptions that underlie modern psychological theory.

Browning, D. S., Jobe, T., & Evison, I. S. (1990). *Religious and ethical factors in psychiatric practice*. New York: Nelson-Hall.
For those interested in both religious and ethical issues in psychiatric clinical practice.

Fuller, R. C. (2001). *Spiritual but not religious*. New York: Oxford University Press.
Might be especially helpful for those who are not interested in the major religious traditions but are open to increasing spirituality in their lives.

Griffith, J. L., & Griffith, M. E. (2001). *Encountering the sacred in psychotherapy: How to talk with people about their spiritual lives*. New York: Guilford Press.
A good introduction to integrating spirituality into psychotherapy.

Hartz, G. W. (2005). *Spirituality and mental health: Clinical applications*. Binghamton, NY: Haworth Pastoral Press.

An easy-to-read, brief book about the relationship between spirituality and mental health services. It is primarily for mental health professionals and includes a description of a group treatment model used at the Palo Alto Veterans Administration Hospital, where the author is employed.

Hood, R. W. (Ed.). (1995). *Handbook of religious experience*. Birmingham, AL: Religious Education.

Offers helpful insights into religious experiences among various faith traditions as well as useful overviews of several psychological perspectives on religious experiences.

Hood, R. W., Jr., Spilka, B., Hunsberger, B., & Gorsuch, R. (1996). *The psychology of religion: An empirical approach*. New York: Guilford Press.

One of the best research-based texts on psychological research on religion.

James, W. (1902). *The varieties of religious experience*. Cambridge, MA: Harvard University Press.

A classic text that is frequently referenced in the psychology and religion field. It is likely to be of more interest to professionals than to most clients.

Jung, C. G. (1938). *Psychology and religion*. New Haven, CT: Yale University Press.

Also a classic text that is frequently referenced in the psychology and religion field. Like James (1902), it is likely to be more of interest to professionals than to most clients.

McLennan, S. (2001). *Finding your religion: When the faith you grew up with has lost its meaning*. San Francisco: HarperSanFrancisco.

An engaging book that speaks to many who have been dissatisfied with the religious tradition of their youth yet still seek religious–spiritual involvement.

McMinn, M. R., & Dominquez, A. W. (Eds.). (2005) *Psychology and the church*. Hauppauge, NY: Nova Science.

Focuses on the consultation relationship between church organizations and professional psychology, and includes essays that describe professionals' experiences in consulting with a wide range of religious groups.

Miller, W. R. (Ed.). (1999). *Integrating spirituality into treatment: Resources for practitioners*. Washington, DC: American Psychological Association.

A helpful book for clinicians interested in spirituality and psychotherapy integration.

Myers, D. (2000). *The American paradox: Spiritual hunger in a land of plenty*. New Haven, CT: Yale University Press.

A classic text that helps professionals and lay readers better understand the problems with materialism in America and the yearning for spirituality.

Paloutzian, R. F. (1996). *Invitation to psychology of religion*. Boston: Allyn & Bacon.

An excellent introductory book that highlights the research and practice associated with the psychology of religion.

Pargament, K. I. (1997). *The psychology of religious coping: Theory, research, practice*. New York: Guilford Press.

Primarily for professional academics or clinicians who are interested in the research underpinnings of religious coping.

Pargament, K. I. (2007). *Spiritually integrated psychotherapy: Understanding and addressing the sacred*. New York: Guilford Press.

An excellent book by a leader in the field that articulates how to understand the sacred as broadly defined and how to address issues pertaining to the sacred in psychotherapy.

Pargament, K. I., Maton, K. I., & Hess, R. E. (1992). *Religion and prevention in mental health: Research, vision, and action*. New York: Haworth Pastoral Press.

A helpful and now classic book that clearly outlines the research and practice of spirituality and psychotherapy integration.

Richards, P. S., & Bergin, A. E. (Eds.). (2000). *Handbook of psychotherapy and religious diversity*. Washington, DC: American Psychological Association.

Highlights the role of religion in psychotherapy, with chapters describing how individuals from various religious traditions tend to respond to issues such as abortion and euthanasia, and the role of guilt and shame in their faith tradition.

Richards, P. S., & Bergin, A. E. (Eds.). (2004). *Casebook for a spiritual strategy in counseling and psychotherapy*. Washington, DC: American Psychological Association.

A follow-up to their classic 1997 text that provides plenty of clinical examples of spirituality and psychotherapy integration.

Richards, P. S., & Bergin, A. E. (2005). *A spiritual strategy for counseling and psychotherapy* (2nd ed.). Washington, DC: American Psychological Association.

Another classic that provides professional clinicians with a well-researched basis for integrating spirituality and psychotherapy.

Schumaker, J. (Ed.). (1992). *Religion and mental health*. Oxford, England: Oxford University Press.

A scholarly text that highlights religion and mental health.

Shafranske, E. (Ed.) (1996). *Religion and the clinical practice of psychology*. Washington DC: American Psychological Association.

A very useful and classic text that demonstrates the intersection of religion and clinical practice.

Smith, H. (1991). *The world's religions: Our great wisdom traditions*. San Francisco: Harper SanFrancisco.

This classic book is an excellent resource for clients as well as mental health professionals to get a basic understanding of the major religious traditions of the world.

Sperry, L., & Shafranske, E. P. (Eds.). (2005). *Spiritually oriented psychotherapy*. Washington, DC: American Psychological Association.

An edited volume that offers a number of research-based essays on integrating spirituality into psychotherapy.

Spilka, B., & McIntosh, D. N. (Eds.). (1996). *The psychology of religion: Theoretical approaches*. Boulder, CO: Westview.

Highlights many theoretical perspectives influencing current research-focused psychological thought about religion.

Stern, E. M. (Ed.). (1985). *Psychotherapy and the religiously committed patient*. New York: Haworth Pastoral Press.

A collection of essays that focus on psychotherapy with religious people to help therapists use religious beliefs to increase mental health functioning.

Sullivan, J. P. (1998). *On holy ground: The impact of psychotherapists' spirituality on their practice*. New York: University Press of America.

Five respected therapists describe how they use spirituality concepts in their clinical practices.

Walsh, F. (1999). *Spiritual resources in family therapy*. New York: Guilford Press.

Especially helpful for mental health professionals who conduct or are interested in systems and family therapy techniques and models.

Walsh, R. (1999). *Essential spirituality: The seven central practices*. New York: Wiley.

Helps clients (and professionals) learn how to better integrate spirituality into their daily lives.

Wulff, D. M. (1997). *Psychology of religion: Classic and contemporary* (2nd ed.). New York: Wiley.

A popular classic text that gives an excellent overview of psychology and religion.

Physical Health

Dossey, L. (1993). *Healing words: The power of prayer and the practice of medicine*. San Francisco: HarperColllins.

A useful and popular book on the relationship between religion and health that is likely to be of interest to clients as well as therapists.

Koenig, H. G. (1997). *Is religion good for your health? The effects of religion on physical and mental health*. Binghamton, NY: Haworth Pastoral Press.

A brief and easy-to-read book that is ideal for clients who might be interested in the relationship between spirituality and both physical and mental health benefits. It reviews the research evidence in an understandable manner for a lay as well as professional audience.

Koenig, H. G., & Cohen, H. J. (2001). *The link between religion and health: Psychoneuroimmunology and the faith factor*. New York: Oxford University Press.

Examines the notion that religious and spiritual engagement and beliefs affect the immune system in ways that have a variety of health benefits.

Koenig, H. G., McCullough, M. E., & Larson, D. B. (2001). *Handbook of religion and health*. New York: Oxford University Press.

A classic text that discusses the extensive research evidence on religion and health. Ideal for researchers as well as clinicians.

Plante, T. G., & Sherman, A. S. (Eds.). (2001). *Faith and health: Psychological perspectives*. New York: Guilford Press.

Most likely to be of interest to professional researchers as well as clinicians who are interested in the research underpinnings of the relationship between faith and health.

Plante, T. G., & Thoresen, C. E. (Eds.) (2007). *Spirit, science, and health: How the spiritual mind fuels physical wellness*. Westport, CT: Praeger/Greenwood.

 With multidisciplinary essays on various aspects of spirituality and health, this collection would be of interest to clinicians as well as researchers.

Meditation

Easwaran, E. (1991). *Meditation: A simple eight-point program for translating spiritual ideals into daily life*. Tomales, CA: Nilgiri Press. (Original work published 1978)

 Describes the Eight-Point Program that I discussed in chapter 9 of this volume. It is a simple and nondenominational program that has received research and clinical support.

Germer, C. K., Siegel, R. D., & Fulton, P. R. (Eds.). (2005). *Mindfulness and psychotherapy*. New York: Guilford Press.

 Summarizes the integration of mindfulness-based theory and practice into psychotherapy.

Kabat-Zinn, J. (1990). *Full catastrophe living*. New York: Delacourte Press.

 A classic that focuses on mindfulness meditation practices for living, written by a psychologist at the University of Massachusetts Medical Center who is well known for integrating mindfulness meditative practices into health services.

Segal, Z., Williams, M., & Teasdale, J. (2002). *Mindfulness-based cognitive therapy for depression: A new approach to preventing relapse*. New York: Guilford Press.

 Geared for a professional mental health audience, highlighting how to integrate mindfulness-based cognitive–behavioral therapy approaches into treating depression.

Williams, M., Teasdale, J., Segal, Z., & Kabat-Zinn, J. (2007). *The mindful way through depression: Freeing yourself from chronic unhappiness*. New York: Guilford Press.

 A self-help book that uses mindfulness-based cognitive–behavioral interventions to better cope with depressive symptoms. Includes a CD of guided meditations by Jon Kabat-Zinn.

Specific Religious–Spiritual Practices

De Silva, P. (2000). *An introduction to Buddhist psychology* (3rd ed.). New York: Rowman & Littlefield.

 Highlights the Buddhist contribution to modern psychology and integrates Western and Eastern approaches.

Heschel, A. J. (1986). *The wisdom of Heschel*. New York: Farrar, Straus, & Giroux.

 Provides helpful wisdom and reflections from a well-known and respected Jewish theologian and rabbi.

Levine, M. (2000). *The positive psychology of Buddhism and yoga: Paths to a mature happiness*. Mahwah, NJ: Erlbaum.

 Focuses on Buddhism and yoga as they relate to psychology in the Western world and discusses applications to daily life.

Special Topics

Koenig, H. G. (1994). *Aging and God: Spiritual pathways to mental health in midlife and later years*. New York: Haworth Pastoral Press.

   Centers on spirituality in later life and would be of interest to both middle-aged and older clients.

Plante, T. G. (2004). *Do the right thing: Living ethically in an unethical world*. Oakland, CA: New Harbinger.

   Written for laypeople to help readers find easy-to-use principles for living more ethically.

Worthington, E. L., Jr. (1999). *Dimensions of forgiveness: Psychological research and theological perspectives*. New York: Templeton Foundation Press.

   This book focuses on the integration of science and religion as it relates to forgiveness.

Some Additional Books on Religion–Spirituality for the General Reader

   The books that follow have been particularly helpful to me in better understanding contemporary scholarship on religious–spiritual perspectives. They are not written for the mental health and health care professional, as are most of the books previously listed. Many of these books focus on Christian or Jewish themes and traditions. The list is not meant to be exhaustive; it merely reflects texts I have found to be personally helpful in my reading about religion–spirituality in general.

Armstrong, K. (1993). *A history of God: The 4,000 year quest of Judaism, Christianity, and Islam*. New York: Gramercy.

   An excellent and scholarly approach to better understanding the historical, political, and spiritual roots of these three major religious traditions.

Armstrong, K. (2000). *The battle for God: Fundamentalism in Judaism, Christianity, and Islam*. New York: HarperCollins.

   An excellent scholarly book that helps the reader to better understand the historical, political, and religious roots of fundamentalism and traces the role of fundamentalism over time.

Armstrong, K. (2006). *The great transformation: The beginning of our religious traditions*. New York: Anchor Books.

   A first-rate academic approach to better understanding the Axial period of approximately 7,000 BC to 200 BC, which laid the foundations for the current main religious traditions in both the East and West. It emphasizes many of the historical, political, religious, cultural, and geographical factors from the areas now known as China, India, Greece, and the Middle East regions that shaped our religious beliefs and traditions.

Beaudoin, T. (2003). *Consuming faith: Integrating who we are with what we buy*. New York: Sheed & Ward.

An applied theology book that discuss how one's religious beliefs should impact the nature of one's spending habits—helpful for clients interested in applying their faith to their role as consumers.

Beck, C. J. (1993). *Nothing special: Living Zen*. San Francisco: HarperCollins.
A helpful introduction to Zen, with many applications to daily life.

Bokenkotter, T. (1986). *Essential Catholicism: Dynamics of faith and belief*. New York: Image.
An excellent overview of Catholic views, beliefs, and ways of understanding the world and religion.

Borg, M. J. (1989). *The heart of Christianity: Rediscovering a life of faith*. San Francisco: HarperCollins.
An excellent contemporary view of Christianity, with applications for everyday living.

Borg, M. J. (1995). *Meeting Jesus again for the first time: The historical Jesus and the heart of contemporary faith*. San Francisco: HarperCollins.
Articulates what we know (and do not know) about the historical Jesus and the implications this knowledge has for contemporary faith.

Brackley, D. (2004). *The call to discernment in troubled times: New perspectives on the transformative wisdom of Ignatius of Loyola*. New York: Crossroads.
Examines the discernment process of St. Ignatius and applies it to contemporary decision making to help readers achieve better direction for vocational and other life decisions.

Brown, R. E. (1994). *An introduction to New Testament Christology*. New York: Paulist Press.
A scholarly book written for a general audience about what the Bible and other sources say about who Christ is and is not.

Cahill, T. (1996). *How the Irish saved civilization*. New York: Anchor Books.
Explains how the Irish helped to preserve the writings that became the religious and civil foundation during challenging times in Europe.

Cahill, T. (1998). *The gift of the Jews: How a tribe of desert nomads changed the way everyone thinks and feels*. New York: Doubleday.
Shows how the Jewish tradition has influenced current thinking and ways of life.

Cahill, T. (1999). *Desire of the everlasting hills: The world before and after Jesus*. New York: Anchor Books.
This excellent book discusses the history and various forces before and after the time of Jesus to put his words and actions into a political, historical, geopolitical, and religious context.

Carroll, J. (2001). *Constantine's sword: The church and the Jews*. Boston: Houghton Mifflin.
An excellent scholarly book that outlines the relationship between the Christian church and the Jews over centuries and focuses on the influence of Constantine, who made Christianity the official religion of the Roman Empire.

Dreher, D. E. (1990). *The Tao of inner peace*. New York: HarperCollins.
Provides a spiritually focused method to increase inner peace.

Dresner, S. H. (Ed.) (2000). *I asked for wonder: A spiritual anthology of Abraham Joshua Heschel.* New York: Crossroads.

A brief book that reflects the spiritual wisdom of this well-known and respected rabbi.

Ehrman, B. D. (2005). *Misquoting Jesus: The story behind who changed the Bible and why.* San Francisco: HarperCollins.

Documents how the Bible (especially the New Testament) was altered over time by scribes and others in purposeful and accidental ways.

Ellens, J. H. (2004). *The destructive power of religion: Violence in Judaism, Christianity, and Islam: Volume 1. Sacred scriptures, ideology, and violence.* Westport, CT: Praeger Publishers.

Ellens, J. H. (2004). *The destructive power of religion: Violence in Judaism, Christianity, and Islam: Volume 2. Religion, psychology, and violence.* Westport, CT: Praeger Publishers.

Ellens, J. H. (2004). *The destructive power of religion: Violence in Judaism, Christianity, and Islam: Volume 3. Models and cases of violence.* Westport, CT: Praeger Publishers.

Ellens, J. H. (2004). *The destructive power of religion: Violence in Judaism, Christianity, and Islam: Volume 4. Contemporary views on spirituality and violence.* Westport, CT: Praeger Publishers.

A four-volume scholarly edited book series that highlights the relationship between religion and violence over the centuries within various religious traditions.

Friedman, R. E. (1987). *Who wrote the Bible?* New York: Harper and Row.

Discusses the evidence available on who actually wrote the Bible and how understanding who wrote the various parts of the Bible can help one put the document in better historical and religious context.

Gelpi, D. L. (2001). *The firstborn of many: A Christology for converting Christians. Volume I: To hope in Jesus Christ.* Milwaukee, WI: Marquette University Press.

Gelpi, D. L. (2001). *The firstborn of many: A Christology for converting Christians. Volume II: Synoptic narrative Christology.* Milwaukee, WI: Marquette University Press.

A two-volume scholarly book series that provides the historical, philosophical, and theological evidence for understanding Christology (i.e., theological perspectives on Christ).

Harpur, T. (2004). *The pagan Christ: Is blind faith killing Christianity?* New York: Walker.

Discusses the Christ story in the context of other religions, most notably the ancient Egyptian traditions, and highlights the more universal Christ story that can be found in other traditions and times.

Hellwig, M. K. (2002). *Understanding Catholicism* (2nd ed.). New York: Paulist Press.

An easy-to-read, comprehensible description of Catholic beliefs, dogma, and thinking.

Krakauer, J. (2003). *Under the banner of heaven: A study of violent faith.* New York: Anchor Books.

Discusses the history of Mormonism and the story of violence within the tradition.

Layard, R. (2005). *Happiness: Lessons from a new science*. New York: Penguin.
Examines contemporary scholarship on happiness with sections on the relationship between religious–spiritual involvement and happiness.

Mottola, A. (Trans.) (1964). *The spiritual exercises of St. Ignatius: St. Ignatius' profound precepts of mystical theology*. New York: Doubleday.
An English translation of the spiritual exercises of St. Ignatius, which are a useful method for working on spiritual development and discernment.

Nolan, A. (2000). *Jesus before Christianity*. New York: Orbis Books.
A useful and readable book that examines the historical Jesus.

Pagels, E. (1995). *The origin of Satan*. New York: Vintage.
A scholarly yet readable book that explores historical and religious views of Satan and hell.

Pagels, E. (2005). *Beyond belief: The secret gospel of Thomas*. New York: Random House.
A scholarly yet readable book that examines the influence of one of the Gnostic gospels, Thomas, and discusses its implications for on Christianity.

Pelikan, J. (1985). *Jesus through the centuries: His place in the history of culture*. New Haven: Yale University Press.
Provides a helpful understanding of views about Jesus during the past 2,000 years.

Robinson, G. (2000). *Essential Judaism: A complete guide to beliefs, customs, and rituals*. New York: Pocket Books.
Provides a solid, basic understanding of Judaism.

Rolheiser, R. (1999). *The holy longings: The search for a Christian spirituality*. New York: Doubleday.
Examines models of Christian spirituality and how to apply them to life.

Schneiders, S. M. (1999). *The revelatory text: Interpreting the New Testament as sacred scripture*. Collegeville, MN: Liturgical Press.
A scholarly book that examines the New Testament in the context of its historical and cultural origins.

Smith, H. (1991). *The world's religions: Our great wisdom traditions*. San Francisco: HarperCollins.
Provides a solid foundation in the major religious traditions of the world.

Spong, J. S. (2001). *Why Christianity must change or die: A bishop speaks to believers in exile*. San Francisco: HarperCollins.
Discusses how Christianity must adapt to modern understanding and science in a way that can be more spiritual and rewarding.

Spong, J. S. (2002). *A new Christianity for a new world: Why traditional faith is dying and how a new faith is being born*. San Francisco: HarperCollins.
Explores the need for a more contemporary Christianity that grows from its past, focusing more on spirituality than dogma.

Spong, J. S. (2005). *The sins of scripture: Exposing the Bible's text of hate to reveal the God of love*. San Francisco: HarperCollins.

Examines scripture that comments on homosexuality, the role of women, anti-Semitism, and other controversial religious issues and discusses them in context.

Willis, G. (2002). *Why I am a Catholic*. New York: Houghton Mifflin.
Discusses the positive aspects of the Catholic tradition at its best.

Willis, G. (2006). *What Jesus meant*. New York: Penguin.
A brief, readable book that discusses what Jesus likely meant, without the layers of historical, political, and other influences over the years.

Wilson, A. N. (1992). *Jesus: A life*. New York: Fawcett Columbine.
An easy-to-read review of the historical Jesus.

Wright, N. T. (1996). *Jesus and the victory of God: Christian origins and the question of God*. Minneapolis, MN: Fortress Press.
Focuses on the research on the historical Jesus and what the Jesus story may reveal about God.

JOURNAL ARTICLES

There are thousands of superb professional journal articles written on topics related to spirituality and psychotherapy, as broadly defined. The Koenig et al. (2001) text listed previously does an excellent job of reviewing this research. It would not be helpful to list the references here; however, there are several key professional journals that focus on the integration of psychology and religion that the reader may wish to examine online or at a local university library. The journals are as follows:

Journal of Psychology and Christianity
Journal of Psychology & Theology
Journal for the Scientific Study of Religion
The International Journal for the Psychology of Religion
Mental Health, Religion & Culture
Pastoral Psychology

Note that many articles on integrating psychology and religion are published in professional journals that do not focus on that subject. Therefore, the interested reader may wish to search for them by using particular key works in online databases such as PubMed, PsycInfo, PsycArticles, and even Google Scholar. Some examples of relevant key words are *religion*, *spirituality*, *mental health*, *health*, *treatment outcome*, and *meditation*.

APPENDIX: ASSESSMENT

For your use, this appendix provides several of the scales discussed in this chapter. When available, information about norms and references for more information are provided.

Brief Multidimensional Measure of Religiousness/Spirituality[1]

Daily Spiritual Experiences

The following questions deal with possible spiritual experiences. To what extent can you say you experience the following:

1. I feel God's presence.
   1 = *many times a day* 2 = *every day* 3 = *most days*
   4 = *some days* 5 = *once in a while* 6 = *never or almost never*

2. I find strength and comfort in my religion.
   1 = *many times a day* 2 = *every day* 3 = *most days*
   4 = *some days* 5 = *once in a while* 6 = *never or almost never*

3. I feel deep inner peace or harmony.
   1 = *many times a day* 2 = *every day* 3 = *most days*
   4 = *some days* 5 = *once in a while* 6 = *never or almost never*

4. I desire to be closer to or in union with God.
   1 = *many times a day* 2 = *every day* 3 = *most days*
   4 = *some days* 5 = *once in a while* 6 = *never or almost never*

5. I feel God's love for me, directly or through others.
   1 = *many times a day* 2 = *every day* 3 = *most days*
   4 = *some days* 5 = *once in a while* 6 = *never or almost never*

6. I am spiritually touched by the beauty of creation.
   1 = *many times a day* 2 = *every day* 3 = *most days*
   4 = *some days* 5 = *once in a while* 6 = *never or almost never*

---

[1]From *Multidimensional Measurement of Religiousness/Spirituality for Use in Health Research: A Report of the Fetzer Institute/National Institute on Aging Working Group* (pp. 85–88), by Fetzer Institute/National Institute of Aging Working Group, 1999, Kalamazoo, MI: John E. Fetzer Institute. No reprint permission necessary.

Meaning

See note at the end of this section.

Values/Beliefs

7. I believe in a God who watches over me.
   1 = *strongly agree*   2 = *agree* 3 = *disagree* 4 = *strongly disagree*
8. I feel a deep sense of responsibility for reducing pain and suffering in the world.
   1 = *strongly agree*   2 = *agree* 3 = *disagree* 4 = *strongly disagree*

Forgiveness

Because of my religious or spiritual beliefs,

9. I have forgiven myself for things that I have done wrong.
   1 = *always or*   2 = *often*   3 = *seldom*   4 = *never*
      almost always
10. How often do you watch or listen to religious programs on TV or radio?
    1 = *more than once a day* 2 = *once a day*   3 = *a few times a week*

    4 = *once a week*   5 = *a few times* 6 = *once a month*
                                        a month
    7 = *less than once a month*   8 = *never*
11. I have forgiven those who hurt me.
    1 = *always or*   2 = *often* 3 = *seldom*   4 = *never*
       almost always
12. I know that God forgives me.
    1 = *always or*   2 = *often*   3 = *seldom*   4 = *never*
       almost always

Private Religious Practices

13. How often do you pray privately in places other than at church or synagogue?
    1 = *more than*   2 = *once a day*   3 = *a few times a week*
       once a day
    4 = *once a week*   5 = *a few* times 6 = *once a month*
                              times a month
    7 = *less than once a month*   8 = *never*
14. Within your religious or spiritual tradition, how often do you meditate?
    1 = *more than*   2 = *once a day*   3 = *a few times a week*
       once a day

4 = *once a week*   5 = *a few times*   6 = *once a month*
                              a month

7 = *less than once a month*   8 = *never*

15. How often do you read the Bible or other religious literature?
   1 = *more than*   2 = *once a day*   3 = *a few times a week*
       once a day

   4 = *once a week*   5 = *a few times*   6 = *once a month*
                                a month

   7 = *less than once a month*   8 = *never*

16. How often are prayers or grace said before or after meals in your home?
   1 = *at all meals*   2 = *once a day*   3 = *at least once a week*
   4 = *only on special occasions*   5 = *never*

Religious and Spiritual Coping

   Think about how you try to understand and deal with major problems in your life. To what extent is each of the following involved in the way you cope?

17. I think about how my life is part of a larger spiritual force.
    1 = *a great deal*   2 = *quite a bit*   3 = *somewhat* 4 = *not at all*
18. I work together with God as partners.
    1 = *q great deal*   2 = *quite a bit*   3 = *somewhat* 4 = *not at all*
19. I look to God for strength, support, and guidance.
    1 = *a great deal*   2 = *quite a bit*   3 = *somewhat* 4 = *not at all*
20. I feel God is punishing me for my sins or lack of spirituality.
    1 = *a great deal*   2 = *quite a bit*   3 = *somewhat* 4 = *not at all*
21. I wonder whether God has abandoned me.
    1 = *a great deal*   2 = *quite a bit*   3 = *somewhat* 4 = *not at all*
22. I try to make sense of the situation and decide what to do without relying on God.
    1 = *a great deal*   2 = *quite a bit*   3 = *somewhat* 4 = *not at all*
23. To what extent is your religion involved in understanding or dealing with stressful situations in any way?
    1 = *very involved*   2 = *somewhat involved*
    3 = *not very involved*   4 = *not involved at all*

Religious Support

   These questions are designed to find out how much help the people in your congregation would provide if you need it in the future.

24. If you were ill, how much would the people in your congregation help you out?
    1 = *a great deal*   2 = *some*   3 = *a little*   4 = *none*

25. If you had a problem or were faced with a difficult situation, how much comfort would the people in your congregation be willing to give you?
1 = *a great deal* 2 = *some*   3 = *a little*   4 = *none*

Sometimes the contact we have with others is not always pleasant.

26. How often do the people in your congregation make too many demands on you?
1 = *very often* 2 = *fairly often*   3 = *once in*   4 = *never*
                                                        a while

27. How often are the people in your congregation critical of you and the things you do?
1 = *very often* 2 = *fairly often*   3 = *once in*   4 = *never*
                                                        a while

Religious/Spiritual History

28. Did you ever have a religious or spiritual experience that changed your life?
No   Yes
If yes: How old were you when this experience occurred?

29. Have you ever had a significant gain in your faith?
No   Yes
If yes: How old were you when this occurred?

30. Have you ever had a significant loss in your faith?
No   Yes
If yes: How old were you when this occurred?

Commitment

31. I try hard to carry my religious beliefs over into all my other dealings in life.
1 = *strongly agree* 2 = *agree* 3 = *disagree* 4 = *strongly disagree*

32. During the past year, about how much was the average monthly contribution of your household to your congregation or to religious causes?
$_____ OR $_____
Contribution   Contribution
per year   per month

33. In an average week, how many hours do you spend in activities on behalf of your church or activities that you do for religious or spiritual reasons?
If protestant, ask:
Which specific denomination is that? _____

Organizational Religiousness

    34. How often do you go to religious services?
        1 = *more than once a week*   2 = *every week or more often*
        3 = *once or twice a month*   4 = *every month or so*
        5 = *once or twice a year*   6 = *never*

    35. Besides religious services, how often do you take part in other activities at a place of worship?
        1 = *more than once a week*   2 = *every week or more often*
        3 = *once or twice a month*   4 = *every month or so*
        5 = *once or twice a year*   6 = *never*

Religious Preference

    36. What is your current religious preference? _____

Overall Self-Ranking

    37. To what extent do you consider yourself a religious person?
        1 = *very religious*   2 = *moderately religious*
        3 = *slightly religious*   4 = *not religious at all*

    38. To what extent do you consider yourself a spiritual person?
        1 = *very spiritual*   2 = *moderately spiritual*
        3 = *slightly spiritual*   4 = *not spiritual at all*

Meaning: The working group did not feel it was appropriate at this time to include any "religious meaning" items in this measure, as no final decisions have been made regarding this domain. The following items are being considered for a short form of this scale.

    1. The events in my life unfold according to a divine or greater plan.
        1 = *strongly agree* 2 = *agree* 3 = *disagree* 4 = *strongly disagree*
    2. I have a sense of mission or calling in my own life.
        1 = *strongly agree* 2 = *agree* 3 = *disagree* 4 = *strongly disagree*

J. A. Davis, Smith, and Marsden (2005) and Underwood (2006) provided normative information on the scale. In particular, they reported mean scores for general population adults for each of the 6-point Likert scale items in the Daily Spiritual Experiences section of about 4 (1 = *many times a day* and 6 = *never/almost never*), with *SD*s for each item being about 1.5.

Santa Clara Strength of Religious Faith Questionnaire (SCSORF)[2]

    Please answer the following questions about religious faith using the scale below. Indicate the level of agreement (or disagreement) for each statement.

---

[2]From "The Santa Clara Strength of Religious Faith Questionnaire," by T. G. Plante and B. F. Boccaccini, 1997, *Pastoral Psychology, 45,* p. 385. Copyright 1997 by Springer Science + Business Media. Reprinted with permission.

1 = strongly disagree 2 = disagree 3 = agree 4 = strongly agree

_____ 1. My religious faith is extremely important to me.
_____ 2. I pray daily.
_____ 3. I look to my faith as a source of inspiration.
_____ 4. I look to my faith as providing meaning and purpose in my life.
_____ 5. I consider myself active in my faith or church.
_____ 6. My faith is an important part of who I am as a person.
_____ 7. My relationship with God is extremely important to me.
_____ 8. I enjoy being around others who share my faith.
_____ 9. I look to my faith as a source of comfort.
_____ 10. My faith impacts many of my decisions.

To score, add the total scores. They will range from 10 (*low faith*) to 40 (*high faith*).

Plante and Boccaccini (1997) reported that the normative mean for a general sample of college students in the United States is 26 (*SD* = 8) and that scores of 33 or higher are considered evidence of high religiosity and scores below 20 represent not being religious. Plante et al. (1999) further reported a normative mean for substance abuse addicts in recovery of 30 (*SD* = 7).

A brief version of the SCSORF has been developed and validated. These items include the following:

Please answer the following questions about religious faith using the scale below. Indicate the level of agreement (or disagreement) for each statement.

1 = strongly disagree 2 = disagree 3 = agree 4 = strongly agree

_____ 1. I pray daily.
_____ 2. I look to my faith as providing meaning and purpose in my life.
_____ 3. I consider myself active in my faith or church.
_____ 4. I enjoy being around others who share my faith.
_____ 5. My faith impacts many of my decisions.

To score, add the total scores. They will range from 5 (*low faith*) to 20 (*high faith*).

Plante et al. (2002) reported that the normative mean for a general sample of college students in the United States for the brief version of the scale is 14 (SD = 4); for cancer patients, 17 (SD = 3); and for women in general, 16 (SD = 4).

Duke University Religious Index (DUREL)[3]

Please answer the following questions about your religious beliefs and/ or involvement.

> 1 = *more than once a week*   2 = *once a week*   3 = *a few times a month*
> 4 = *a few times a year*   5 = *once a year or less*   6 = *never*

1. How often do you attend church or other religious meetings?

    1   2   3   4   5   6

2. How often do you spend time in private religious activities, such as prayer, meditation, or Bible study?

    1   2   3   4   5   6

The following section contains three statements about religious belief or experience. Please mark the extent to which each statement is true or not true for you.

> 1 = *Definitely true of me*   2 = *Tends to be true*   3 = *Unsure*
> 4 = *Tends not to be true*   5 = *Definitely not true*

3. In my life, I experience the presence of the Divine (i.e., God).

    1   2   3   4   5

4. My religious beliefs are what really lie behind my whole approach to life.

    1   2   3   4   5

5. I try hard to carry my religion over into all other dealings in life.

    1   2   3   4   5

To score:
Subscale 1: Reverse score Item 1 to obtain Frequency of Religious Attendance subscale score.
Subscale 2: Reverse score Item 2 to obtain Frequency of Private Religious Activity subscale score.
Subscale 3: Reverse score Items 3–5 and total to obtain Intrinsic Religiosity subscale score.

---

[3]From "Religion Index for Psychiatric Research: A 5-Item Measure for Use in Health Outcome Studies" [Letter to the editor], by H. G. Koenig, K. Meador, and G. Parkerson, 1997, *The American Journal of Psychiatry, 154*, p. 886. Copyright 1997 by the American Psychiatric Association. Reprinted with permission.

Overall score: For overall religiosity, sum reversed scores for Items 1 through 5 (however, this is not recommended because subscale scores may cancel out the effects of each other).

Koenig, Meador, and Parkerson (1997) did not report established general population norms.

Religious Commitment Inventory—10 (RCI–10)[4]

Read each of the following statements. Using the scale to the right, circle the response that best describes how true each statement is for you.

Not at all true of me 1	Somewhat true of me 2	Moderately true of me 3	Mostly true of me 4	Totally true of me 5

1. I often read books and magazines about my faith. 1 2 3 4 5
2. I make financial contributions to my religious organization. 1 2 3 4 5
3. I spend time trying to grow in understanding of my faith. 1 2 3 4 5
4. Religion is especially important to me because it answers many questions about the meaning of life. 1 2 3 4 5
5. My religious beliefs lie behind my whole approach to life. 1 2 3 4 5
6. I enjoy spending time with others of my religious affiliation. 1 2 3 4 5
7. Religious beliefs influence all my dealings in life. 1 2 3 4 5
8. It is important to me to spend periods of time in private religious thought and reflection. 1 2 3 4 5
9. I enjoy working in the activities of my religious affiliation. 1 2 3 4 5
10. I keep well informed about my local religious group and have some influence in its decisions. 1 2 3 4 5

To score, add the total score that will range from 10 (*low commitment*) to 50 (*high commitment*)

Worthington et al. (2003) reported that the normative mean for a general sample of adults in the United States is 26 (*SD* = 12) and that scores of 38 or higher are considered evidence of high religiosity.

---

[4]From "The Religious Commitment Inventory—10: Development, Refinement, and Validation of a Brief Scale for Research and Counseling," by E. L. Worthington Jr., N. G. Wade, T. L. Hight, J. S. Ripley, M. E. McCullough, J. W. Berry, et al., 2003, *Journal of Counseling Psychology*, 50, p. 96. Copyright 2003 by the American Psychological Association.

Brief RCOPE[5]

The following items deal with ways you coped with a negative event in your life. There are many ways to try to deal with problems. These items ask what you did to cope with this negative event. Obviously different people deal with things in different ways, but we are interested in how you tried to deal with it. Each item says something about a particular way of coping. We want to know to what extent you did what the item says. How much or how frequently. Don't answer on the basis of what worked or not—just whether or not you did it. Use these response choices. Try to rate each item separately in your mind from the others. Make your answers as true FOR YOU as you can. Circle the answer that best applies to you.

1 = *not at all*   2 = *somewhat*   3 = *quite a bit*   4 = *a great deal*

(+)	1. Looked for a stronger connection with God.	1 2 3 4
(+)	2. Sought God's love and care.	1 2 3 4
(+)	3. Sought help from God in letting go of my anger.	1 2 3 4
(+)	4. Tried to put my plans into action together with God.	1 2 3 4
(+)	5. Tried to see how God might be trying to strengthen me in this situation.	1 2 3 4
(+)	6. Asked forgiveness for my sins.	1 2 3 4
(+)	7. Focused on religion to stop worrying about my problems.	1 2 3 4
(–)	8. Wondered whether God had abandoned me.	1 2 3 4
(–)	9. Felt punished by God for my lack of devotion.	1 2 3 4
(–)	10. Wondered what I did for God to punish me.	1 2 3 4
(–)	11. Questioned God's love for me.	1 2 3 4
(–)	12. Wondered whether my church had abandoned me.	1 2 3 4
(–)	13. Decided the devil made this happen.	1 2 3 4
(–)	14. Questioned the power of God.	1 2 3 4

(+) Positive religious coping item
(–) Negative religious coping item

To score, add the total; score for the first seven positive religious coping items (score range from 7 to 28) and then add the total score for the last seven negative religious coping items (score range from 7 to 28).

[5]From "The Many Methods of Religious Coping: Initial Development and Validation of the RCOPE," by K. I. Pargament, H. G. Koenig, and L. Perez, 2000, *Journal of Clinical Psychology*, 56, p. 543. Copyright 2000 by Wiley. Reprinted with permission.

Pargament, Koenig, and Perez (2000) did not have established general population norms available.

Additional Measures Professionals May Wish to Be Aware Of

Spiritual Well-Being Scale

The Spiritual Well-Being Scale (Paloutzian & Ellison, 1982) is a 20-item survey using two subscales that include religious well-being (e.g., "I believe that God loves me and cares about me"), and existential well-being (e.g., "I feel good about my future"). The existential well-being part of the questionnaire is generally unrelated to religion and spirituality and likely better reflects positive mental health or general life satisfaction (Koenig et al., 2001). Thus, for the purposes of this book, the use of the 10-item religious well-being subscale may be adequate for clinical and research needs for those interested in religious–spiritual dimensions in their assessment procedures. Although especially popular in nursing care and research, it has demonstrated adequate reliability and validity (Hill et al., 2007; Sherman et al., 2001).

Intrinsic Religious Motivation Scale

The Intrinsic Religious Motivation Scale (Hoge, 1972) is a 10-item instrument that assesses religious motivation rather than religious behavior (e.g., "My religious beliefs are what really lie behind my whole approach to life") and can be used with a variety of faith traditions. It includes 7 items that assess intrinsic qualities such as prayer and 3 items that evaluate extrinsic dimensions such as church attendance. The scale demonstrates adequate reliability and validity as well (Hoge, 1972; Koenig et al., 2001; Koenig, Moberg, & Kvale, 1988; Sherman et al., 2001).

Revised Religious Orientation Scale

The Revised Religious Orientation Scale (Gorsuch & McPherson, 1989) is 14-item scale that has been reworked from previous questionnaires (Allport & Ross, 1967; Gorsuch & Venable, 1983) and highlights two measures including intrinsic (e.g., "I enjoy reading about my religion") and extrinsic (e.g., "I go to church because it helps me to make friends") religious motivation. The scale demonstrates adequate reliability and validity in a variety of studies (Gorsuch & McPherson, 1989; Koenig et al., 2001; Schaefer & Gorsuch, 1991; Sherman et al., 2001).

Religious Doubts Scale

The Religious Doubts Scale (Altemeyer, 1988) is a 10-item scale that assesses religious doubt and has demonstrated adequate reliability and validity mostly assessed in college student settings.

Mysticism Scale

Mysticism Scale (Hood, 1975) is a 32-item scale that assesses self-reported mystical experiences applicable to people who either do or do not associate with a particular religious tradition or faith community. The questionnaire highlights two subscales including a 20-item general mysticism scale that examines experiences of unity, mood, inner subjectivity and so forth as well as a 12-item scale that evaluates religious interpretations of these experiences. Reliability and validity of the measure is adequate (Burris, 1999; Koenig et al., 2001).

Religious Problem-Solving Scales

The Religious Problem-Solving Scale (Pargament et al., 1998) consists of 36-items that assess three religious approaches to solving problems. The questionnaire assesses whether the individual assumes an active or passive approach toward problem solving and whether primary responsibility is attributed to self or to God. The scale has shown adequate reliability and validity as well (Friedel & Pargament, 1995; N. A. Harris & Spilka, 1990; Pargament et al., 1998).

Religious Practices Scales

Although many research studies and clinicians can simply ask clients whether they regularly attend religious–spiritual services, several brief questionnaires have been developed to better understand the nature of religious behavior and practice. *The Religious Involvement Inventory* (Hilty & Morgan, 1985) is a 14-item questionnaire that focuses on church involvement, whereas *The Spirituality Religiosity Scale* (Koenig, Smiley, & Gonzales, 1988) evaluates the frequency of church service attendance as well as engagement with other religious group activities such as study groups, Sunday school, religious education classes, and so forth.

CONCLUSION

Although I have focused on scales that can be used with people who identify with most any religious tradition or perhaps no tradition at all, there are numerous scales available that are specifically designed for a particular religious or faith community. Most of these scales tend to be appropriate for Christian populations (and especially Protestant or evangelical communities) yet there are several that focus on Jewish (e.g., the 10-item Jewishness Scale; Ressler, 1997), Hindu or Muslim (e.g., the 10-item Hassan Religiosity Scale; Haasan & Khalique, 1981), and Buddhist communities (e.g., the Buddhist Beliefs and Practices Scale; Emavardhana & Tori, 1997).

REFERENCES

Alcoholics Anonymous World Services. (1955). *The story of how many thousands of men and women have recovered from alcoholism* (2nd ed.). New York: Author.

Alcoholics Anonymous World Services. (1977). *Alcoholics Anonymous: The twelve steps and twelve traditions* (3rd ed.). New York: Author.

Alcoholics Anonymous World Services. (1990). *Alcoholics Anonymous 1989 membership survey.* New York: Author.

Allen, J. (2004). Clergy sexual abuse in the American Catholic Church: The view from the Vatican. In T. G. Plante (Ed.), *Sin against the innocents: Sexual abuse by priests and the role of the Catholic Church* (pp. 13–24). Westport, CT: Praeger/Greenwood.

Allport, G. W. (1950). *The individual and his religion: A psychological interpretation.* New York: Macmillan.

Allport, G. W., & Ross, J. M. (1967). Personal religious orientation and prejudice. *Journal of Personality and Social Psychology, 5,* 432–443.

Altemeyer, B. (1988). *Enemies of freedom: Understanding right-wing authoritarianism.* San Francisco: Jossey-Bass.

Ameling, A. (2000). Prayer: An ancient healing practice becomes new again. *Holistic Nursing Practice, 14,* 40–48.

American Association for Marriage and Family Therapy. (2001). *AAMFT code of ethics.* Alexandria, VA: Author.

American Psychological Association. (2002). Ethical principles of psychologists and code of conduct. *American Psychologist, 57,* 1060–1073.

American Psychological Association. (2003). Guidelines on multicultural education, training, research, practice, and organizational change for psychologists. *American Psychologist, 58,* 377–402.

American Psychological Association. (2008). *Graduate study in psychology: 2008.* Washington, DC: Author

American Society on Aging. (2008). *About FORSA.* Retrieved October 16, 2008, from http://www.asaging.org/networks/FORSA/about.cfm

Andresen, J. (2000). Meditation meets behavioral medicine. *Journal of Consciousness Studies, 7,* 17–74.

Ano, G. A. (2005). *Spiritual struggles between vice and virtue: A brief psychospiritual intervention.* Unpublished doctoral dissertation, Bowling Green State University, Bowling Green, OH.

Armstrong, K. (1993). *A history of God: The 4,000 year quest of Judaism, Christianity, and Islam.* New York: Gramercy.

Armstrong, K. (2000). *The battle for God: Fundamentalism in Judaism, Christianity, and Islam.* New York: HarperCollins.

Armstrong, K. (2006). *The great transformation: The beginning of our religious traditions*. New York: Anchor.

Association of American Medical Colleges. (1999). *Contemporary issues in medicine: Communication in medicine* (Report III). Washington, DC: Author.

Association for Transpersonal Psychology. (n.d.). *About ATP*. Retrieved October 16, 2008, from http://www.atpweb.org/about_atp.asp

Azhar, M. Z., Varma, S. L., & Dharap, A., S. (1994). Religious psychotherapy in anxiety disorder patients. *Acta Psychiatrica Scandinavica, 90*, 1–3.

Baer, R. A. (2003). Meditation training as a clinical intervention: A conceptual and empirical review. *Clinical Psychology: Science and Practice, 10*, 125–143.

Ball, R. A., & Goodyear, R. K. (1991). Self-reported professional practices of Christian psychologists. *Journal of Psychology and Christianity, 10*, 144–153.

Bandura, A. (1986). *Social foundations of thought and action*. Englewood Cliffs, NJ: Prentice Hall.

Bandura, A. (2003). On the psychosocial impact and mechanisms of spiritual modeling. *The International Journal for the Psychology of Religion, 13*, 167–174.

Banks, C. (1997). The imaginative use of religious symbols in subjective experiences of anorexia nervosa. *Psychoanalytic Review, 84*, 227–236.

Barbour, I. (2000). *When science meets religion*. San Francisco: HarperCollins.

Barr, C. (1995). Panic disorder: The fear of fearful feelings. *Journal of Psychology and Christianity, 14*, 112–125.

Benson, H. (1976). *The relaxation response*. New York: HarperTorch.

Benson, H. (1996). *Timeless healing: The power and biology of belief*. New York: Scribner.

Berkman, L. F., & Syme, S. L. (1979). Social networks, host resistance, and mortality: A nine-year follow-up study of Alameda County residents. *American Journal of Epidemiology, 109*, 186–204.

Bilgrave, D. P., & Deluty, R. H. (2002). Religious beliefs and political ideologies as predictors of psychotherapeutic orientations of clinical and counseling psychologists. *Psychotherapy, 39*, 245–260.

Blaine, B., & Croker, J. (1995). Religiousness, race, and psychological well-being: Exploring social psychological mediators. *Personality and Social Psychology Bulletin, 21*, 1031–1041.

Bormann, J. E., Gifford, A. L., Shively, M., Smith, T. L., Redwine, L., Kelly, A., et al. (2006). Effects of spiritual mantram repetition on HIV outcomes: A randomized controlled trial. *Journal of Behavioral Medicine, 29*, 359–376.

Bormann, J. E., & Oman, D. (2007). Mantram or holy name repetition: Health benefits from a portable spiritual practice. In T. G. Plante & C. E. Thoresen (Eds.), *Spirit, science, and health: How the spiritual mind fuels physical wellness* (pp. 94–114). Westport, CT: Praeger/Greenwood.

Bormann, J. E., Smith, T. L., Becker, S., Gershwin, M., Pada, L., Grudzinski, A. H., & Nurmi, E. A. (2005). Efficacy of frequent, mantram repetition on stress, spiritual well-being, and quality of life in veterans: A pilot study. *Journal of Holistic Nursing, 23*, 395–414.

Borysenko, J., & Borysenko, M. (1994). *The power of the mind to heal: Renewing body, mind, and spirit*. Carson, CA: Hay House.

Brawer, P. A., Handal, P. J., Fabricatore, A. N., Roberts, R., & Wajda-Johnston, V. A. (2002). Training and education in religious/spirituality within APA-accredited clinical psychology programs. *Professional Psychology: Research and Practice, 33*, 203–206.

Burris, C. T. (1999). The Mysticism Scale: Research Form D [review]. In P. C. Hill & R. W. Hood Jr. (Eds.), *Measures of religiosity* (pp. 363–367). Birmingham, AL: Religious Education Press.

Campion, J., & Bhugra, D. (1997). Experiences of religious healing in psychiatric patients in South Asia. *Social Psychiatry and Psychiatric Epidemiology, 32*, 215–221.

Centers for Disease Control and Prevention. (2000). *Eleven leading causes of death, United States: 1998, all races, both sexes*. Washington, DC: Author.

Centers for Disease Control and Prevention. (2001). *Deaths/mortality*. Washington, DC: Author.

Centers for Disease Control and Prevention. (2004). *National vital statistics report*. Washington, DC: Author.

Chaddock, T. P., & McMinn, M. R. (1999). Values affecting collaboration among psychologists and evangelical clergy. *Journal of Psychology & Theology, 27*, 319–328.

Clements, R. (1998). Intrinsic religious motivation and attitudes toward death among the elderly. *Current Psychology: Developmental, Learning, Personality, and Social, 17*, 237–248.

Cole, B. S., & Pargament, K. I. (1998). Re-creating your life: A spiritual/psychotherapeutic intervention for people diagnosed with cancer. *Psycho-Oncology, 8*, 395–407.

Collins, G. R. (1977). *The rebuilding of psychology: An integration of psychology and Christianity*. Wheaton, IL: Tyndale House.

Cosar, B., Kocal, N., Arikan, Z., & Isik, E. (1997). Suicide attempts among Turkish psychiatric patients. *Canadian Journal of Psychiatry, 42*, 1072–1075.

Davis, N., Clance, P., & Gailis, A. (1999). Treatment approaches for obese and overweight African American women: A consideration of cultural dimensions. *Psychotherapy, 36*, 27–35.

Davis, J. A., Smith, T. W., & Marsden, P. V. (2005). *General social surveys, 1972–2004*. Chicago: National Opinion Research Center.

Dawkins, R. (2006). *The God delusion*. New York: Houghton Mifflin.

Delaney, H. D., Miller, W. R., & Bisono, A. M. (2007). Religiosity and spirituality among psychologists: A survey of clinicians members of the American Psychological Association. *Professional Psychology: Research and Practice, 38*, 538–546.

DiBlasio, F. A. (1992). Forgiveness in psychotherapy: Comparison of older and younger therapists. *Journal of Psychology and Christianity, 11*, 181–187.

Diener, E., Suh, E. M., Lucas, R. E., & Smith, H. L. (1999). Subjective well-being: Three decades of progress. *Psychological Bulletin, 125,* 276–302.

Division 36 of the American Psychological Association. (2008). *Mission statement.* Retrieved October 16, 2008, from http://www.apa.org/divisions/div36/mission.html

Donahue, M. J., & Benson, P. L. (1995). Religion and the well-being of adolescents. *Journal of Social Issues, 51,* 145–160.

Dossey, L. (1993). *Healing words: The power of prayer and the practice of medicine.* San Francisco: HarperCollins.

Dreher, D. E., & Plante, T. G. (2007). The calling protocol: Promoting greater health, joy, and purpose in life. In T. G. Plante & C. E. Thoresen (Eds.), *Spirit, science, and health: How the spiritual mind fuels physical wellness* (pp. 129–142). Westport, CT: Praeger/Greenwood.

D'Souza, R., Rich, D., Dimond, I., Godfrey, K., & Gleeson, D. (2002). An open randomized control trial of a spiritually augmented cognitive behaviour therapy in patients with depression and hopelessness. *Proceedings of the 37th Royal Australian and New Zealand College of Psychiatrists and Congress, 36*(Suppl.), A9.

Dwyer, J. W., Clarke, L. L., & Miller, M. K. (1990). The effects of religious concentration and affiliation on county cancer mortality rates. *Journal of Health and Social Behavior, 31,* 185–202.

Easwaran, E. (1991). *Meditation: A simple eight-point program for translating spiritual ideals into daily life.* Tomales, CA: Nilgiri Press. (Original work published 1978)

Ellis, A. (1971). *The case against religion: A psychotherapist's view.* New York: Institute for Rational Living.

Ellison, C. G. (1998). Introduction to symposium: Religion, health, and well-being. *Journal for the Scientific Study of Religion, 37,* 692–694.

Emavardhana, T., & Tori, C. D. (1997). Changes in self concept, ego defense mechanisms, and religiosity following seven-day Vipassana meditation retreats. *Journal for the Scientific Study of Religion, 36,* 194–206.

Emmons, R. A., & McCullough, M. E. (2003). Counting blessings versus burdens: Experimental studies of gratitude and subjective well-being. *Journal of Personality and Social Psychology, 84,* 377–389.

Enright, R. D., Freedman, S., & Rique, J. (1998). The psychology of interpersonal forgiveness. In R. D. Enright & J. North (Eds.), *Exploring forgiveness* (pp. 46–62). Madison: University of Wisconsin Press.

Fetzer Institute/National Institute of Aging Working Group. (1999). *Multidimensional measurement of religiousness/spirituality for use in health research: A report of the Fetzer Institute/National Institute on Aging Working Group.* Kalamazoo, MI: John E. Fetzer Institute.

Fischer, L., & Richards, P. S. (1998). *Religion and guilt in childhood.* San Diego, CA: Academic Press.

Flinders, T., Oman, D., & Flinders, C. L. (2007). The eight-point program of passage meditation: Health effects of a comprehensive program. In T. G. Plante & C. E.

Thoresen (Eds.), *Spirit, science, and health: How the spiritual mind fuels physical wellness* (pp. 72–93). Westport, CT: Praeger/Greenwood.

Frame, M. W. (2003). *Integrating religion and spirituality into counseling: A comprehensive approach*. Belmont, CA: Wadsworth.

Freud, S. (1961). *The future of an illusion* (J. Strachey, Ed. & Trans.). New York: Norton. (Original work published 1927)

Frick, E., Riedner, C., Fegg, M. J., Hauf, S., & Borasio, G. D. (2006). A clinical interview assessing cancer patients' spiritual needs and preferences. *European Journal of Cancer Care, 15*, 238–243.

Friedel, L. A., & Pargament, K. I. (1995, August). *Religion and coping with crises in the work environment*. Paper presented at the annual convention of the American Psychological Association, New York, NY.

Friend, T. (1995, September 20). Patient calls Ornish program miraculous. *USA Today*, pp. 1–2.

Fuller, R. C. (2001). *Spiritual but not religious*. New York: Oxford University Press.

Gallup, G., Jr., (2002). *The Gallup poll: Public opinion 2001*. Wilmington, DE: Scholarly Resources.

Gallup, G., Jr., & Jones, T. (2000). *The next American spirituality: Finding God in the twenty-first century*. Colorado Springs, CO: Cook Communications.

Gallup, G., Jr., & Lindsay, D. M. (1999). *Surveying the religious landscape: Trends in U.S. beliefs*. Harrisburg, PA: Morehouse.

Garret, C. (1996). Recovery from anorexia nervosa: A Durkheimian interpretation. *Social Science & Medicine, 43*, 1489–1506.

Germer, C. K., Siegel, R. D., & Fulton, P. R. (Eds.). (2005). *Mindfulness and psychotherapy*. New York: Guilford Press.

Gillis, J. S., & Mubbashar, M. H. (1995). Risk factors for drug abuse in Pakistan: A replication. *Psychological Reports, 76*, 99–108.

Goleman, D. (1988). *The meditation mind*. Los Angeles: Tarcher.

Gorsuch, R. L., & McPherson, S. E. (1989). Intrinsic/extrinsic measurement: I/E-Revised and single-item scales. *Journal of the Scientific Study of Religion, 28*, 348–354.

Gorsuch, R. L., & Venable, G. D. (1983). Development of an age universal I-E scale. *Journal of the Scientific Study of Religion, 22*, 181–187.

Hackney, C. H., & Sanders, G. S. (2003). Religiosity and mental health: A meta-analysis of recent studies. *Journal for the Scientific Study of Religion, 42*, 43–55.

Hage, S. M. (2006). A closer look at the role of spirituality in psychology training. *Professional Psychology: Research and Practice, 37*, 303–310.

Harrington, V., Lackey, N. R., & Gates, M. F. (1996). Needs of caregivers of home and hospice care patients. *Cancer Nursing, 19*, 118–125.

Harris, N. A., & Spilka, B. (1990). *The sense of control and coping with alcoholism: A multidimensional approach*. Paper presented at the meeting of the Rocky Mountain Psychological Association, Tucson, AZ.

Harris, S. (2005). *The end of faith: Religion, terror, and the future of reason*. New York: Norton.

Hartz, G. W. (2005). *Spirituality and mental health: Clinical applications*. Binghamton, NY: Haworth Pastoral Press.

Hassan, M. K., & Khalique, A. (1981). Religiosity and its correlates in college students. *Journal of Psychological Researches, 25*, 129–136.

Hayes, S. C. (2005). *Get out of your mind and into your life: The new acceptance and commitment therapy*. Oakland, CA: New Harbinger.

Hayes, S. C., Follete, V. M., & Linehan, M. M. (2004). *Mindfulness and acceptance: Expanding the cognitive-behavioral tradition*. New York: Guilford Press.

Heschel, A. J. (1986). *The wisdom of Heschel*. New York: Farrar, Straus, & Giroux.

Hill, P. C., Kopp, K. J., & Bollinger, R. A. (2007). A few good measures: Assessing religion and spirituality in relation to health. In T. G. Plante & C. E. Thoresen (Eds.), *Spirit, science, and health: How the spiritual mind fuels physical wellness* (pp. 25–38). Westport, CT: Praeger/Greenwood.

Hill, T. D., Ellison, C. G., Burdette, A. M., & Musick, M. A. (2007). Religious involvement and healthy lifestyles: Evidence from the survey of Texas adults. *Annals of Behavioral Medicine, 34*, 217–222.

Hilty, D. M., & Morgan, R. L. (1985). Construct validation for the Religious Involvement Inventory: Replication. *Journal of the Scientific Study of Religion, 24*, 75–86.

Hinton, J. (1999). The progress of awareness and acceptance of dying assessed in cancer patients and their caring relatives. *Palliative Medicine, 13*, 19–35.

Hitchens, C. (2007). *God is not great: How religion poisons everything*. New York: Twelve Books.

Hoge, D. R. (1972). A validated intrinsic religious motivation scale. *Journal for the Scientific Study of Religion, 11*, 369–376.

Holtz, T. (1998). Refugee trauma versus torture trauma: A retrospective controlled short study of Tibetan refugees. *Journal of Nervous and Mental Diseases, 186*, 24–34.

Hood, R. W., Jr. (1975). The construction and preliminary validation of a measure of reported mystical experience. *Journal of the Scientific Study of Religion, 14*, 29–41.

Hopson, R. E. (1996). The 12-step program. In E. P. Shafranske (Ed.), *Religion and the clinical practice of psychology* (pp. 533–558). Washington, DC: American Psychological Association.

Hummer, R. A., Rogers, R. G., Nam, C. B., & Ellison, C. G. (1999). Religious involvement and U.S. adult mortality. *Demography, 36*, 272–285.

International Association of Pastoral Counselors. (n.d.). *International Association of Pastoral Counselors*. Retrieved October 16, 2008, from http://www.angelfire.com/tx6/anglican

Ita, D. (1995). Testing of a causal model: Acceptance of death in hospice patients. *Omega, 32*, 81–82.

Jacobs-Pilipski, M. J., Winzelberg, A., Wilfley, D. E., Bryson, S. W., & Taylor, C. B. (2005). Spirituality among young women at risk for eating disorders. *Eating Behaviors, 6,* 293–300.

Jahangir, F. (1995). Third force therapy and its impact on treatment outcome. *The International Journal for the Psychology of Religion, 5,* 125–129.

James, W. (1890). *Principles of psychology.* New York: Holt.

James, W. (1936). *The varieties of religious experience: A study in human nature.* New York: Modern Library. (Original work published 1902)

John Jay College of Criminal Justice. (2004). *The nature and scope of the problem of sexual abuse of minors by Catholic priests and deacons in the United States.* New York: Author.

Jones, S. L. (1994). A constructive relationship for religion with the science and profession of psychology: Perhaps the boldest model yet. *American Psychologist, 49,* 184–199.

Jones, S. L., Watson, E. J., & Wolfram, T. J. (1992). Results of the Rech conference survey on religious faith and professional psychology. *Journal of Psychology & Theology, 20,* 147–158.

Jung, C. G. (1938). *Psychology and religion.* New Haven, CT: Yale University Press.

Kabat-Zinn, J. (1990). *Full catastrophe living.* New York: Delacourte Press.

Kabat-Zinn, J. (1994). *Wherever you go, there you are.* New York: Hyperion.

Kabat-Zinn, J. (2003). Mindfulness-based interventions in context: Past, present, and future. *Clinical Psychology: Research and Practice, 10,* 144–156.

Kabat-Zinn, J., & Skillings, A. (1992). *Sense of coherence and stress hardiness as outcome measures of a mindfulness-based stress reduction program: Three-year follow-up.* Unpublished manuscript, University of Massachusetts Medical Center, Boston.

Kaplan, M., Marks, G., & Mertens, S. (1997). Distress and coping among women with HIV infection: Preliminary findings from a multiethnic sample. *American Journal of Orthopsychiatry, 37,* 80–91.

Kazanigian, M. A. (1997). The spiritual and psychological explanation for experience. *The Hospice Journal, 12,* 17–27.

Keating, T. (1981). *The heart of the world: An introduction to contemplative Christianity.* New York: Crossroad Publishing.

Keating, T., Pennington, B., & Clarke, T. (1978). *Finding grace at the center.* Petersham, MA: St. Bede's.

Kendler, K. S., Gardner, C. O., & Prescott, C. A. (1997). Religion, psychopathology, and substance use and abuse: A multi-measure, genetic-epidemiologic study. *The American Journal of Psychiatry, 154,* 322–329.

Kernberg, O. F. (2003). Sanctioned social violence: Part II. A psychoanalytic view. *International Journal of Psychoanalysis, 84,* 953–968.

Keyes, C. L. M., & Haidt, J. (2003). *Flourishing: Positive psychology and the life well-lived.* Washington, DC: American Psychological Association.

Koenig, H. G. (1995). Religion and older men in prison. *International Journal of Geriatric Psychiatry, 10,* 219–230.

Koenig, H. G. (1997). *Is religion good for your health? The effects of religion on physical and mental health.* Binghamton, NY: Haworth Pastoral Press.

Koenig, H. G. (2007). Religion and depression in older medical inpatients. *American Journal of General Psychiatry, 15,* 282–291.

Koenig, H. G., McCullough, M. E., & Larson, D. B. (2001). *Handbook of religion and health.* New York: Oxford University Press.

Koenig, H. G., Meador, K., & Parkerson, G. (1997). Religion Index for Psychiatric Research: A 5-item measure for use in health outcome studies [Letter to the editor]. *The American Journal of Psychiatry, 154,* 885–886.

Koenig, H. G., Moberg, D. O., & Kvale, J. N. (1988). Religious activities and attitudes of older adults in a geriatric assessment clinic. *Journal of the American Geriatric Society, 36,* 362–374.

Koenig, H. G., Smiley, M., & Gonzales, J. A. P. (1988). *Religion, health, and aging: A review and theoretical integration.* Westport, CT: Greenwood.

Koocher, G., & Keith-Speigal, P. (2008). *Ethics in psychology and the mental health professions: Standards and cases* (3rd ed.). New York : Oxford University Press.

Krause, N. (2003a). Praying for others, financial strain, and physical health status in late life. *Journal for the Scientific Study of Religion, 42,* 377–391.

Krause, N. (2003b). Religious meaning and subjective well-being in late life. *The Journals of Gerontology: Series B. Psychological Sciences and Social Sciences, 58*(Suppl.), 160–170.

Krause, N. (2004). Assessing the relationships among prayer expectancies, race, and self-esteem in late life. *Journal for the Scientific Study of Religion, 43,* 395–408.

Kremer, H., & Ironson, G. (2007). Spirituality and HIV/AIDS. In T. G. Plante & C. E. Thoresen (Eds.), *Spirit, science, and health: How the spiritual mind fuels physical wellness* (pp. 176–190). Westport, CT: Praeger/Greenwood.

Kulik, J. A., & Mahler, H. I. M. (1989). Social support and recovery from surgery. *Health Psychology, 8,* 221–238.

Lampton, C., Oliver, G. J., Worthington, E. L., Jr., & Berry, J. W. (2005). Helping Christian college students become more forgiving: An intervention study to promote forgiveness as part of a program to shape Christian character. *Journal of Psychology & Theology, 33,* 278–290.

Langston, C. A. (1994). Capitalizing on and coping with daily-life events: Expressive responses to positive events. *Journal of Personality and Social Psychology, 67,* 1112–1125.

Larson, D. B., Lu, F. G., & Swyers, J. P. (1996). *Model curriculum for psychiatry residency training programs: Religion and spirituality in clinical practice.* Rockville, MD: National Institute for Healthcare Research.

Lee, B. Y., & Newberg, A. B. (2005). Religion and health: A review and critical analysis. *Zygon, 40,* 443–468.

Lehman, C. (1993, January 30). Faith-based counseling gains favor. *The Washington Post*, pp. B7–B8.

Leigh, J., Bowen, S., & Marlatt, G. A. (2005). Spirituality, mindfulness, and substance abuse. *Addictive Behavior, 30*, 1335–1341.

Levin, J. (1994). Investigating the epidemiologic effects of religious experience. In J. Levin (Ed.), *Religion in aging and health: Theoretical foundations and methodological frontiers* (pp. 3–17). Thousand Oaks, CA: Sage.

Levin, J. (1997). The role of the Black church in community medicine. *Journal of the National Medical Association, 76*, 477–483.

Levin, J., & Taylor, R. (1998). Panel analyses of religious involvement and well-being in African-Americans: Contemporaneous vs. longitudinal effects. *Journal for the Scientific Study of Religion, 37*, 695–709.

Lindgren, K. N., & Coursey, R. D. (1995). Spirituality and mental illness: A two-part study. *Psychosocial Rehabilitation Journal, 18*, 93–111.

Linehan, M. (1993). *Cognitive-behavior treatment of borderline personality disorder*. New York: Guilford.

Lopez, S. J., & Snyder, C. R. (Eds.). (2003). *Positive psychological assessment: A handbook of models and measures*. Washington, DC: American Psychological Association.

Lotufo-Neto, F. (1996). The prevalence of mental disorders among clergy in San Paulo, Brazil. *Journal of Psychology & Theology, 24*, 313–322.

Luks, A. (1993). *The healing power of doing good*. New York: Ballantine Books.

Marks, L. (2005). Religion and bio-psycho-social health: A review of and conceptual model. *Journal of Religion and Health, 44*, 173–186.

Marlatt, G. A., & Kristeller, J. L. (1999). Mindfulness and meditation. In W. R. Miller (Ed.), *Integrating spirituality into treatment: Resources for practitioners* (pp. 67–84). Washington, DC: American Psychological Association.

Marsden, P., Karagianni, E., & Morgan, J. F. (2007). Spirituality and clinical care in eating disorders: A qualitative study. *International Journal of Eating Disorders, 40*, 7–12.

Martin, M. (2003, November/December). Bridging the mental health/spirituality divide. *Behavioral Health Management*, 40–41.

Maslow, A. H. (1964). *Religions: Values and peak experiences*. New York: Viking.

Masters, K. S. (2007). Prayer and health. In T. G. Plante & C. E. Thoresen (Eds.), *Spirit, science, and health: How the spiritual mind fuels physical wellness* (pp. 11–24). Westport, CT: Praeger/Greenwood.

Masters, K. S., Spielmans, G. I., & Goodson, J. T. (2006). Are there demonstrable effects of distant intercessory prayer? A meta-analytic review. *Annals of Behavioral Medicine, 32*, 337–342.

McClain, C., Rosenfeld, B., & Breitbart, W. (2003, May 10). Effect of spiritual well-being on end-of-life despair in terminally ill cancer patients. *The Lancet, 361*, 1603–1607.

McCourt, J., & Waller, G. (1996). The influence of socio-cultural factors on the eating psychopathology of Asian women in British society. *European Eating Disorders Review, 4*, 73–83.

McCullough, M. E. (1995). Prayer and health: Conceptual issues, research review, and research agenda. *Journal of Psychology & Theology, 25*, 15–29.

McCullough, M. E., Hoyt, W. T., Larson, D. B., Koenig, H. G., & Thoresen, C. E. (2000). Religious involvement and mortality: A meta-analytic review. *Health Psychology, 19*, 211–221.

McCullough, M. E., & Larson, D. B. (1999). Prayer. In W. R. Miller (Ed.), *Integrating spirituality into treatment: Resources for practitioners* (pp. 85–110). Washington, DC: American Psychological Association.

McCullough, M. E., Pargament, K. I., & Thoresen, C. E. (Eds.). (2000). *Forgiveness: Theory, research, and practice*. New York: Guilford Press.

McLennan, S. (2001). *Finding your religion: When the faith you grew up with has lost its meaning*. San Francisco: HarperSanFrancisco.

McMinn, M. R., Aikins, D. C., & Lish, R. A. (2003). Basic and advanced competence in collaborating with clergy: Survey findings and implications. *Professional Psychology: Research and Practice, 34*, 197–202.

McMinn, M. R., Chaddock, T. P., Edwards, L. C., Lim, R. K. B., & Campbell, C. D. (1998). Psychologists collaborating with clergy: Survey findings and implications. *Professional Psychology: Research and Practice, 29*, 564–570.

McMinn, M. R., & Dominquez, A. W. (2005). *Psychology and the church*. Hauppauge, NY: Nova Science.

McNichols, K. Z., & Feldman, D. B. (2007). Spirituality at the end of life: Issues and guidelines for care. In T. G. Plante & C. E. Thoresen (Eds.), *Spirit, science, and health: How the spiritual mind fuels physical wellness* (pp. 191–206). Westport, CT: Praeger/Greenwood.

Merton, T. (1969). *The climate of monastic prayer*. Kalamazoo, MI: Cistercian.

Merton, T. (1973). *Contemplation in a world of action*. Garden City, NY: Image Books.

Michalak, L., Trocki, K., & Bond, J. (2007). Religion and alcohol in the U.S. National Alcohol Survey: How important is religion for abstention and drinking? *Drug and Alcohol Dependence, 87*, 268–280.

Mickley, J., Carson, V., & Soeken, L. (1995). Religion and adult mental health: State of the science in nursing. *Issues in Mental Health Nursing, 16*, 345–360.

Mickley, J., Pargament, K., Brant, C., & Hipp, K. (1998). God and the search for meaning among hospice caregivers. *The Hospice Journal, 13*, 1–17.

Miller, J. J., Fletcher, K., & Kabat-Zinn, J. (1995). Three-year follow-up and clinical implications of a mindfulness-based stress reduction intervention in the treatment of anxiety disorders. *General Hospital Psychiatry, 17*, 192–200.

Miller, J. P. (1994). *The contemplative practitioner: Meditation in education and the professions*. Westport, CT: Bergin & Garvey.

Miller, L., Warner, V., Wickramaratne, P., & Weissman, M. (1997). Religiosity and depression: Ten-year follow-up of depressed mothers and offspring. *Journal of the American Academy of Child & Adolescent Psychiatry, 36*, 1416–1425.

Miller, W. R. (1998). Researching the spiritual dimensions of alcohol and other drug problems. *Addiction, 93,* 979–990.

Miller, W. R. (Ed.). (1999). *Integrating spirituality into treatment: Resources for practitioners.* Washington, DC: American Psychological Association.

Miller, W. R., & Thoresen, C. E. (2003). Spirituality, religion and health: An emerging research field. *American Psychologist, 58,* 24–35.

Mills, B. A., Bersamina, R. B., & Plante, T. G. (2007). The impact of college student immersion service learning trips on coping with stress and vocational identity. *The Journal for Civic Commitment, 9,* 1–8.

Milstein, G., Manierre, A., Susman, V. L., & Bruce, M. L. (2008). Implementation of a program to improve the continuity of mental health care through clergy outreach and professional engagement (C.O.P.E.). *Professional Psychology: Research and Practice, 39,* 218–228.

Mitchell, J., Lannin, D. R., Mathews, H. F., & Swanson, M. S. (2002). Religious beliefs and breast cancer screening. *Journal of Women's Health, 11,* 907–915.

Mottola, A. (Trans.). (1964). *The spiritual exercises of St. Ignatius: St. Ignatius' profound precepts of mystical theology.* New York: Doubleday.

Murray-Swank, N. A. (2003). *Solace for the soul: An evaluation of a psychospiritual intervention for female survivors of sexual abuse.* Unpublished doctoral dissertation, Bowling Green State University, Bowling Green, OH.

Murray-Swank, N. A., & Pargament, K. I. (2005). God, where are you? Evaluating a spiritually-integrated intervention for sexual abuse. *Mental Health, Religion & Culture, 8,* 191–203.

Myers, D. (2000a). *The American paradox: Spiritual hunger in a land of plenty.* New Haven, CT: Yale University Press.

Myers, D. (2000b). The friends, funds, and faith of happy people. *American Psychologist, 56,* 227–238.

National Association of Social Workers. (1999). *Code of ethics of the National Association of Social Workers.* Washington, DC: Author.

Ng, F. (2007). The interface between religion and psychosis. *Australasian Psychiatry, 15,* 62–66.

Niebuhr, R. (1987). Epilogue: A view of life from the sidelines. In R. M. Brown (Ed.), *The essential Reinhold Niebuhr: Selected essays and addresses* (pp. 250–258). New Haven, CT: Yale University Press.

Norcross, J. C. (2002). *Psychotherapy relationships that work: Therapist contributions and responsiveness to patients.* London: Oxford University Press.

Norcross, J. C. (2006). Integrating self-help into psychotherapy: Sixteen practical suggestions. *Professional Psychology: Research and Practice, 37,* 683–693.

Norcross, J. C., Sayette, M. A., & Mayne, T. J. (2008). *Insider's guide to graduate programs in clinical and counseling psychology: 2008/2009 edition.* New York: Guilford Press.

Oman, D., & Driskill, J. D. (2003). Holy name repetition as a spiritual exercise and therapeutic technique. *Journal of Psychology and Christianity, 22,* 5–19.

Oman, D., Shapiro, S. L., Thoresen, C. E., Flinders, T., Driskill, J. D., & Plante, T. G. (2007). A college course for learning from community-based and traditional spiritual models: A randomized evaluation. *Pastoral Psychology, 55,* 473–493.

Oman, D., Shapiro, S. L., Thoresen, C. E., Plante, T. G., & Flinders, T. (2008). Meditation lowers stress and supports forgiveness among college students: A randomized controlled trial. *Journal of American College Health, 56,* 569–578.

Oman, D., & Thoresen, C. E. (2003). Spiritual modeling: A key to spiritual and religious growth? *The International Journal for the Psychology of Religion, 13,* 149–165.

Oman, D., & Thoresen, C. E. (2005). Do religion and spirituality influence health? In R. F. Paloutzian & C. L. Park (Eds.), *Handbook of the psychology of religion and spirituality* (pp. 435–459). New York: Guilford Press.

Oman, D., & Thoresen, C. E. (2007). How does one learn to be spiritual? The neglected role of spiritual modeling in health. In T. G. Plante & C. E. Thoresen (Eds.), *Spirit, science, and health: How the spiritual mind fuels physical wellness* (pp. 39–56). Westport, CT: Praeger/Greenwood.

Ornish, D. (1990). *Dr. Dean Ornish's program for reversing heart disease: The only system scientifically proven to reverse heart disease without drugs or surgery.* New York: Ballantine Books.

Paloutzian, R. F., & Ellison, C. W. (1982). Loneliness, spiritual well-being, and quality of life. In L. A. Peplau & D. Perlman (Eds.), *Loneliness: A sourcebook of current theory, research and therapy* (pp. 224–237). New York: Wiley Interscience.

Paloutzian, R. F., & Park, C. L. (2005). Integrative themes in the current science of the psychology of religion. In R. F. Paloutzian & C. L. Park (Eds.), *Handbook of the psychology of religion and spirituality* (pp. 3–20). New York: Guilford Press.

Pardini, D., Plante, T. G., Sherman, A., & Stump, J. E. (2000). Religious faith and spirituality in substance abuse recovery: Determining the mental health benefits. *Journal of Substance Abuse Treatment, 19,* 347–354.

Pargament, K. I. (1997). *The psychology of religious coping: Theory, research, practice.* New York: Guilford Press.

Pargament, K. I. (2007). *Spiritually integrated psychotherapy: Understanding and addressing the sacred.* New York: Guilford Press.

Pargament, K. I., Koenig, H. G., & Perez, L. (2000). The many methods of religious coping: Initial development and validation of the RCOPE. *Journal of Clinical Psychology, 56,* 519–543.

Pargament, K. I., McCarthy, S., Shah, P., Ano, G., Tarakeshwar, N., Wachholtz, A. B., et al. (2004). Religion and HIV: A review of the literature and clinical implications. *Southern Medical Journal, 97,* 1201–1209.

Pargament, K. I., Smith, B. W., Koenig, H. G., & Perez, L. (1998). Patterns of positive and negative religious coping with major life stressors. *Journal for the Scientific Study of Religion, 37,* 711–725.

Peele, S. (1997). Utilizing culture and behavior in epidemiological models of alcohol consumption and consequences for Western nations. *Alcohol and Alcoholism, 32,* 51–64.

Philips, R. L., & Snowdon, D. A. (1983). Association of meat and coffee use with cancers of the large bowel, breast, and prostate among Seventh-Day Adventists: Preliminary results. *Cancer Research, 43*(Suppl.), 2403–2408.

Plante, T. G. (1999). A collaborative relationship between professional psychology and the Roman Catholic Church: A case example and suggested principles for success. *Professional Psychology: Research and Practice, 30*, 541–546.

Plante, T. G. (2003). Priests behaving badly: What do we know about priest sex offenders? *Journal of Sexual Addiction and Compulsivity, 9*, 93–97.

Plante, T. G. (2004). *Do the right thing: Living ethically in an unethical world.* Oakland, CA: New Harbinger.

Plante, T. G. (2007). Spirituality, religion, and health: Ethical issues to consider. In T. G. Plante & C. E. Thoresen (Eds.), *Spirit, science, and health: How the spiritual mind fuels physical wellness* (pp. 207–218). Westport, CT: Praeger/Greenwood.

Plante, T. G., & Aldridge, A. (2005). Psychological patterns among Roman Catholic clergy accused of sexual misconduct. *Pastoral Psychology, 54*, 73–80.

Plante, T. G., & Boccaccini, B. F. (1997). The Santa Clara Strength of Religious Faith Questionnaire. *Pastoral Psychology, 45*, 375–387.

Plante, T. G., Lackey, K., & Hwang, J. (in press). The impact of immersion trips on development of compassion among college students. *Journal of Experiential Education.*

Plante, T. G., & Sharma, N. (2001). Religious faith and mental health outcomes. In T. G. Plante & A. C. Sherman (Eds.), *Faith and health: Psychological perspectives* (pp. 240–261). NewYork: Guilford Press.

Plante, T. G., & Sherman, A. C. (Eds.). (2001). *Faith and health: Psychological perspectives.* New York: Guilford Press.

Plante, T. G., & Thoresen, C. E. (Eds.). (2007). *Spirit, science, and health: How the spiritual mind fuels physical wellness.* Westport, CT: Praeger/Greenwood.

Plante, T. G., Vallaeys, C. L., Sherman, A. C., & Wallston, K. A. (2002). The development of a brief version of the Santa Clara Strength of Religious Faith Questionnaire. *Pastoral Psychology, 48*, 11–21.

Plante, T. G., Yancey, S., Sherman, A., Guertin, M., & Pardini, D. (1999). Further validation for the Santa Clara Strength of Religious Faith Questionnaire. *Pastoral Psychology, 48*, 11–21.

Powell, L., Shahabi, L., & Thoresen, C. E. (2003). Religion and spirituality: Linkages to physical health. *American Psychologist, 58*, 36–52.

Puchalski, C. (2004). Spirituality in health: The role of spirituality in critical care. *Critical Care Clinics, 20*, 487–504.

Pulchalski, C., & Rommer, A. L. (2001). Taking a spiritual history allows clinicians to understand patients more fully. *Journal of Palliative Medicine, 3*, 129–137.

Rachels, J., & Rachels, S. (2007). *The elements of moral philosophy* (5th ed.). New York: McGraw-Hill.

Rajarathinam, R. M., & Muthusamy, R. (1996). Pattern of substance abuse in Salem: A three year study. *International Medical Journal, 3*, 309–312.

Reese, D., & Brown, D. (1997). Psychosocial and spiritual care in hospice: Differences between nursing, social work, and clergy. *Hospice Journal, 12,* 29–41.

Ressler, W. H. (1997). Jewishness and well-being: Specific identification and general psychological adjustment. *Psychological Reports, 81,* 515–518.

Richards, P. S., & Bergin, A. E. (1997). *A spiritual strategy for counseling and psychotherapy.* Washington, DC: American Psychological Association.

Richards, P. S., & Bergin, A. E. (Eds.). (2004). *Casebook for a spiritual strategy in counseling and psychotherapy.* Washington, DC: American Psychological Association.

Richards, P. S., & Bergin, A. E. (2005). *A spiritual strategy for counseling and psychotherapy* (2nd ed.). Washington, DC: American Psychological Association.

Richards, P. S., Hardman, R. K., & Berrett, M. E. (2000). *Spiritual renewal: A journal of faith and healing.* Orem, UT: Center for Change.

Richards, P. S., Hardman, R., Frost, H., Berrett, M., Clark-Sly, J., & Anderson, D. (1997). Spiritual issues and interventions in treatment of patients with eating disorders. *Eating Disorders: The Journal of Treatment and Prevention, 5,* 261–279.

Rogers, C. R. (1980). *A way of being.* New York: Houghton Mifflin.

Rose, E. M., Westfeld, J. S., & Ansley, T. N. (2001). Spiritual issues in counseling clients' beliefs and preferences. *Journal of Counseling Psychology, 30,* 118–134.

Russell, S. R., & Yarhouse, M. A. (2006). Religion/spirituality within APA-accredited psychology predoctoral internships. *Professional Psychology: Research and Practice, 37,* 430–436.

Rye, M., & Pargament, K. I. (2003). *Coping with divorce: A journey toward forgiveness.* Unpublished manuscript, University of Dayton, Dayton, OH.

Rye, M., Pargament, K. I., Pan, W., Yingling, D. W., Shogren, K. A., & Ito, M. (2005). Can group interventions facilitate forgiveness of an ex-spouse? A randomized clinical trial. *Journal of Consulting and Clinical Psychology, 73,* 880–892.

Schaefer, C. A., & Gorsuch, R. L. (1991). Psychological adjustment and religiousness: The multivariate belief-motivation theory of religiousness. *Journal for the Scientific Study of Religion, 30,* 448–461.

Seeman, T. E., Dubin, L. F., & Seeman, M. (2003). Religiosity/spirituality and health: A critical review of the evidence for biological pathways. *American Psychologist, 58,* 53–63.

Seligman, M. E. P. (2002). *Authentic happiness.* New York: Simon & Schuster.

Seligman, M. E. P., & Csikszentmihalyi, M. (2000). Positive psychology: An introduction. *American Psychologist, 55,* 5–14.

Seligman, M. E. P., Steen T. A., Park, N., & Peterson, C. (2005). Positive psychology progress: Empirical validation of interventions. *American Psychologist, 60,* 410–421.

Shafranske, E. P. (2000). Religious involvement and professional practices of psychiatrists and other mental health professionals. *Psychiatric Annals, 30,* 525–532.

Shafranske, E. P. (2001). The religious dimensions of patient care within rehabilitation medicine: The role of religious attitudes, beliefs, and professional practices.

In T. G. Plante & A. C. Sherman (Eds.), *Faith and health: Psychological perspectives* (pp. 311–338). New York: Guilford Press.

Shafranske, E. P., & Malony, H. N. (1990). Clinical psychologists' religious and spiritual orientations and their practice of psychotherapy. *Psychotherapy, 27*, 72–78.

Shafranske, E. P., & Malony, H. N. (1996). Religion and the clinical practice of psychology: A case for inclusion. In E. P. Shafranske (Ed.), *Religion and the clinical practice of psychology* (pp. 561–586). Washington, DC: American Psychological Association.

Shapiro, S. L., Schwartz, G. E. R., & Bonner, G. (1998). The effects of mindfulness-based stress reduction on medical and pre-medical students. *Journal of Behavioral Medicine, 21*, 581–599.

Shapiro, S. L., Schwartz, G. E. R., & Santerre, C. (2002). Meditation and positive psychology. In C. R. Snyder & S. J. Lopez (Eds.), *The handbook of positive psychology* (pp. 632–645). New York: Oxford University Press.

Shapiro, S. L., & Walsh, R. (2007). Meditation: Exploring the farther reaches. In T. G. Plante & C. E. Thoresen (Eds.), *Spirit, science, and health: How the spiritual mind fuels physical wellness* (pp. 57–71). Westport, CT: Praeger/Greenwood.

Sheldon, K. M., & King, L. (2001). Why positive psychology is necessary. *American Psychologist, 56*, 216–217.

Sherman, A. C., Plante, T. G., Simonton, S., Adams, D., Burris, K., & Harbison, C. (1999). Assessing religious faith in medical patients: Cross-validation of the Santa Clara Strength of Religious Faith Questionnaire. *Pastoral Psychology, 48*, 129–142.

Sherman, A. C., & Simonton, S. (2007). Spirituality and cancer. In T. G. Plante & C. E. Thoresen (Eds.), *Spirit, science, and health: How the spiritual mind fuels physical wellness* (pp. 157–175). Westport, CT: Praeger/Greenwood.

Sherman, A. C., Simonton, S., Adams, D. C., Latif, U., Plante, T. G., Burris, S. K., & Poling, T. (2001). Measuring religious faith in cancer patients: Reliability and construct validity of the Santa Clara Strength of Religious Faith Questionnaire. *Journal of Psycho-Oncology, 10*, 436–443.

Shooka, A., Al-Haddad, M., & Raees, A. (1998). OCD in Bahrain: A phenomenological profile. *International Journal of Social Psychiatry, 44*, 147–154.

Shreve-Neiger, A. K., & Edelstein, B. A. (2004). Religion and anxiety: A critical review of the literature. *Clinical Psychology Review, 24*, 379–397.

Siegrist, M. (1996). Church attendance, denomination, and suicide ideology. *Journal of Social Psychology, 136*, 559–566.

Sloan, R. P., Bagiella, E., & Powell, T. (1999, February 20). Religion, spirituality, and medicine. *The Lancet, 353*, 664–667.

Sloan, R. P., Bagiella, E., & Powell, T. (2001). Without a prayer: Methodological problems, ethical challenges, and misrepresentations in the study of religion, spirituality, and medicine. In T. G. Plante & A. C. Sherman (Eds.), *Faith and health: Psychological perspectives* (pp. 339–354). New York: Guilford Press.

Smith, D. P., & Orlinsky, D. E. (2004). Religious and spiritual experience among psychotherapists. *Psychotherapy, 4,* 144–151.

Smith, H. (1991). *The world's religions: Our great wisdom traditions.* San Francisco: HarperSanFrancisco.

Snyder, C. R., & Lopez, S. J. (2007). *Positive psychology: The scientific and practical explorations of human strengths.* Thousand Oaks, CA: Sage.

Sperry, L., & Shafranske, E. P. (Eds.). (2005). *Spiritually oriented psychotherapy.* Washington, DC: American Psychological Association.

Spohn, W. C. (2000). *Go and do likewise: Jesus and ethics.* New York: Continuum.

Stewart, C. (2001). The influence of spirituality on substance abuse of college students. *Journal of Drug Education, 31,* 343–351.

Stroebe, W., & Stroebe, M. (1996). The social psychology of social support. In E. T. Higgins & A. W. Kruglanski (Eds.), *Social psychology: Handbook of basic principles* (pp. 597–621). New York: Guilford Press.

Sue, D. W., Bingham, R. P., Porche-Burke, L., & Vasquez, M. (1999). The diversification of psychology: A multicultural revolution. *American Psychologist, 54,* 1061–1069.

Sugisawa, H., Shibata, H., Hougham, G. W., Sugihara, Y., & Liang, J. (2002). The impact of social ties on depressive symptoms in U.S. and Japanese elderly. *Journal of Social Issues, 58,* 785–804.

Tan, S.-Y. (1996). Religion in clinical practice: Implicit and explicit integration. In E. P. Shafranske (Ed.), *Religion and the clinical practice of psychology* (pp. 365–387). Washington, DC: American Psychological Association.

Tan, S.-Y. (2003). Inner healing prayer. *Christian Counseling Today, 11,* 20–22.

Tan, S.-Y. (2007). Use of prayer and scripture in cognitive-behavioral therapy. *Journal of Psychology and Christianity, 26,* 101–111.

Task Force on Promotion and Dissemination of Psychological Procedures. (1995). Training in and dissemination of empirically validated psychological treatments: Report and recommendations. *Clinical Psychologist, 48,* 3–23.

Thearle, M. J., Vance, J., Najman, J., Embelton, G., & Foster, W. (1995). Church attendance, religious affiliation and parental responses to sudden infant death, neonatal death and stillbirth. *Omega, 31,* 51–58.

Thoresen, C. E. (2007). Spirituality, religion, and health: What's the deal? In T. G. Plante & C. E. Thoresen (Eds.), *Spirit, science, and health: How the spiritual mind fuels physical wellness* (pp. 3–10). Westport, CT: Praeger/Greenwood.

Trenholm, P., Trent, J., & Compton, W. C. (1998). Negative religious conflict as a predictor of panic disorder. *Journal of Clinical Psychology, 54,* 59–65.

Tsang, J., & McCullough, M. E. (2003). Measuring religious constructs: A hierarchical approach to construct organization and scale selection. In S. J. Lopez & C. R. Snyder (Eds.), *Positive psychological assessment: A handbook of models and measures* (pp. 345–360). Washington, DC: American Psychological Association.

Underwood, L. G. (2006). Ordinary spiritual experience: Qualitative research, interpretive guidelines, and population distribution for the Daily Spiritual Experience Scale. *Archive for the Psychology of Religion, 28,* 181–218.

Vaughn, F. (1995). *Shadows of the sacred: Seeing through spiritual illusion*. Wheaton, IL: Quest.

Vitz, P., & Mango, P. (1997). Kernbergian psychodynamics and religious aspects of the forgiveness process. *Journal of Psychology & Theology, 25*, 72–80.

Von Staden, H. (Trans.) (1996). In a pure and holy way: Personal and professional conduct in the Hippocratic oath. *Journal of the History of Medicine and Allied Sciences, 51*, 406–408.

Wachholtz, A. B. (2005). *Does spirituality matter? Effects of meditative content and orientation on migraneurs*. Unpublished doctoral dissertation, Bowling Green State University, Bowling Green, OH.

Wachholtz, A. B., & Pargament, K. I. (2005). Is spirituality a critical ingredient of meditation? Comparing the effects of spiritual meditation, secular meditation, and relaxation on spiritual, psychological, cardiac, and pain outcomes. *Journal of Behavioral Medicine, 28*, 369–384.

Wachholtz, A. B., & Pearce, M. (2007). Compassion and health. In T. G. Plante & C. E. Thoresen (Eds.), *Spirit, science, and health: How the spiritual mind fuels physical wellness* (pp. 115–128). Westport, CT: Praeger/Greenwood

Wade, N. G., & Worthington, E. L., Jr. (2006). Religiously tailored interventions in explicitly Christian therapy: An initial effectiveness study. *Psychotherapy Research, 17*, 91–105.

Wahass, S., & Kent, G. (1997). Coping with auditory hallucinations: A cross-cultural comparison between Western (British) and non-Western (Saudi Arabian) patients. *The Journal of Nervous and Mental Disease, 185*, 664–668.

Walls, P., & Williams, R. (2004). Accounting for Irish Catholic ill health in Scotland: A qualitative exploration of some links between religion, class, and health. *Sociology of Health and Illness, 26*, 527–556.

Walsh, J. (1995). The impact of schizophrenia on clients' religious beliefs: Implications for families. *Families in Society, 76*, 551–558.

Walsh, R. (1999). *Essential spirituality: The seven central practices*. New York: Wiley.

Walsh, R., & Shapiro, S. L. (2006). The meeting of meditative disciplines and Western psychology: A mutually enriching dialogue. *American Psychologist, 61*, 227–239.

Walters, J., & Neugeboren, B. (1995). Collaboration between mental health organizations and religious institutions. *Psychiatric Rehabilitation Journal, 19*, 51–57.

Wasserman, I., & Stack, S. (1993). The effect of religion on suicide: An analysis of cultural context. *Omega: Journal of Death and Dying, 27*, 295–305.

Watson, J. B. (1983). *Psychology from the standpoint of a behaviorist*. Dover, NH: Frances Pinter. (Original work published 1924)

Wilcock, A., Van Der Arend, H., Darling, K., Scholz, J., Siddaly, R., Snigg, C., & Stephens, J. (1998). An exploratory study of people's perceptions and experiences of well-being. *British Journal of Occupational Therapy, 61*, 75–82.

Worthington, E. L., Jr. (1989). *Marriage counseling: A Christian approach to counseling couples*. Downers Grove, IL: InterVarsity Press.

Worthington, E. L., Jr. (1990). Marriage counseling: A Christian approach to counseling couples. *Counseling and Values, 35,* 3–15.

Worthington, E. L., Jr. (2004). *Experiencing forgiveness: Six practical sessions for becoming a more forgiving Christian.* Unpublished manuscript, Virginia Commonwealth University, Richmond.

Worthington, E. L., Jr., Berry, J., & Parrott, L. (2001). Unforgiveness, forgiveness, religion, and health. In T. G. Plante & A. C. Sherman (Eds.), *Faith and health: Psychological perspectives* (pp. 107–138). New York: Guilford Press.

Worthington, E. L., Jr., Kurusu, T. A., McCullough, M. E., & Sandage, S. J. (1996). Empirical research on religion and psychotherapeutic processes and outcomes: A 10-year review and research prospectus. *Psychological Bulletin, 119,* 448–487.

Worthington, E. L., Jr., Sandage, S. J., & Berry, J. W. (2000). Group interventions to promote forgiveness: What researchers and clinicians ought to know. In M. E. McCullough, K. I. Pargament, & C. E. Thoresen (Eds.), *Forgiveness: Theory, research, and practice* (pp. 228–254). New York: Guilford Press.

Worthington, E. L., Jr., & Scherer, M. (2004). Forgiveness is an emotion-focused coping strategy that can reduce health risks and promote health resilience: Theory, review, and hypotheses. *Psychology and Health, 19,* 385–405.

Worthington, E. L., Jr., & Wade, N. G. (1999). The social psychology of unforgiveness and forgiveness and implications for clinical practice. *Journal of Social and Clinical Psychology, 18,* 385–418.

Worthington, E. L., Jr., Wade, N. G., Hight, T. L., Ripley, J. S., McCullough, M. E., Berry, J. W. et al. (2003). The Religious Commitment Inventory—10: Development, refinement, and validation of a brief scale for research and counseling. *Journal of Counseling Psychology, 50,* 84–96.

Young, J. S., Cashwell, C., Wiggins-Frame, M., & Belaire, C. (2002). Spiritual and religious competencies: A national survey of CACREP-accredited programs. *Counseling and Values, 47,* 22–33.

INDEX

Graduate Theological Union, 178
Gratitude, 92–93. *See also* Forgiveness, gratitude, and kindness
Grieving process, religious–spiritual engagement and, 20–21

Happiness, religious–spiritual involvement and, 19
Health
    cleaner living and, 17
    integration of religion–spirituality and, 14. *See also* Mental health benefits of integrated therapy
    and religiosity, 26–27
    religious/spiritual, 54
    resource books on, 193–194
    spirituality and, 3, 4
Hinduism
    mantras in, 74
    meditative practices/techniques in, 34
    spiritual models in, 95
Hippocratic Oath, 88
HIV/AIDS group treatment approach, 153

Illness, group treatment program for, 153. *See also* Chronic illness
Implicit approach to integration, 67–68
Inflexibility, religious–spiritual, 110–111, 117, 119
In-group/out-group conflicts, 26
Inspirational reading, in Eight-Point Program, 156
Intake forms, 55, 56
Integration of religion–spirituality into psychotherapy, 13–14
    art of, 175–176
    cultural considerations in, 44–45
    current level of, 148
    ethical precautions for, 42–45
    and health effects of religion–spirituality, 14
    research supporting, 15
    resources for, 110
    specific recommendations about, 110
    using external tools in, 100–102
Integrity, 38, 107–109
    case study of, 161–163
    in RRICC model, 90, 104
Internal benefits of religion–spirituality, 32
Internal religious–spiritual tools, 65–81
    bibliotherapy, 78–80
    case example for, 80–81

and implicit/explicit approaches to psychotherapy, 67–68
meaning, purpose, and calling in life, 75–77
meditation, 72–75
prayer, 69–72
and problematic attitudes of clinicians, 68–69
and spiritually and psychologically minded services, 66–67
International Association for the Psychology of Religion, 184
International Association of Pastoral Counselors, 187
Interpersonal relationships
    clinical observation of, 57
    and sacredness of life, 42
Interventions. *See* Religious–spiritual interventions
Interviewing, clinical, 58–61
Intolerance
    of ambiguity, 69
    from inflexibility, 110–111
Intrinsic religiosity, 18
Intrinsic Religious Motivation Scale, 210
Islam. *See also* Muslims
    meditative practices/techniques in, 34, 73
    spiritual models in, 95

James, William, 5, 32, 69
Jargon, 137–138
Jesuits, 99, 100
Jesus, as spiritual model, 96
Jews. *See also* Judaism
    cultural differences among, 44, 57–58
    language of, 57
    overgeneralizations about, 111
    religious orthodoxy of, 51
    risk of depressive symptoms in, 20
    victimized by religious influence/leaders, 123, 126
John Templeton Foundation, 14
Journal article resources, 199
Judaism. *See also* Jews
    ethical values and behavior in, 38
    formal prayers in, 70
    meditative practices/techniques in, 34, 73
    particular affiliations within, 50

Kabala, 55

Myopia, spiritual, 68
Mysticism Scale, 211

Narcotics Anonymous, 150
National Institutes of Health (NIH), 14
National Multicultural Conference and Summit (1999), 14
Negative outcomes in research, 26–27
Networks, collaborative, 179
Neurotic guilt, religious–spiritual involvement and, 22
NIH (National Institutes of Health), 14
Nonreligious clients
    in valuing self and others case study, 166–168
    working with, 118–120

Obesity, 25
One-point attention, in Eight-Point Program, 155
Opening Your Heart program, 151
Ornish, Dean, 151
Overconfidence of therapists, 69
Overeaters Anonymous, 25, 150
Overenthusiasm, spiritual, 69
Overgeneralizations, 111, 124

Pargament, K. I., 5, 67
Passage meditation, 154–155
Patient referrals, 43
Personality disorders, 24–25
Positive psychology, 13, 15, 75, 76
Prayer, 33–34, 69–72
    in AA program, 151
    in anxiety case study, 159–160
    as both internal and external practice, 66
    centering, 35, 74
    in clergy sexual abuse case study, 169
    with clients, 70–71
    Serenity Prayer, 41, 98
    types of, 70
Prejudice, 43
Principles, 32
Productive life with chronic illness case study, 161–163
Professional organizations, 183–189
Psychological mind-set, 67
Psychologists, religion–spirituality of, 10–13
Psychology
    evolution and maturation of, 27
    integration of religion and, 13–16

positive, 13, 15, 75, 76
    scientific/secular viewpoint of, 12–13
Psychology of religion, 180
Psychology of Religion Web site, 189
Psychotic disorders, 24
Purpose in life. See Meaning, purpose, and calling in life
Putting others first, in Eight-Point Program, 156

Quality of service, 143

Ramakrishna, Sri, 30
Randomized clinical trials, 177
RCI–10. See Religious Commitment Inventory—10
RCOPE, 64
REACH model, 92
Readings. See Bibliotherapy
Reciprocity, when collaborating with clergy, 135–136
Re-Creating Your Life, 152
Referrals, 132, 135, 141, 143
Relaxation response, 155
Religion(s)
    common aspects of, 30
    comparative, 180
    defined, 4, 5
    differences among, 31–32
    health benefits of, 13–16
    psychology of, 180
    specific intrafaith affiliations within, 50–51
Religion–spirituality, 3–4, 9–28
    and anxiety, 21–22
    assessment of. See Assessment of religious–spiritual influences
    and depression/suicidal ideation, 20–21
    and eating disorders, 26
    integration of psychology and, 13–16. See also Integration of religion–spirituality into psychotherapy
    mental health associations with, 18–26
    methodological issues in research on, 16–18
    of most Americans, 10
    of most psychologists, 10–13
    and negative outcomes of religious involvement, 26–27, 113–114
    and personality disorders, 24–25
    in psychotherapy, 6
    and psychotic disorders, 24

Scientific viewpoint of psychology, 12–13
SCSORF. *See* Santa Clara Strength of Religious Faith Questionnaire
Secular humanism, 32
Secular viewpoint of psychology, 12–13
Self-acceptance. *See* Acceptance of self and others
Self-esteem, religious–spiritual involvement and, 19
Self-help literature, 36, 78
Self-image, sacredness of life and, 42
Serenity Prayer, 41, 98
Services, community. *See* Attending community services and rituals
Seventh-Day Adventists, 17
Sexoholics Anonymous, 150
Sexual abuse
    case study of religious–spiritual tools in overcoming, 168–172
    by priests, 40–41, 123
SHI. *See* Spirituality and Health Institute, Santa Clara University
SIG. *See* Spirituality and Health Special Interest Group
Signature strengths, 75, 76
Signs of religious affiliation, 55, 57–58
Slowing down, in Eight-Point Program, 155
Smith, Huston, 30–31
Smriti, 78
Social justice, 39–40, 94–95. *See also* Volunteerism and charity
    benefits of, 94
    in call toward integrity/community case study, 162–163
    harm caused by, 94–95
    in valuing self and others case study, 167–168
Social networking, 85
Social support, 19–20. *See also* Attending community services and rituals
Society for the Scientific Study of Religion, 185
Society of Behavioral Medicine (SBM), 14. *See also* Spirituality and Health Special Interest Group
Solace for the Soul, 152
Spiritual association, in Eight-Point Program, 156
Spiritual bias, 68
Spiritual cockiness, 69
Spiritual direction, 76, 157–160
Spiritual health and maturity, 54

Spiritual identity, 52–53
Spiritual inflexibility, 117, 119
Spiritual interventions. *See* Religious–spiritual interventions
Spirituality. *See also* Religion–spirituality
    defined, 4–5
    and health, 3, 4
    of most Americans, 10
Spirituality and Health Institute (SHI), Santa Clara University, 178, 185–186
Spirituality and Health Special Interest Group (SIG, SBM), 110, 178, 184
The Spirituality Religiosity Scale, 211
Spiritual mind-set, 67
Spiritual models. *See* Learning from spiritual models
Spiritual myopia, 68
Spiritual overenthusiasm, 69
Spiritual Renewal, 152
Spiritual timidity, 68
Spiritual Well-Being Scale, 210
Sruti, 78
Stanford University, 178
Stereotypes, 43–44, 57
Stressors on clergy, 137
Structure in life. *See* Attending community services and rituals
Substance abuse, 22–23
Successful research, learning from, 177–178
Suicidal ideation, religious–spiritual engagement and, 21
Supernatural context. *See* Being part of something larger than oneself
Symbols, religious, 55, 57

Talmud, 89
Taoism, 34
Therapists. *See* Mental health professionals
Timidity, spiritual, 68
TM. *See* Transcendental meditation
Tolerance, supporting, 110–111
Tools from religious–spiritual thought, 29–46
    acceptance of self and others, 51, 97–98
    appreciating the sacredness of life, 42, 99–100
    attending community services and rituals, 36–37, 84–86
    being part of something larger than oneself, 41–42, 98–99

ABOUT THE AUTHOR

Thomas G. Plante, PhD, ABPP, is a professor of psychology at Santa Clara University and adjunct clinical associate professor of psychiatry and behavioral sciences at Stanford University School of Medicine. He also directs the Spirituality and Health Institute at Santa Clara University and serves on the National Review Board of the U.S. Council of Catholic Bishops. Born and raised in Rhode Island, he received his ScB degree in psychology from Brown University, his MA and PhD degrees in clinical psychology from the University of Kansas, and his clinical internship and postdoctoral fellowship in clinical and health psychology from Yale University. He has authored, coauthored, edited, or coedited 11 books, including *Sin Against the Innocents: Sexual Abuse by Priests and the Role of the Catholic Church* (2004); *Bless Me Father for I Have Sinned: Perspectives on Sexual Abuse Committed by Roman Catholic Priests* (1999); *Faith and Health: Psychological Perspectives* (2001); *Do the Right Thing: Living Ethically in an Unethical World* (2004); *Contemporary Clinical Psychology* (1999, 2005); *Mental Disorders in the New Millennium* (Vols. 1, 2, and 3; 2006); and, most recently, *Spirit, Science, and Health: How the Spiritual Mind Fuels Physical Wellness* (2007). He also has published more than 150 journal articles and book chapters. His areas of clinical and research interests focus on faith and health outcomes, psychological issues among Catholic clergy and laypersons, ethical decision making, stress and coping, and the psychological benefits of physical exercise. He has been featured in numerous media outlets, including *Time* magazine, the *New York Times, USA Today,* NBC, PBS, the British Broadcasting Company, National Public Radio, and CNN, among many others. On April 1, 2002, *Time* referred to him as one of the three leading American Catholics. He maintains a private practice as a licensed psychologist in Menlo Park, California.